Applied Language Study: New Objectives and New Methods

Applied Language Study: New Objectives and New Methods

Contributors

Angela Chambers et al.

www.aurisreference.com

Applied Language Study: New Objectives and New Methods

Contributors: Angela Chambers et al.

Published by Auris Reference Limited

www.aurisreference.com

United Kingdom

Applied Language Study: New Objectives and New Methods

ISBN: 978-1-78154-722-9

British Library Cataloguing in Publication Data
A CIP record for this book is available from the British Library

Printed in the United Kingdom

Contents

List of Abbreviations

APT	Association pattern technique
BBS	Bhutan Broadcasting Service
DAP	Democratic Action Party
DPM	Deputy Prime Minister
GDP	gross domestic product
HVM	Hierarchical value map
HVMs	Hierarchical value maps
ICT	Information and Communication Technology
PKR	People's Justice Party
SSCI	Science Citation Index Social
SNSs	Social network services

List of Contributors

Joergen Oerstroem Moeller
Visiting Senior Fellow, ISEAS Yusof Ishak Institute, Singapore
Singapore Management University & Copenhagen Business School, Singapore
Honorary Alumnus, University of Copenhagen, Copenhagen, Denmark

Kurt Lang Gladys Engel Lang
University of Washington

Lhamo T
Public Policy Program, National Graduate Institute for Public Policy, Tokyo 106-0032, Japan

Oyama T
Professor of Public Policy Analysis, National Graduate Institute for Public Policy, Tokyo 106-0032, Japan

Feifei Han
Department of Sci-Tech Communication and Policy, University of Science and Technology of China, Hefei, China

Zhangzhi Ge
School of Public Affairs, University of Science and Technology of China, Hefei, China

Rongting Zhou
Department of Sci-Tech Communication and Policy, University of Science and Technology of China, Hefei, China

Célestin Messanga Obama
Department of Advertisement, Advance School of Mass Communication, University of Yaoundé 2, Yaoundé, Cameroon

Brittany L. Pavolik
Department of Communications Media, Indiana University of Pennsylvania, Indiana, PA, USA

Mark J. Piwinsky
Department of Communications Media, Indiana University of Pennsylvania, Indiana, PA, USA

Lacey A. Fulton
Department of Communication, Clarion University, Clarion, PA, USA

Sara Chinnasamy
University Technology Mara, Selangor, Malaysia

Izyan Roslan
University Technology Mara, Selangor, Malaysia

Jean-François Nguegan
University of Yaoundé II, Advance School of Mass Communication (AS-MAC), Yaoundé, Cameroon

Thomas Essono
University of Yaoundé II, Advance School of Mass Communication (AS-MAC), Yaoundé, Cameroon

Jingqian Tang
Library of Jinan University, Guangzhou, China

Denise Avancini Alves
Pontifical Catholic University of Rio Grande do Sul (PUCRS), Porto Alegre, Brazil
Federal University of Rio Grande do Sul (UFRGS), Porto Alegre, Brazil

Maria Helena Weber
Federal University of Rio Grande do Sul (UFRGS), Porto Alegre, Brazil

Valene Bummara
School of Journalism & Mass Communication, Texas State University, San Marcos, TX, USA

Jinbong Choi
Department of Media & Communication, Sungkonghoe University, Seoul, South Korea

Sang Hee Kwon
Sungkyunkwan University, Seoul, Korea

Min Kyung Cha
Sungkyunkwan University, Seoul, Korea

Seo Young Lee
Yonsei University, Seoul, Korea

Marianne Paimre
Department of Law, University of Tartu, Tartu, Estonia

Fatma Gürses
Department of Journalism, University of Kastamonu, Kastamonu, Turkey

Tai-Li Wang
The Graduate Institute of Journalism, National Taiwan University, Taiwan

Kazi Nazmul Huda
Department of Business Administration, Southern University Bangladesh, Chittagong, Bangladesh

Abul Kalam Azad
Department of Communication & Journalism, University of Chittagong, Chittagong, Bangladesh

Israel Udomisor
The Department of Mass Communication, University of Maiduguri, Maiduguri, Nigeria

Anthony Paul Udoh
The Department of Communication Art, University of Uyo, Uyo, Nigeria

Preface

Sometimes called applied linguistics, the field of applied language study (ALS) is devoted to the study of particular domains of language learning and use, such as foreign language learning and teaching, bi- and multilingualism, translation and interpretation, communication in professional contexts, or intercultural communication. The text *Applied Language Study: New Objectives and New Methods* presents the research methods for applied language studies, and combines the application of second language theories to the practice of learning, teaching, and assessing second languages. The aim of first chapter is to examine a number of aspects of course design in corpora and language learning involving direct access by learners, focusing not on the training of corpus linguists but rather on the popularization of corpus consultation by a wide spectrum of learners. Strategy use and language performance by second language learners in Nigeria have been discussed in second chapter. Third chapter presents findings of a study of recognition vocabulary knowledge as a predictor of written academic English proficiency (AEP) and overall academic achievement in an English medium higher education program in an English-as-a-foreign-language (EFL) context. Fourth chapter highlights key problematic issues, especially in light of the increasingly diverse student bodies, and highlights potential solutions for the European language context. An empirical study of content-based instruction applied in non-English-majored graduate English teaching in the post-massification has been presented in fifth chapter. The linguistic study of language has been introduced in sixth chapter. Seventh chapter deals with the study of language and language acquisition. Eighth chapter examines the use of communication strategies in monologues and dialogues by Malaysian healthcare trainees with limited English proficiency during communication strategy training. The effect of listening to comic strip stories on incidental vocabulary learning among Iranian EFL learners has been evaluated in ninth chapter. A critical review of common vocabulary learning strategies in Iranian EFL classrooms has been presented in tenth chapter. Eleventh chapter explores how students' informal language learning experiences with English find their way into the formal context of content-based language teaching (CLIL). Last chapter discusses the language ideologies of voluntary learners of Swedish and Hungarian in two contexts where these languages are historical minority languages.

Chapter 1

INTEGRATING CORPUS CONSULTATION IN LANGUAGE STUDIES

Angela Chambers

University of Limerick

ABSTRACT

Alongside developments in language research, the potential of corpora as a resource in language learning and teaching has been evident to researchers and teachers since the late 1960s. Despite publications which emphasise the benefits of corpus consultation for language learners (Bernardini, 2002; Kennedy & Miceli, 2001), there is little evidence to suggest that direct corpus consultation is coming to be seen as a complement or alternative to consultation of a dictionary, course book, or grammar by the majority of learners. There is thus a need for research to underpin the integration of corpora and concordancing in the language-learning environment.

This study begins with an account of published research relating to course design and structure in the area of corpus consultation by language learners. The focus then narrows to the initial training of learners in corpus consultation, using as an example a course involving undergraduate students on several language degree programmes. The results of the students' consultation of the corpora are examined, including choice of search word(s), analytical skills, the problems encountered, and their evaluation of the activity. The results reveal how corpus consultation can complement traditional language-learning resources, while also raising questions concerning its integration in the language-learning environment.

INTRODUCTION

Since large computerised corpora of English were created in the 1960s, there has been a steady increase in the number of publications devoted to their use in the context of language teaching and learning. The pioneering work of Johns

(1986) and Tribble and Jones (1990) was followed by an explosion of studies devoted to various aspects of the use of corpora in language learning in various contexts, for example the publications resulting from the TALC (Teaching and Language Corpora) conferences on teaching and language corpora (see, e.g., Burnard & McEnery, 2000; Kettemann & Marko, 2002). From the early 1990s onward, corpora were clearly being consulted by language teachers, and also by learners, at least in courses run by researchers and enthusiasts, and this activity was gaining in popularity by a process which McEnery and Wilson (1997, p. 5) describe as percolation. This has created a need for research to underpin this new development, focusing on aspects such as the type of corpora to be consulted, large or small, general or domain-specific, tagged or untagged.

Other pedagogic issues also require investigation, such as the advantages of direct access to corpora as opposed to mediation by the teacher through the preparation of corpus-based worksheets, the strategies which learners need to acquire to benefit from direct consultation, and, last but not least, the means by which this new activity can best be integrated into the language-learning environment. Some of these issues are already receiving considerable attention from researchers, with a number of studies recommending the use of small corpora tailored to the learners' needs (Aston, 1997; Roe, 2000), while others champion large corpus concordancing (Bernardini, 2000; Cheng, Warren, & Xun-feng, 2003). Direct access to corpora by learners is the subject of a number of studies (see, e.g., Bernardini, 2002; Chambers & O'Sullivan, 2004; Kennedy & Miceli, 2001, 2002), with a cautionary note from Johns (1997, p. 113) recommending the use of corpus results mediated by the teacher as a first stage. While there is already a substantial and increasing body of research in several aspects of direct corpus consultation by learners, there is still considerable scope for developments, particularly in the area of course design and structure, concerning how one can successfully integrate corpus consultation into a programme of language study in higher education.

The publications on corpus consultation quoted in this study give varying amounts of information on the types of course structure within which they are operating, including the aims of their courses and the time allotted to them. But all this is presented as a given, understandably so, as the studies do not aim to investigate issues arising from course design and structure. The aim of this study is to examine a number of aspects of course design in corpora and language learning involving direct access by learners, focusing not on the training of corpus linguists but rather on the popularisation of corpus consultation by a wide spectrum of learners. After a brief overview of the types of courses which are described in the studies referred to above and other similar publications, one example will be examined in more detail, namely a section of a second-year undergraduate course on language and technology which aims to encourage the learners to use corpora as a resource in their language learning alongside other resources such as the dictionary, course book, and grammar. The course aims, structure, content, and assessment will be briefly described, paying particular attention to the training provided in concordancing and corpus analysis, the corpus resources used, the students' choice of an aspect of the language to be studied, the strategies which they require to benefit from the corpus consultation, their success or otherwise in analysing the results, and their evaluation of the activity. This will enable us to draw some conclusions concerning the factors which favour the integration of corpora and concordancing into the language-learning environment and the obstacles which remain to be surmounted.

COURSE DESIGN IN CORPORA AND LANGUAGE LEARNING

Within the disciplinary area of language studies, corpora and corpus-based methods are increasingly used outside language learning per se, in areas such as the teaching of literature (see, e.g., Kettemann, 1995; Louw, 1997) and of translation (see, e.g., Bowker, 1998; Zanettin, 2001). This section, however, will include only research concerning those wishing to learn about language either as linguistic researchers or language learners. Fligelstone (1993, p. 98) proposes what he terms a simple framework for assessing "the factors relevant to good teaching practice," grouping corpus-related activities into three categories:

TEACHING ABOUT (i.e., teaching about corpora/corpus linguistics)

TEACHING TO EXPLOIT (i.e., teaching students to exploit corpus data)

EXPLOITING TO TEACH (i.e., exploiting corpus resources in order to teach)

Even from reading only the small selection of studies of direct corpus consultation by learners referred to above, it is clear that there is considerable variation in the nature of the courses on which they are based, ranging from courses clearly designed as part of a programme of study in linguistics, to a limited amount of training included in a language course so that the learners can benefit from consulting a corpus. Davies (2000), for example, uses corpora of historical and dialectal texts when teaching an advanced course in Spanish linguistics. Similarly, the description of Paul Thompson's (2004) postgraduate module in corpora in applied linguistics in the University of Reading clearly situates it within the discipline of corpus linguistics. At the other end of the scale, in the sense not of being inferior but of having very different aims and therefore content, certain courses, mostly at undergraduate level, include a very limited amount of training in corpus consultation with the practical aim of enabling the learners to consult corpora to improve their language skills. A comparison of one such course, part of a second-year undergraduate module at the University of Limerick, and the Reading postgraduate course, reveals both the similarities and differences between them (see Table 1).

Table 1. General and Specialised Courses

	Undergraduate Year 2	Postgraduate
Course	Part of course/ Core	Complete course/ Specialist option
Hours	9	20
Corpus resources	Small	Small + large
Corpus creation	No	Yes
Corpus analysis	Yes	Yes
Tagging	No	Yes
Assessment	3,000-word essay	3/4,000-word essay

While both courses include lectures on corpus linguistics and on the analysis of corpora, alongside practical laboratory sessions, the postgraduate course is a specialist option embedded within the already specialised context of masters programmes in Applied Linguistics and ELT. It is allotted time to allow for greater depth of study and familiarisation with the tagging of corpora, while the core undergraduate teaching is, as we shall see, part of a second-year module and is obliged to make room for other aspects of technology and language study, also considered as core elements of the degree programme. It is this situation which creates the challenge of popularising corpus consultation, informing students of its potential benefits and giving them the skills to benefit from it in a very limited amount of time, as well as providing access to resources for future use and guidelines on how best to benefit from them.

Before examining the undergraduate course in more detail, it is important to note that the publications relating to corpus consultation by learners do not all fit neatly into the two types of course described in Table 1, or into one of Fligelstone's three categories. Several other studies contain elements of both the postgraduate and undergraduate courses, supporting Fligelstone's (1993, p. 98) comment that there is a certain amount of interaction between his three categories. Aston (1997, p. 61), for example, notes that the analysis of small corpora for language-learning purposes can serve as a useful starting point for students who may later wish to move on to the analysis of larger corpora in a research context. Dodd (1997), referring to the use of unedited corpus data with advanced students at undergraduate and postgraduate level, comments, At this level, several teaching aims are likely to coincide. These include improving the practical proficiency of the learner, improving the learner's formal knowledge about the language (and about language in general), and giving the student an insight into the work of the descriptive grammarian. (p. 132)

In another context, Cheng et al. (2003) are able to devote a much more substantial amount of classroom and laboratory contact hours over two semesters to corpus design and analysis than their Limerick counterparts. Corpora and concordancing are taught by them as a substantial part of second-year undergraduate courses on Information Technology and Discourse Analysis, within an English language major undergraduate programme. Their aims include both research in corpus linguistics and the practical benefits of language learning, firstly, placing the students "in the role of language researchers finding out for themselves about the English language" (p. 178), and secondly, at the same time encouraging them "to reflect on their experiences as language learners and English language majors from this form of data-driven learning" (p. 178). The much greater amount of time available to them enables them to introduce the students to work with larger corpora and to move further into the study of corpus linguistics as a discipline than the shorter undergraduate course. In the context of popularising corpus consultation, however, the Limerick course is interesting by its very limitation, in that it can be seen as a component of a course which one could reasonably envisage being included in all undergraduate language degree programmes. Kennedy and Miceli (2001, 2002) are very possibly examples of other researchers working within similar parameters, in that there is no evidence in their publications that the degree programmes involved have a noticeable bias towards Information Technology or Discourse Analysis, as in the case of Cheng et al. Looking at the variety of course design and structure within the publications which study corpus consultation by learners, it seems clear, without in any way undermining the validity of Fligelstone's framework, that the range of courses or parts of courses devoted to direct access to corpora can be situated on a continuum rather than within a clearly defined category.

CORPUS CONSULTATION AT POPULARISATION LEVEL

While a limited amount of training in corpus consultation at undergraduate level may be the first step in a career as a corpus linguist, it seems reasonable to assume that the majority of those undertaking such a course have at this stage no ambition to become experts in corpus linguistics, any more than they desire to become lexicographers when using the dictionary or materials designers when learning from a course book. Their interest is thus most likely to be aroused if they perceive the activity as being of benefit to their language learning. Thus, while a small number of graduates of the Limerick course are active in research involving corpus-based methods, the main aim of the course is to encourage all students to consult corpora as part of their language learning.

Corpora and concordancing are included in a second-year module on language and technology, which aims to introduce students to the major pedagogical, professional and research applications of technology in modern languages and to enable them to integrate these into their studies. Corpora and concordancing is one of four components, each of which is taught for 3 weeks, with one lecture and a 2-hour session in a computer laboratory. For the module assessment students submit two 3000-word essays, selecting any two of the areas covered. While there is some variation in the students' choice of topics from year to year, the essays are more or less equally divided between the four areas, namely introduction to technology and language learning, WELL (Web-enhanced language learning) evaluation and personalisation of language technologies, corpora and concordancing, and machine translation. The students taking the module come from a variety of different courses. Most are following either the BA in Applied Languages or the BA in Applied Languages with Computing in which it is a core module; some take it as an optional module on the BA in Languages and Cultural Studies; others are exchange students, mostly from France, Germany, Romania, and Spain. All of these students are studying at least one language to degree level, some are studying two, and a number are studying three, including English, French, German, Irish, and Spanish. This brings together a relatively diverse community of university language learners in the module, making it a suitable terrain for an evaluation of the potential for popularising corpus consultation.

The lectures on corpora and concordancing include an introduction to corpus linguistics and an account of the types of research based on corpora, focusing in particular on the use of corpora in language learning. In the laboratory sessions, using Wordsmith Tools (Scott, 1999), students receive training in the use of the software and guidance on corpus consultation and analysis. Within the general aim of the module to encourage students to integrate technology into their studies, the classes on corpora and concordancing are intended to show how corpora can be used a resource for language learning alongside their more traditional counterparts, the course book, grammar, and dictionary. It is emphasised that corpora can complement these resources, and, as we shall see, the students particularly appreciate the access to a large number of examples, and to language use which one describes as "authentic, up to date, and relevant." The laboratory sessions also provide guidance on the use of the corpora for problem-solving activities, and students are encouraged to bring examples of their written work to the classes and to try to improve them through corpus consultation. They are given advice on the selection of appropriate search words, for example the choice of a noun as a search word in order to find what verbs accompany it. (For a more detailed analysis of the strategies used by students in corpus consultation and the type of guidance provided by the teacher, see Chambers & O'Sullivan, 2004, and Kennedy & Miceli, 2001.)

The fact that five languages are involved makes the choice of the corpora used for training purposes a difficult one. After experimenting with a number of options, it was decided to create what we call "training corpora" in the five languages involved. Version 1 of these corpora includes for each language a journalistic corpus of 100,000 words and a corpus of academic writing of 50,000 words (published research articles and parts of masters and doctoral theses). In 2003 only the journalistic corpora were available. Each contained articles on a wide variety of topics, including current affairs, editorials, reviews, and sport, collected in 2002-2003 from two newspapers, in the case of French, for example, Le Monde and L'Humanité, and in the case of English, The Irish Times and The Independent (the Irish newspaper of that name). While the limited size was determined largely by time and resources, and while it is intended to expand the size for future cohorts, it is interesting to note that certain other researchers with experience of using corpora with undergraduate learners also choose to use very small training corpora. Kennedy and Miceli (2001, p. 79), for example, created sub-corpora of 50,000 words from their corpus of approximately 570,000 words for initial training in corpus analysis, and Gavioli (2001, p. 108) comments that 50,000 words is a lot for a learner. Dodd's (1997, p. 131) comment that "a modest corpus of a million or so words is certainly enough to make a valuable teaching aid" may well provide some common ground between those aware of the difficulties experienced by undergraduate students analysing a corpus for the first time, and the champions of large corpus concordancing such as Bernardini (2000, 2002).

Large corpora clearly provide superior resources for the study of language, providing many examples of a much larger proportion of the words in a language than their smaller counterparts. They do, however, present a number of disadvantages for beginners with limited time available for training, in particular long waiting times for searches for common words. In addition, the need to cope with examples from several sub-corpora in different genres would further complicate what is already a challenging task for the learners. In the particular context of this course, providing training in five languages using large corpora, all different in size, content, and means of access, would clearly be impossible. As we have seen, however, researchers working in one language only also show a strong preference for using small corpora for initial training, suggesting that their experience of the reality of using corpora in the classroom or computer laboratory has led them to the conclusion that using small corpora is most likely to succeed. It is also interesting to note that the exceptions to this, namely Bernardini (2000) and Cheng et al. (2003), are working in more specialised contexts at undergraduate level (translation, and information technology and discourse analysis, respectively) and have more time available for training over a much longer period. This is not to suggest that the learners in this and similar studies should be limited to using small corpora throughout their degree programmes and beyond. As we shall see, this study raises questions concerning the resources, support, and guidance provided as a follow-up to this type of introductory training.

The theoretical and pedagogical basis of this course is firmly situated within what Benson (2001) terms technology-based and teacher-based approaches to learner autonomy, favouring "independent interaction with educational technologies" and emphasising "the role of the teacher [...] in the practice of fostering autonomy among learners" (p. 111). Thus, although considerable guidance is given in the choice of the aspect of the language which they may wish to analyse for the assessed coursework, that choice is theirs. As the aim is to encourage them to see corpora as a resource in language learning alongside the course book, dictionary, and grammar, they were asked to choose a problem which they had encountered in their language work and to compare the usefulness of the corpus with what they could learn from a course book or grammar. In the lectures they were introduced to the concept of lexical grammar, and it was made clear that they could investigate not just traditional grammatical concepts, but common words where the corpus, despite its limited size, might reveal relevant lexico-grammatical patterns which students at this level might not master and where a grammar or course book are of little or no use.

A number of examples were given, including "la question" in French and "time" in English. None of the students chose this option, perhaps because it seemed easier to choose an aspect of the language which was clearly identified in the course book or grammar, or perhaps because, influenced by traditional language-teaching methods, it seemed more beneficial to them to identify traditional aspects of grammar which were problematical for them in their language work and to see what they could learn from the corpus. As we shall see, however, from their traditional grammatical starting points, they often made discoveries which were lexico-grammatical rather than solely grammatical in nature, thus benefiting from the corpus-based approach. The choices of the 14 students who submitted essays for this part of the course in 2003 were as follows:

Table 2. Essay Topics

Language	Essays	Topics
English	3	Verb + to + infinitive/Verb + gerund
		Since
		Come/phrasal verb
French	8	*En* (3)
		Pour
		Connaître/savoir
		Negation
		Celui/ceux/celle/celles
		Pronominal verbs
Irish	1	*Is*
Spanish	2	*Ser/estar*
		Hasta

Given the variety of languages and topics, it is not possible to give a detailed individual analysis of all 14 students' work within the limited scope of this study. The analysis will therefore be limited to comments on the success or otherwise of the students' analyses, with particular reference to the strategies they used and their evaluation of the activity. As it is interesting to observe the relationship between the students' analyses, strategies, and evaluation, a number of individual students' work will be used as starting points, with examples from others added subsequently to illustrate points common to many of the essays. It is important to note that there was very considerable variation in the amount of learning resulting from the corpus consultation. In one case, for example, a student did not reduce the 837 occurrences of the search word through random selection, and the analysis consisted solely of isolated comments on individual expressions which she noticed among the 837 results. In this case, poor corpus consultation and analysis skills were clearly an obstacle to the learning experience. This, however, was the exception rather than the rule, and the great majority of the students benefited from the activity. The cases examined in more detail below represent varying degrees of success. (Essays involving Irish and Spanish are not included here, as the author has no knowledge of these languages and had to rely on assistance from colleagues in assessing them.)

To examine how successful the students were in this activity, it is important to ask the question, What did they learn from the corpus? Clearly, given the limited size of the corpora, the concept of the language learner as researcher cannot be applied in any literal sense although, as we shall see, discovery learning is possible. In the lectures, following Dodd (1997, pp. 135-136), two possible methods of analysis were suggested: deductive and inductive. In the deductive method, which I presented as the easier of the two and the more appropriate for initial work on a small corpus, the grammar or the course book would be studied first, and the student would then apply the rules to the concordance results and compare the two resources. A student adopting the more demanding inductive approach would try to infer the rules from the concordance results, only attempting this if a large number of results was obtained. Of the 14 students, 9 chose the latter method, perhaps suggesting that they found the inductive approach more natural or more interesting when using corpus data. It is difficult to draw firm conclusions on this subject, however, as it is possible that they simply decided to present their results in this way. A clear example of how the inductive method was presented is found in the study of verb + to + infinitive and verb + gerund. Only 49 examples of the first were found, along with 41 of the second. The student inferred rules from these, which she[1] subsequently confirmed in the grammar of her choice, commenting that the grammar included far fewer examples. She noted that only one area covered in the grammar did not appear at all in her concordance, namely the use of go + gerund to describe a recreational activity, for example to go fishing, boating, birdwatching, and so forth. She did, however, discover «to go missing» in the corpus, which was not covered in the grammar, illustrating the role of the corpus as a source of serendipitous discoveries, as noted by Johns (1988, p. 21) and Bernardini (2000, p. 225). This led her to reflect on why the corpus did not include examples of go + gerund to refer to recreational activities, which she attributed not to its limited size but to its nature, concluding that it was a better resource for «formal language use» than for what she termed «everyday language,» recommending the addition of magazine articles to remedy this. Her conclusion was similar to that of the majority of the students, namely that the grammar is useful for explaining rules and -- especially -- exceptions, but that the corpus complements it, giving a much larger number of up-to-date examples that are easier to remember, and sometimes giving information which is not found in the grammar.

A clear example of the deductive approach was found in the study of *connaître* and *savoir.* More interestingly, this student's essay also reveals how a learner can derive benefit from corpus consultation without realising the full potential of the activity. With careful use of the wildcard, the student found most of the 75 examples of all forms of the lemma *savoir*and of the

50 of *connaître.* Following a brief presentation of how this area, which was problematic for her, was covered in two grammars, she proceeded to analyse the concordance results. The analysis of the occurrences of *savoir* focuses on several of the colligational contexts in which it is used, including *savoir* as noun, *savoir que, savoir ce que, savoir* + infinitive, *savoir* + noun, *faire savoir, savoir si, savoir à quel point,* in all a much richer presentation than is found in the grammar. Expressions such as *à savoir, reste à savoir,*and *en savoir gré,* which are found in the corpus, remain unexplored by the student, as does the use of the conditional tense, where the meaning changes from *savoir* in the sense of "to possess knowledge" and is used as a modal, as in the examples below.

de dollars sur dix ans. Ce plan	*ne sau-rait*	*cependant s'apparenter à un quelconque*
la brutalité qui éviscère et méprise	*ne sau-raient*	*en être absentes. Les petits marins*
au creux du crâne ! Bobby Lapointe	*ne sau-rait*	*être absent d'un tel répertoire,*
avec une drôle de langueur. On	*ne sau-rait,*	*pour vous mettre en bouche, citer tous*
les joies de la libre entreprise	*ne sau-raient*	*dissimuler l'absence de com-passion*

The analysis of *connaître* provides another example of how a student can benefit from corpus consultation while not realising the full potential of the activity for discovery learning. While most of the 50 results confirm the explanation in the grammars that *connaître* is used in the sense of being acquainted with something or some one, in 9 the subject is not a person, and the sense is rather to experience, as in the examples below.

Véritable foire aux idées, il a	*connu,*	*depuis sa création, en 2001, un succès*
mondiaux, à Davos, le Forum social	*con-naîtra*	*un temps fort particulier: le*
salaire moyen est de 30 cents. Le pays	*con-naît*	*à nouveau la sécheresse, après deux ans*
ce n'est pas l'unique cause. Le pays	*con-naît*	*une sécheresse très impor-tante, une des*

Champagne-Ardennes et l'Île-de-France ont	*connu*	*un véritable enfer, qui a provoqué*
guérilla, et le Kosovo pourrait	*con-naître*	*une dangereuse radicalisa-tion. Il est*
montre la voie. La capitale toscane a	*connu*	*durant cinq jours un événement qui*
des " sages " n'a visiblement pas	*connu*	*un grand succès auprès des technocrates*
SPORTS Affaires : le foot fran-çais ne	*con-naît*	*pas de trêve Football. Fer-nandez*

This use of *connaître,* which would be very appropriate in student essays in French, received no comment. The expression "*on connaît la chanson,*" which has nothing to do with singing but rather has the sense of "the same old story" also remained unexplored. Despite this, the student fulfilled her objective of using this exercise to solve her difficulty in distinguishing between the uses of these two verbs, particularly appreciating the example of both in one concordance line: "*les gens qui me connaissent savent que ma joie est tout intérieure.*" She concluded that the best problem-solving strategy for her consisted of an initial consultation of a grammar followed by a study of the much greater variety of examples of actual language use in the corpus, well illustrated in this case by her analysis of the occurrences of *savoir.* Although this essay reveals limited corpus consultation skills, it is interesting in the context of popularising corpus consultation in that the student still benefits from the activity, just as learners with limited dictionary skills still find solutions in the dictionary to some of the problems they encounter.

To complete the individual case-studies, it is interesting to compare the three essays on the preposition *en* in French, good examples of Kennedy and Miceli›s comment on «the fatal lure of prepositions» (2001, p. 83) and also good illustrations of the students› independence of mind and autonomy in choosing to ignore the lecturer›s advice to avoid selecting very common words such as this as search words. These students will be referred to as Students 1, 2, and 3. Student 1, deciding to analyse about 130 of the 1,530 occurrences, randomly selected 240, as she wished to remove the «obvious patterns» which she had observed during an initial trawl of all the results, namely *en* + year/season/month, *en* + country/continent/province, *en* + gerund, and *en* + number. Having eliminated these, she then concentrated her analysis on the remaining 136 occurrences. She observed that, in addition to the grammatical functions listed in the grammar book and dictionary which she consulted, the concordance revealed examples of expressions such as *la mise en* + noun,*en tout* + noun, and *en plein* + noun, information which, she noted, was not referred to in any structured way in either the dictionary or the grammar. The concordance results then aroused her interest in phrasal verbs, so she returned to the 1,530 occurrences, sorted them alphabetically, and studied the 91 phrasal verbs which this revealed. *S›en sortir, s›en prendre, s›en tenir,* and *s›en aller* proved to be the most common, none of which was given in the dictionary or grammar, although both gave examples of seven phrasal verbs with*en,* all of which were present in the corpus with the exception of *s›en ficher.* Like her colleague who had studied English verbs, she reflected that *s›en ficher* was understandably absent from this corpus, as the verb is "reserved for the spoken language." Despite such a successful journey of discovery in the corpus, she noted in what was generally a very positive conclusion that she found a number of aspects of the whole activity tedious, tiring, and laborious, in particular counting frequencies, deleting what she considered irrelevant concordances such as Aix-en-Provence, and reading from a screen.

Student 2 analysed a random sample of 300 occurrences of *en.* She began by analysing the use of *en* + gerund, noting that it would have been interesting if it had been possible to compare the use of the gerund with and without *en.* (This is possible albeit a little laborious.) Concluding the analysis of *en* + gerund, she observed, "While this aspect of grammar can be covered quite successfully without concordancing, the use of the software can certainly help cement in the learner›s mind that which has already been covered.» This student also noted the presence of phrasal verbs with *en,* but chose not to explore that discovery. She emphasised rather that the concordance results not only provided more examples than the grammar book, they acted as a sort of extension of it, in that, for example, while the grammar covered simple expressions of time such as *en quatre semaines,* the concordance also included related expressions such as *en l›espace de quatre semaines.* The discovery of phrases such as *mettre en* + noun and *la mise en* + noun was highlighted by the student as "one of the most interesting discoveries made from this concordance." Indeed, this may suggest that the students were right to ignore the lecturer's advice concerning prepositions, as it would be hard to discover these phrases unless one knew in advance that they existed or was given the search words by the teacher. This student was particularly proud to discover several examples of a category not covered in the grammar book, namely *en* meaning "as" in the sense of "in the role of": "*Cécile Brune, en amante anglaise*;" "*Anne Kessler, en beauté chlorotique.*" Finally, the student noted that *en* is used as a preposition in a large number of adverbial and prepositional expressions, while the grammar gives only seven examples. As the student noted, "By quite a great deal this is the area in which the concordancer has proven itself to be the most useful, easily surpassing how the topic is dealt with in the selected grammar.» This student›s conclusion is extremely positive, with the corpus and concordancer clearly appreciated as a much richer learning environment than the grammar.

The third student who analysed *en,* also selecting 300 occurrences for analysis, found the experience much less worthwhile and stimulating, and it is important to note that differences in level of linguistic or analytical skills cannot provide the explanation for this. While Student 2 found the examples of *en* + gerund a useful complement to the examples in the grammar, Student 3 preferred the "very basic and easy to understand" examples in the grammar (all three students used the same grammar). Interestingly, this was the only student in the group who found the truncated concordance lines frustrating: "I did not find the concordance helpful in establishing these rules as the full context is not given." The generally very competent level of her corpus consultation skills suggests that she was aware of the possibility of accessing the full text in each case, but understandably did not consider this a realistic activity to undertake for each and every example. Only in the case of the adverbial and prepositional expressions and phrases did Student 3 accept the superiority of the concordance, as it provided many more than the seven examples in the grammar. Her conclusion, like that of most students, is that the combination of grammar and concordance is the ideal method, but, exceptionally in this case, that view is expressed in an almost grudging manner:

I have concluded that the latter [the grammar] proved far more suitable in helping me to understand this point of grammar. I did although obtain a great deal of useful expressions that I know are up to date and widely used by native speakers from the concordance list.

The considerable variations in three learners› reactions to the very same activity cannot be analysed in any greater detail here, as no detailed information is available on their motivation or learning styles. The negative reaction of Student 3, however, is interesting in that it may suggest that not all learners will experience the interest and exhilaration which is evident in the reactions of many learners to the discoveries they make from corpus consultation.

The five brief case studies exemplify the main features of the 11 essays analysed here. In relation to the success or otherwise of the attempts at corpus analysis and the strategies used, there was a considerable amount of variation in the students› ability to explore the corpus to see what, if anything, it could add to the presentation in the course book or grammar, ranging from complete mastery and enjoyment of the exploratory nature of the activity, to a mechanical analysis of the results which added little to the student›s knowledge of the language, at times missing points which seem worth commenting on. Basic command of the software did not seem to be at issue in the great majority of cases, although some obvious strategies were missed. *S'**, for example, was not used in the study of pronominal verbs, although using *se* still provided a considerable amount of data for analysis. In general, however, all these students showed the ability to use Wordsmith Tools (Scott, 1999) sufficiently well to derive some benefit from their analysis of the results. It would seem rather that differences in motivation or learning styles may explain the considerable variation in the success of the activity. In addition to the variation in analytical ability, there was also considerable variation in the students' ability to reflect on the nature and limitations of the corpus, an ability which came easily to some students, but was totally lacking in others.

STUDENT EVALUATION

The students' evaluation of the activity in the final section of their essays reveals several clearly recurring patterns. Unlike Widdowson (2000, p. 7), these students do not call into question the authenticity of the concordance results, despite a brief reference by the lecturer to this view. As one student wrote, "the French used in these articles is authentic, up to date, and relevant." The word "real" is also used to describe the corpus, in contrast to the invented examples in course books and grammars, which are described by one student as "unreal and sometimes stupid." The up-to-date nature of the contents, relating to news from just a few months previously, was appreciated by many students. For a number of them, this authenticity and familiarity made for what one termed "easy memorizing." However, while most were happy to accept the limited size of the corpus for their first attempt at corpus consultation, a few queried the choice of texts, revealing a preference for "simple colloquial language out of magazines or novels." The rich learning environment created by a large number of examples was also appreciated, in contrast to the limited number of examples given in course books, dictionaries, and grammars. As one student wrote, "The sheer amount of entries given by the software was impressive, and it made learning about the choice made [demonstrative pronouns in French] much quicker and easier when there were numerous examples to look at."

The positive features of discovery learning are mentioned by a number of the students. As one Erasmus student wrote: "Working out lexical or grammatical patterns on his or her own may help the learner to memorise problematic aspects better than it would be the case when 'spoonfed' with rules." Furthermore, although the term is not used, a sense of empowerment is evident in some of the positive evaluations. As Student 2 concluded, "I discovered that achieving results from my concordance was a highly motivating and enriching experience. I've never encountered such an experience from a textbook." These positive reactions suggest that corpora and concordancing certainly have their place in a language-learning environment focusing on learner autonomy and discovery learning.

Even where students' overall reactions were positive, however, they did not hesitate to express strongly worded views on the disadvantages. Firstly, none saw the corpus and concordancer as replacing the grammar book or course book. Indeed there was a general consensus in their conclusions that the grammar still had its place, with two students concluding strongly in its favour. As one expressed it, "old friends are still best." A third, who studied "since" in English, while greatly appreciating the corpus consultation, remained faithful to the grammar book as the ultimate authority, innocently destroying the whole edifice of descriptive corpus linguistics: "Besides, a grammar book can confirmed [sic] to us if the grammar structures employed in a text are really right or if there is a mistake." Secondly, the limitations of the small corpus were noted by a number of students, in the case of phrasal verbs with "come" for example, although as a result of the choice of very common words, few students made this criticism. It will possibly be solved in this course in the near future, if the size of the corpora and the variety of the texts increases. It will be interesting to see, however, if this influences in any way the third criticism, namely the students' perception of the analysis of the results as tedious, time-consuming, and laborious. It is possible that a larger resource will encourage them to choose less commonly occurring terms, in particular to avoid prepositions, but the task of classifying and counting will still have to be undertaken.

It is difficult to reach a firm conclusion here, however, as prepositions are a common source of problems for learners in a number of languages, English and French for example. Fourthly, several students included in their section on disadvantages, comments on the need for training and appropriate analytical skills, showing uncertainty as to whether or not they had reached a sufficient level. As one student (one of the negative conclusions) noted, "In order to really derive any benefit from the use of corpora and concordancing, one would need quite intensive training and much practice." Fifthly, a number of students mentioned in their section on the disadvantages that the benefits of direct corpus consultation were limited to advanced students, and would be of no use to beginners because of their lack of comprehension of the text surrounding the search word. (This limitation could, of course, be solved by creating an appropriate corpus.) Finally, the lack of availability of corpora was cited by several students as a disadvantage. As they had been provided with an extensive list of available corpora in several languages, with easily accessible links through the module Web page, this perceived disadvantage raises important questions which go beyond the issue of course design and lead us to ask what learning environment is necessary for learners if corpus consultation is to be integrated into their language learning. This issue will be dealt with in the following section.

SUGGESTIONS FOR FURTHER RESEARCH

Although the earliest attested use of corpora in the language classroom was as early as 1969, according to McEnery and Wilson (1997, p. 12) who refer to Peter Roe's use of it in Aston University, Birmingham, research focusing on the extent to which learners actually benefit from corpus consultation and analysis is relatively recent. Chambers (2004) has identified 12 studies since the early 1990s, including four quantitative studies (Cobb, 1997; Gaskell & Cobb, 2004; Stevens, 1991; and Yoon & Hirvela, 2004) and nine[2] qualitative studies including the present article (Bernardini, 2000, 2002; Chambers & O›Sullivan, 2004; Cheng et al., 2003; Johns, 1997; Kennedy & Miceli, 2001, 2002;[3] Sun, 2003; Yoon & Hirvela, 2004). While French (Chambers & O›Sullivan, 2004) and Italian (Kennedy & Miceli, 2001, 2002) are included in these publications alongside the languages involved in the present study, the majority of the studies involve learners of English. Although the results of these experiments are largely positive, they raise a number of issues which point the way for future research. Firstly, they focus on the context of university education, understandably as they can all be classed as action research, with the students of the researchers forming the subjects of the experiment, as in this article. There is thus a need for studies involving other sectors of education, possibly in the form of concordances prepared by the teacher rather than direct access.

Secondly, they mainly use written corpora as a resource, leaving scope for investigations of the use of spoken corpora. Braun (in press) describes an initiative in which an extract from a spoken corpus is used as the basis for a language class, with concordances of specific items which are encountered providing additional examples. The learners› activities and reactions are not, however, included in her study.

Thirdly, the existing publications raise several issues which merit further study: for example, the benefit of direct consultation of corpora by learners as opposed to consultation of concordances provided by teachers; the learner strategies used in corpus consultation and analysis, and the teacher›s role in providing guidance; the role of corpus consultation in specific areas of second language acquisition such as the acquisition of vocabulary, grammar, and writing skills; and the role of the corpus alongside other resources. Although the existing studies involve a variety of research methods, including accounts of the activities undertaken by the learners and presentations of the results of their work with the corpora, learner evaluations of the activity, sometimes but not always questionnaire-based, observations by the researcher, trialling, and think-aloud protocol, there are few examples of each of these, and there is thus a need for more quantitative and qualitative studies. Finally, there is clearly scope for studies involving languages other than English, particularly now that corpora are available in several languages.

The increasing availability of vast corpora and their potential in language learning raises the fundamental issue of the ease with which learners can access these resources and benefit from them. There is as yet little evidence to suggest that the learners in the various studies cited here move on to regular corpus consultation in the course of their degree programme.

This situation suggests that classroom-based activity, which has so far provided the setting for all of the publications related to direct corpus consultation by language learners cited in this study, cannot on its own lead to any large-scale integration of corpus consultation into language studies. In addition to this, the student evaluations quoted above suggest that they do not easily make the transition from an initial training course, however much they appreciate it and benefit from it, to regular corpus consultation using the large Web-based corpora which are available. University language resource centres or the writing centres common in universities in the United States of America may provide a solution here, as they can serve as repositories of resources suitable for learners, and also as providers of learner training and guidance. This is not to say that each individual centre should have to create its own resources. Learners› needs are sufficiently similar in many universities for shared resources to be appropriate. And it is possible that the most appropriate resources for all but the most proficient students in corpus consultation and analysis will not be the huge corpora of hundreds of millions of words which have been created for research purposes, but of corpora created for learners, such as BNC Baby to give one example (Burnard, 2004). This four million word corpus, extracted from the British National Corpus and consisting of one million words each of written academic and journalistic English, fiction and spoken English, is part of a project involving the Oxford Text Archive and the Open University in the UK. Similarly, one-million word corpora of written academic and journalistic French are currently being created at the University of Limerick, and will be deposited with the Oxford Text Archive, the journalistic corpus in May 2005 and the academic corpus in 2006. If resources such as these and other relevant corpora were replicated in other languages, learners could benefit from accessing them independently and using them alongside the traditional resources of dictionary, course book, and grammar. Centres providing resources and guidance, which are at least as important as the classroom in a language-learning environment which aims to promote learner autonomy, could then become the focus for future research projects involving corpus consultation by learners.

CONCLUSION

The example of this course, together with the evidence from several other publications on related topics cited in this study, suggests that corpus consultation as a language-learning activity has many positive features, particularly in a language-learning environment which favours learner autonomy and discovery learning. It is, however, the disadvantages noted by these learners which are of particular interest here, as they provide a list of problems to be solved. Issues relating to the size and nature of the corpus are no doubt the easiest to remedy, although a delicate balancing act is required to ensure that the size of the corpus used for initial training does not unduly increase what they already perceive as the laborious and tedious analytical work, even when only a randomly selected concordance of about 150 occurrences is involved.

An increased allocation of time for training could provide the answer, although probably not within the context of most language degree programmes, where the curriculum is already under pressure from the competing disciplines of literature, cultural studies, area studies, linguistics, and language learning per se. Finally, as we have seen in the previous section, corpora and concordancing is an area where the whole language-learning environment has a role to play, not just the classroom but also facilities for independent and collaborative learning, and where there is thus ample scope for further research and development.

NOTES

1. As only one of the students was male, all students are referred to as «she» to preserve their anonymity.
2. Yoon and Hirvela›s analysis, being both quantitative and qualitative, is included in both categories.
3. Two reports based on different aspects of the same study.

ACKNOWLEDGMENTS

I am indebted to my colleague Íde O›Sullivan for creating the French corpus used here, for providing the laboratory-based training in corpus consultation and analysis to the students, and for co-ordinating the creation of the other corpora. I am also grateful to my colleagues Núria Borrull, Jean Conacher, Fiona Farr, Mairead Moriarty, and Seosamh MacMuirí for their work on the corpora in English, Irish, German, and Spanish. Finally I would like to thank the editors and reviewers for their constructive comments on an earlier version of this article.

ABOUT THE AUTHOR

Angela Chambers is professor of applied languages and director of the Centre for Applied Language Studies in the University of Limerick, Ireland. She has co-edited two books on computer assisted language learning. Her current research focuses on the role of corpora in language learning.

E-mail: Angela.Chambers@ul.ie

REFERENCES

1. Aston, G. (1997). Small and large corpora in language learning. In B. Lewandowska-Tomaszczyk & J. P. Melia (Eds.), *Practical applications in language corpora* (pp. 51-62). Lodz, Poland: Lodz University Press.
2. Benson, P. (2001). *Teaching and researching autonomy in language learning.* London: Longman.
3. Bernardini, S. (2000). Systematising serendipity: Proposals for concordancing large corpora with language learners. In L. Burnard & T. McEnery (Eds.), *Rethinking language pedagogy from a corpus perspective* (pp. 225-234). Frankfurt: Peter Lang.
4. Bernardini, S. (2002). Exploring new directions for discovery learning. In B. Kettemann & G. Marko (Eds.), *Teaching and learning by doing corpus analysis* (pp. 165-182). New York: The Edwin Mellen Press.
5. Bowker, L. (1998). Using specialised monolingual native-language corpora as a translation resource: A pilot study. *Meta, 43*(4), 631-651. Retrieved December 9, 2004, fromhttp://www.erudit.org/revue/meta/1998/v43/n4/002134ar.pdf
6. Braun, S. (in press). From pedagogically relevant corpora to authentic language learning contents. *ReCALL, 17*(1), 47-64.
7. Burnard, L. (Ed.). (2004). *BNC Baby* [CD-Rom]. Oxford, England: Research and Technology Service, Oxford University. Available at http://www.natcorp.ox.ac.uk/babyinfo.html
8. Burnard, L., & McEnery, T. (Eds.). (2000). *Rethinking language pedagogy from a corpus perspective: Papers from the Third International Conference on Teaching and Language Corpora.* Frankfurt: Peter Lang.
9. Chambers, A. (2004). Popularising corpus consultation among language learners and teachers. Paper presented at TALC (Teaching and Language

Corpora) conference, University of Granada.

10. Chambers, A. & O'Sullivan, Í. (2004). Corpus consultation and advanced learners' writing skills in French. *ReCALL, 16*(1), 158-172.
11. Cheng, W., Warren, M., & Xun-feng, X. (2003). The language learner as language researcher: Putting corpus linguistics on the timetable. *System, 31*(2), 173-186.
12. Cobb, T. (1997). Is there any measurable learning from hands on concordancing? *System 25*(3), 301-315.
13. Davies, M. (2000). Using multi-million word corpora of historical and dialectal Spanish texts to teach advanced courses in Spanish linguistics. In L. Burnard & T. McEnery (Eds.),*Rethinking language pedagogy from a corpus perspective* (pp. 173-185). Frankfurt: Peter Lang.
14. Dodd, B. (1997). Exploiting a corpus of written German for advanced language learning. In A. Wichmann, S. Fligelstone, T. McEnery, & G. Knowles (Eds.), *Teaching and language corpora* (pp. 131-145). London: Longman.
15. Fligelstone, S. (1993). Some reflections on the question of teaching, from a corpus linguistics perspective. *ICAME, 17*, 97-109.
16. Gaskell, D., & Cobb, T. (2004). Can learners use concordance feedback for writing errors. *System 32*(3), 301-319.
17. Gavioli, L. (2001). The learner as researcher: Introducing corpus concordancing in the classroom. In G. Aston (Ed.), *Learning with corpora* (pp. 108-137). Houston, TX: Athelstan.
18. Johns, T. (1986). Micro-concord: A language learner›s research tool. *System, 14*(2), 151-162.
19. Johns, T. (1988). Whence and whither classroom concordancing. In T. Bongaerts, P. De Haan, S. Lobbe, & H. Wekker (Eds.), *Computer applications in language learning* (pp. 9-27). Dordrecht, The Netherlands: Foris.
20. Johns, T. (1997). Contexts: The background, development, and trialling of a concordance-based CALL program. In A. Wichmann, S. Fligelstone, T. McEnery, & G. Knowles (Eds.),*Teaching and language corpora* (pp. 100-115). London: Longman.
21. Kennedy, C., & Miceli, T. (2001). An evaluation of intermediate students› approaches to corpus investigation. *Language Learning & Technology, 5*(3), 77-90. Retrieved December 9, 2004, from http://llt.msu.edu/vol5num3/kennedy/
22. Kennedy, C., & Miceli, T. (2002). The CWIC project: Developing and

using a corpus for intermediate Italian students. In B. Kettemann & G. Marko (Eds.), *Teaching and learning by doing corpus analysis* (pp. 183-192). New York: The Edwin Mellen Press.

23. Kettemann, B. (1995). Concordancing in stylistics teaching. In W. Grosser, J. Hogg, & K. Hubmeyer, (Eds.), *Style: Literary and non-literary. Contemporary trends in cultural stylistics* (pp. 307-318). New York: The Edwin Mellen Press.

24. Kettemann, B., & Marko, G. (Eds.). (2002). *Teaching and learning by doing corpus analysis.* Amsterdam; New York: Rodopi.

25. Louw, B. (1997). The role of corpora in critical literary appreciation. In A. Wichmann, S. Fligelstone, T. McEnery, & G. Knowles, (Eds.), *Teaching and language corpora* (pp. 240-251). London: Longman.

26. McEnery, T., & Wilson, A. (1997). Teaching and language corpora. *ReCALL, 9*(1), 5-14.

27. Roe, P. (2000). The ASTCOVEA German Grammar in conText Project. In B. Dodd (Ed.), *Working with German corpora* (pp. 199-216). Birmingham, England: University of Birmingham Press.

28. Scott, M. (1999). *Wordsmith Tools version 3.* Oxford, England: Oxford University Press.

29. Stevens, V. (1991). Concordance-based vocabulary exercises: A viable alternative to gap-fillers. In T. Johns & P. King (Eds.), *Classroom concordancing: English Language Research Journal 4* (pp. 47-63). Birmingham, England: Centre for English Language Studies, University of Birmingham.

30. Sun, Y-C. (2003). Learning process, strategies and Web-based concordancers: A case-study. *British Journal of Educational Technology, 34*(5), 601-613.

31. Thompson, P. (2004). The University of Reading master's program in applied linguistics [Web page]. Retrieved December 9, 2004, fromhttp://www.rdg.ac.uk/AcaDepts/cl/slals/maal.htm

32. Tribble, C., & Jones, G. (1990). *Concordances in the classroom: A resource book for teachers.* Harlow, England: Longman.

33. Widdowson, H. G. (2000). On the limitations of linguistics applied. *Applied Linguistics, 21*(1), 3-25.

34. Yoon, H., & Hirvela, A. (2004). ESL student attitudes towards corpus use in L2 writing. *Journal of Second Language Writing, 13,* 257-283.

35. Zanettin, F. (2001). Swimming in words: Corpora, translation, and language learning. In G. Aston (Ed.), *Learning with corpora* (pp. 177-197). Houston, TX: Athelstan.

Chapter 2

STRATEGY USE AND LANGUAGE PERFORMANCE BY SECOND LANGUAGE LEARNERS IN NIGERIA

Laz Chinedu Ogenyi

The Use of English Unit, School of General Studies, University of Nigeria, Nsukka, Nigeria

ABSTRACT

It is commonly believed that Nigerian students perform very poorly in the English language. Many reasons adduced to be the causative variables for students' poor performance in the English language are located away from the students themselves. What the above scenario portends is that no effort has been made to find out the strategies which the students themselves use in their efforts to learn the English language; it also implies that no effort has been made to find out the relationship between such strategies and the level of students' performance in the target language. The problem which this study addressed was not only to evaluate the language learning strategies which the sampled study population use in their efforts to learn English, but also to determine the extent to which their mean achievement scores in English depend on their use of various language learning strategies. The study was carried out using a descriptive survey research design. Its population consisted of Senior Secondary School (SSS) form II students in three states of south-east- ern Nigeria. Random sampling technique was used to select a total of one thousand, four hundred and one (1401: 747 = males, 654 = females) students used for the study. Two sets of instrument were used to collect data for the investigation: appraisal instrument (cloze test), and questionnaire. Two research questions and corresponding two null hypotheses were formulated to guide the study. Results of the study revealed that 1) the greatest proportion of the Igbo learners of English in SSS II (84.3%) made use of socio-affective language learning strategy, while cognitive strategy had the lowest proportion of users (50.9%); 2) there was a significant difference, in the English language performance, between the users and non-users of the various language learning strategies.

THEORETICAL BACKGROUND/INTRODUCTION

In the literature, different scholars use various terms to refer to the concept: learner strategies, learning strategies, and language learning strategies (http://iteslj.org/Articles/Lessard-Clouston-Strategy.html). These terms are used interchangeably in this work. Generally speaking, strategies are specific plans and methods of approaching a problem or task. Attempts to define learning strategies are situated in psychology, within the theories of cognition. In the context of language learning, researchers have defined language learning strategies as the thoughts and actions of learners who are attempting to increase their learning comprehension, and retention (Rivera-Mills & Plonsky, 2007: p. 1) . Nunan has posited that language learning strategies are the mental and communicative procedures learners use in order to learn and use a language (171). Lessard-Clouston explains language learning strategies as "specific actions, behaviour, steps, or techniques that students (often intentionally) use to improve their progress in developing second language skills" (12).

It is apparent from the foregoing that language learning strategies have to do with the input learners of a language make in order to comprehend, store, retrieve, process, and use linguistic data. Drawing from the above, I define language learning strategies as the goals, conscious and unconscious mental actions, language acquisition processes, skills, learning plans which second language learners adopt in their efforts to acquire and use their second language. Learner strategies are thus performance-related, application-specific, subject to different levels of achievements, and usually lead to language learning success. Experts such as Lessard-Clouston (1997) , Ellis (2005) , and Steinberg and Sciarini (2006) are in accord that successful language learners frequently use the following components of strategies: verification, inductive processing, deductive reasoning, practice, memorization, and monitoring.

Different researchers have sought different tags to classify learner strategies. The categorization seems to revolve from social, linguistic, creative, and meta-cognitive to affective, compensation and socio-affective strategies. Learner characteristics inherent in cognitive strategies, according to Otagburuagu quoting O'Malley and Chamot, include:

Repetition, resourcing, translation, grouping, deduction, recombination, imagery, auditory representation, key word, contextualization, elaboration, transfer, (and) inferencing (English as a Second Language, 108- 110). Meta-cognitive strategies involve functional planning, and thinking about production and comprehension. In addition, learners who use these strategies are said to be engaged in directed and selective attention, self-man- agement and monitoring, delayed production, note-taking and self-evaluation. Research by renowned figures in the field gave rise to a new group of learner strategies referred to as socio-affective strategies—those that take consideration issues such as co-operation, classroom interaction, question for clarification, and learning environment (Cohen 1; O'Malley & Chamot, cited in Otagburuagu (1999) English as a Second Language, 110; Rivera-Mills & Plonsky, 2007: pp. 1-2). Nunan's (1991) classification of language learning strategies followed a different slant from those of the other scholars before him. He matched each of the five categories of his learner strategies with macro and micro-skills, and in some cases gave examples of tasks. The five categories of Nunan's language learning strategies include:

Strategy Skills Involved

1) Cognitive—classification, predicting, inducing, taking notes, concept mapping, inferencing, discriminating, and diagramming;
2) Interpersonal—co-operating, and role-playing;
3) Linguistic—conversational patterns, practicing, using context, summarizing, selected listening, and skimming;
4) Affective—personalizing, self-evaluating, reflecting; and
5) Creative—brainstorming.

David Nunan qtd. in Otagburuagu, E. J. English as a Second Language: A Perceptual Approach. Owerri: Intercontinental Educational Books & Publishers, 1999, 111-114).

Two other features that make Nunan's language learning strategies distinctive are: firstly, his linguistic skills mean the same thing as language skills, because the characteristics of this type of LLS, and their tasks relate more to listening, speaking, reading, and writing. Secondly, brainstorming is given a special status by categorizing it as a creative strategy.

Oxford differentiates between direct and indirect strategies, which she sorts into six separate sets. Under the direct strategies, she lists:

Memory, which creates mental linkages, and assists in entering information into long-term memory, and retrieving same when needed for communication;

Cognitive, which is used for forming, analyzing, and revising internal mental models and for receiving and producing messages in the target language; and

Compensation strategy, which is employed for guessing; it is also needed to overcome any gaps in knowledge of the target language (http://iteslj.org/

Articles/Lessard-Clouston-strategy.httml). Under the indirect strategies, she classifies:

Meta-cognitive: This helps learners "execute control" through planning, arranging, focusing, and evaluating their learning;

Affective which is adopted when one wants to encourage one's self. It also enables learners to control feelings, motivations, and attitudes related to language learning. In the opinion of Macaro (2006) , affective strategy requires the knowledge of oneself as a learner through recurrent monitoring of one's learning (328); and

Social strategy constitutes Oxford's third type of indirect LLS. It facilitates interaction with others. Within social strategy is found such features as asking questions, co-operating and empathizing with others (Oxford, cited in Lessard-Clouston, 4).

It is therefore obvious that language learning strategies, especially when used by informed students, place students at the centre of the second language classroom enabling them to make pedagogically sound decisions concerning their own learning. One can rightly assert that language learning strategies are facilitative criteria for language learning, especially in second language situations. The general feeling of the majority of stakeholders in the education sector in Nigeria is that students' performances in both internal and external examinations are not only poor, but reprehensible. Osakwe (1998/99) corroborates this fact when she succinctly writes:

In recent time in Nigeria, it has been discovered that adolescents do not perform as well as they should in school… Several research findings have actually shown that students perform very poorly in English… In a research conducted by Prof Akere… of the University of Lagos, it was discovered that out of 195,840 students who sat for English in the West African Examinations Council's SSCE of a particular year, only 12,383 (6.3%) had a credit pass in the subject (138-139).

The general poor performance, in the researcher's thinking, implies that students are not competent in the English language. This view is informed by a commonly held belief that competence in the English language skills enhances students' good performance in English and other subjects. Reading, one of the four language skills, is regarded as a tool skill in the sense that a child's progress in other subjects depends substantially on his reading ability (cf. Nwosu-Izuwa, 2002; Ezeokoli, 2004; Ogenyi, 2008b). Osakwe (1998/99) cites Mohammed's study of Senior Secondary School Certificate Examination results of a five-year period where it was observed that there was an alarming close correlation between failure in English and failure in the other subjects. Mohammed was quoted to have observed that the correlation "seems to lend strong support that many failures in subjects are really failures in English" (Mohammed qtd. in Osakwe, 1998/99: p. 139).

The World Bank (1995) report, in addition to Osakwe's reason (1998/99) for students' poor performance, locates the following as the causative variables in the low level, in performance, of Nigerian students and graduates: inadequate financing, insufficient and irrelevant learning materials, including old and outdated equipment, books and journals, poorly trained and paid teaching staff, unplanned expansion of enrolment leading to over-supply of graduates, and irrelevant curriculum. Results of other studies point to the curriculum designers and implementers, policy makers, decay in the educational sector, incessant closure of universities, and strikes among others, as the causes of students' poor performance (Kolapo, 2008: p. 1; Akwanya, 2; Onukaogu, 2002: pp. 182-183; Otagburuagu (1997) , Teaching and Learning, 4).

What the above scenario portends is that the causative variables are located away from the students themselves. There has been no effort, as far as this researcher knows, to find out how the students themselves try to acquire the target language, English, and according to Firth and Wagner, one of the ways of approaching the study of second language acquisition is to understand how non-primary acquisition takes place (789). This calls attention to the language learning strategies (LLS) which the Nigerian students use in their endeavour to learn and use the English language in their second language environment. This is important because scholars in the field believe that learners who fail to do well in language learning have been known to adopt bad language learning strategies (Cohen, 1; Lessard-Clouston, 2; Nunan, 171; Rivera-Mills & Plonsky, 2007: pp. 3-4). There is paucity of research on the assessment of the strategies students of Igbo origin use in learning their second language (L2), and also on the relationship between such strategies and the level of the students' performance in the English language. Even though the World Bank (1995) study identified major areas of the decline in the university education, the real problem may have its roots at the Senior Secondary School level, especially when one considers such critical issues as transfer of training and learning. Based on this, it becomes reasonable for research efforts to be rigorously directed on this level of learners. The necessity of this is highlighted by the fact that it is at this level that the potential undergraduates are given adequate foundation in the use of English. In addition, an evaluation of learners' strategy repertoire is an important measure which will help both the teachers and learners to know the strategies that are useful and effective for particular language tasks, thereby increase the learners' learning potential, autonomy, and overall success.

Problem of the Study

The problem which this study addressed was not only to determine the percentage of the Igbo learners of English who were in SSS II in south-eastern Nigeria that made use of different language learning strategies; the study further ascertained the extent to which the mean achievement scores, in English, of Igbo learners of English in SSS II depended on their use of various language learning strategies.

The Study Design

The procedure that was adopted in this study is consistent with the features of survey research, which is defined as: "The method of collecting information by asking a set of pre-formulated questions in a predetermined sequence in a structured questionnaire to a sample of individuals drawn from a defined population so as to be representative of that population" (www.mori.com/rmu/glossary.shtml).

To guide the study, two research questions were designed as follows:

Research Question 1:

What proportion of the Igbo learners of the English language in Senior Secondary School II (SSS II) uses the various language learning strategies (LLS) in learning English as a second language?

Research Question 2:

To what extent do the mean achievement scores in the English of the Igbo learners of English in SSS II depend on their use of various language learning strategies?

Arising from the foregoing, and also to guide the investigation, the following null hypotheses were formulated:

Ho1: There is no significant difference between the proportion of the Igbo learners of English who use the various language learning strategies and those who do not use them.

Ho2: There in no significant difference between the mean achievement scores in the English language of the Igbo learners of English who use various language learning strategies and those who do not.

The Study Population and Sampling Procedure

The study population consisted of the same Senior Secondary School (SSS) form II students that the researcher used in an earlier published study. This study and that one were carried out simultaneously in three (3) out of the five

(5) States of south-eastern geopolitical Zone of Nigeria. The three States—Ebonyi, Enugu, and Imo—were purposively chosen. They were considered, as it were, true representatives of the two (2) old Igbo States— Anambra and Imo. Enugu and Imo States represented the old Anambra and old Imo States respectively; Ebonyi is an offshoot of communities drawn from both the old Anambra and old Imo States. There are similarities in the educational systems and attitudes towards education in these states. Typically, education is highly prized. High value is placed on effort, which is viewed as being directly linked to high education achievement (cf. Grant & Dweck, 2001; Woodrow, 2006).

Senior Secondary School form II (SSS II) students were considered appropriate for the study, because they were very close to "examination class": it was expected that the period of anticipation of moving to the final stage of secondary school examinations would predispose them to using more strategies, other things being equal.

Twelve (12) schools, four (4) each, were randomly sampled from the three selected States. Two of the sampled schools in each State were government owned and the other two privately owned. Two of such schools were also randomly sampled from both urban and rural areas of each of the chosen States.

The study used the proportionate stratified random sampling technique in sampling students from the above mentioned states and student cohort. However, the sampling technique was used only in schools where the population of the SSS II students was more than one hundred (100). All the SSS II students in schools where the students' population was less than one hundred were used; seven schools fell under this category. These criteria gave rise to a total of one thousand, four hundred and one (1401) students that were used for the study, comprising seven hundred and forty-seven (747) males and six hundred and fifty-four (654) females (Table A1). Their ages ranged between fifteen (15) and nineteen (19) years with an average of seventeen (17) years.

Research Instruments

Design of the Instruments

Two sets of instruments were used to collect the data for the investigation. One of the instruments was appraisal instrument which was in the form of cloze test. Cloze tests measure the readers' ability to decode "interrupted" or "mutilated" messages by making the most acceptable substitutions from all the contextual clues available. Decoding is a well known feature of proficient reading. The cloze test questions incorporated relevant topics in the Senior Secondary School II English language syllabus in the area of the study. In constructing the questions, I considered their objectivity, clarity, and suitability to the level of students. The questions tested the mean achievement scores of the sampled students on reading skill. The design was cognizance that there were some other language skills, but chose reading skill, because of all the language skills, reading can be regarded as a "tool skill", in the sense that a learner's progress in other language skills depends considerably on his ability to read. Reading and writing are higher order language skills, but the former occupies the most important position in language learning. Ezeokoli agrees with this point when he writes: "In spite of the multiple or elastic meaning of literacy, reading and writing remain basic literacy skills for acquiring other literacy skills; but perhaps reading stands out as the most basic (sic) tool for learning and human survival" (318). Reading experts describe the concept variously. In the opinion of Gwete, reading is "... the gateway to education..." (32); Onukaogu (2002) describes it as "the fulcrum of literacy" (292). Dike also avers that "... reading is not only the best but also the only way to master a language, whether it is a first or second language. Through wide reading, individuals build foundations for independent learning and gain awareness of the broad uses of reading for information and pleasure" (17).

It is therefore obvious that learners who cannot, and do not read will not get educated linguistically, because in addition to the facts fore stated, "Reading helps to keep the individual on a pedestal in which he vicariously enters the textual world of authors, and shares the diversity of experiences embodied in such works" (Ogenyi, 137). Increase in both the depth and breath of vocabulary knowledge needed for unambiguous oral and written expressions depends on reading. In addition to developing vocabulary, reading helps the reader/learner to make inferences, classify issues, observe situations, criticize matters, identify relationships, differentiate styles, draw conclusions, and make generalizations all of which are needed in effective learning and use of the English language in a second language environment. Based on the foregoing significant roles of reading over the other three language skills, it was considered a more appropriate skill for assessing the study subjects.

The cloze test instrument which was used for the study had the features of the structuralist, the integrative, and the communicative approaches to testing. One of the characteristics of the structuralist approach to testing is that "the skills of listening, speaking, reading, and writing are... separated from one another... because it is considered essential to test one thing at a time"(Heaton, 1988: p. 15) . Again, reliability forms an integral part of structuralist testing. Although integrative tests do not seek to separate language skills into neat divisions in order to improve test reliability, they "are best characterized by the use of cloze testing" (Heaton, 1988: p. 16) ; thus, lies their relevance in this study. Like the structuralist approach to testing, communicative tests do measure different language skills. The attempt to measure different language skills is based on a view of language referred to as "the divisibility hypothesis" (Heaton, 1988: p. 19) . It is further explained that communicative testing results in an attempt to obtain different profiles of learners' performance in the language, which also explains its usefulness in the present study. Communicative evaluation also emphasizes on test contents to be totally relevant for a particular group of testees. This criterion was met by the test items used in this study, since they were drawn from the Senior Secondary School form II English language syllabus.

The second instrument was questionnaire the contents of which elicited responses on the participants' use of the various language learning strategies (LLS) of Oxford and Burrystock's (2008) standardized Strategy Inventory for Language Learning (SILL) (http://homepage.wtuc.edu.tw/sill.php) which was used for the study. The questionnaire items addressed issues that boarder on cognitive, linguistic, meta-cognitive, affective, compensation, and socio-affective language learning strategies in that order. Self-reporting data on the use of these language learning strategies were collected from the sampled population used for the study. The use of questionnaire to elicit the participants' strategy use is validated by Macaro's assertion as follows:

The methodology for eliciting learner strategy use... is at an acceptable level of validity and reliability. Questionnaires... provide the broad picture... and effectively yield insights into skill-specific or task-spe- cific strategy use... The claims of effectiveness are made by both L2 researchers and by researchers operating in other fields related to cognitive processing (321).

ELICITATION TECHNIQUE

Both the elicitation task mode and elicitation task focus were used to gather data on the student's language performance ability. The task mode was reading. The subjects were required to read and answer (respond to) cloze test questions. The task focus was on both natural communication task and linguistic manipulation task. The natural communication task tested the participants' subconscious use of the grammar rules required to convey an idea or a message. The linguistic manipulation task was, on the other hand, used to focus the subjects' attention on performing conscious linguistic manipulation; i.e., to test the students' meta-linguistic awareness, or their conscious knowledge and manipulation of the rules and forms of the English language. The tasks (communicative & manipulative) were structured, since the researcher intended to ask specific questions in order to elicit target linguistic knowledge within a limited time span. It is important to note that the usage of these tasks is interrelated, as none is used in complete exclusion of the other.

Validation of the Research Instruments

Face and content validities of the appraisal instruments and the questionnaire were established. Practitioners knowledgeable in the field of second language learning examined, read, made suggestions and certified that the instruments were indeed appropriate and reflected their various intents.

Also, the use of SSS II English language syllabus for the data base of the appraisal items/questions added to the content validity. The questions were unambiguous, and this made them answerable in a dichotomous manner; that, too, contributed to the items' validity.

Administration of the Study Instruments

The administration of the research instruments on the study subjects took place towards the end of the schools' second term of 2008/2009 academic session. However, the time and dates of administration varied at different schools. On arrival at each school, I went to the Principle, introduced myself and my mission. Some of the school authorities demanded to go through the instruments before allowing their administration on their students.

The administration of the instruments took place during school period and under examination condition: I distributed the instruments, waited on the students to respond to the questionnaire and answer the cloze test questions, and collected the instruments after one hour, twenty minutes. This led to no loss of the instruments distributed. In some of the schools where I did not arrive on time, I had to wait for the students to finish the examination they had already begun to write before my arrival. The administration of the instruments lasted for four weeks.

Method of Data Analysis

As was done in the earlier published study that was executed at the same time with this one, the scores of the individuals on the various items were summed up for each sub-scale of the inventory. The means and standard deviations of the scores were computed for each sub-scale and used to analyse the data for the two research questions. A variety of statistical tools was used in testing the two corresponding null hypotheses at 0.05 levels of significance. Specifically, chi square test of significance was used to test hypothesis 1. A two-way analysis of variance (ANOVA) test was run to test the data that were generated for, and used in hypothesis 2.

Data Presentation and Interpretation

The results of the data that were collected are presented and interpreted hereunder:

Research Question 1:

What proportion of the Igbo learners of the English language in SSS II uses the various language learning strategies in learning English as a second language?

Table 1 shows that the order of decreasing use of the various language learning strategies is socio-affective, meta-cognitive, affective, linguistic, compensation and cognitive with their respective mean ratings (MRs) of 84.3, 79.8, 57.7, 57.5, 51.9 and 50.9. In other words, the greatest proportion of students (84.3) uses socio-affec- tive language learning strategy, while the least proportion (50.9) uses cognitive. The table indicates that four of the strategy types—cognitive, linguistic, affective, and compensation are averagely used with the mean ratings of 50.9%, 57.5%, 57.7% and 51.9% respectively.

Research Question 2:

To what extent do the mean achievement scores in English of the Igbo learners of English in SSS II depend on their use of the various language learning strategies?

Evidence in Table 2 shows that the mean achievement score for the students who use cognitive language learning strategy is 46.49, as against 30.81 for those who do not make use of the same strategy. For those who use linguistic language learning strategy, it is 45.62 against 29.56 for those who do not use it; for meta-cognitive, it is 39.10 for those who use it as against 37.55 for the non-users; for affective, it is 45.65 for those who use as against 29.41 for those who do not use it; for compensation, 45.11 for those who use as against 31.98 for those who do not use; and for socio-affective, it is 39.69 for those who use as against 33.95 for those who do not use it. In other words, there appears to be consistent difference between those who use and the students who do not make use of each of the various language learning strategies, suggesting that the mean achievement scores in English appear to be dependent on the use of each of the language learning strategies.

Ho1:

There is no significant difference between the proportion of the Igbo learners of English who use the various language learning strategies and those who do not use them.

As observed in Table 3, the number of users of:

1) Cognitive language learning strategy is 713 as against 688 for those

who do not use it. This represents 50.9% of the sampled population as shown in Table 1. The chi square in respect of this value which is 0.446 at 1 df. is not significant at 0.05 levels.

2) Linguistic language learning strategy is 805 for the users, as against the 596 for those who do not use it. This represents 57.5% of the study subjects as shown in Table 1. The chi square in respect of this value which is 31.18 at 1 df. is significant at 0.05 levels.

3) Meta-cognitive language learning strategy is 1118 for the users, as against 283 for those who do not use the strategy. This represents 79.8% of the study population as shown in Table 1 fore presented. The chi square in respect of this value which is 497.66 at 1 df. is significant at 0.05 levels.

4) Affective language learning strategy stands at 809 for the users against 592 for the non-users. This repre- sents 57.7% of the students as shown also in Table 1. The chi square in respect of this value which is 36.61 at 1 df. is significant at 0.05 levels.

5) Compensation language learning strategy is 727 for those who use the strategy as against 674 for those who do not use it. This represents 51.9% of the study sample as shown in Table 1. The chi square in respect of this value which is 2.01 at 1 df. is not significant at 0.05 levels.

6) Socio-affective language learning strategy is 1181 and 220 for those who use the learner strategy and those who do not use it respectively. This represents 84.3% of the students used for the study as shown in Table 1. The chi square in respect of this value which is 659.19 at 1 df. is significant at 0.05 levels.

From the foregoing, it is seen that for the compensation and cognitive language learning strategies, the difference between the proportion of the users and non-users, in each case, is not significant. In other words, the

Table 1. Proportion/percentage of Igbo learners of English who uses the various language learning strategies (LLS).

Types of LLS	Number of users	Percentage
Cognitive	713	50.9
Linguistic	805	57.5
Meta-cognitive	1118	79.8
Affective	809	57.7
Compensation	727	51.9
Socio-affective	1181	84.3

Table 2. Mean achievement scores of Igbo learners of English that use the various language learning strategies (by use/do not use of LLS).

		Mean achievement scores	
		Use	**Do not use**
Types of LLS	Cognitive	46.49	30.81
	Linguistic	45.62	29.56
	Meta-cognitive	39.10	37.55
	Affective	45.65	29.41
	Compensation	45.11	31.98
	Socio-affective	39.69	33.95

Table 3. Chi square test of the proportion of Igbo learners of the English language in SSS II that makes use of the various language learning strategies.

Types of LLS	Use/do not use	Observed	Expected	Chi square	Df	Sig.	Sig. @ 0.05 level
Cognitive	Use	713	700.50	0.446	1	0.504	Not Sig.
	Do not use	688	700.50				
Linguistic	Use	805	700.50	31.18	1	0.00	Sig.
	Do not use	596	700.50				
Meta-cognitive	Use	1118	700.50	497.66	1	0.00	Sig.
	Do not use	283	700.50				
Affective	Use	809	700.50	33.61	1	0.00	Sig.
	Do not use	592	700.50				
Compensation	Use	727	700.50	2.01	1	0.16	Not Sig.
	Do not use	674	700.50				
Socio-affective	Use	1181	700.50	659.19	1	0.00	Sig.
	Do not use	220	700.50				

difference between those who use and those who do not use both compensation and cognitive language learning strategies, as earlier observed in Table 1, is real difference which means that the difference is not attributable to chance error. This confirms the earlier observed results in Table 1where it was seen that the lowest proportion of students uses cognitive language learning strategy followed by compensation strategy. Similarly, in each of the other four language learning strategies—linguistic, meta-cognitive, affective, and socio-affective—the difference between those who use and those who do not use, as earlier observed, is significant. In other words, the difference is real and not attributable to chance error, nor arose by chance.

Ho2:

There is no significant difference between the mean achievement scores in the English language of the Igbo learners of English who use the various language learning strategies and those who do not.

ANOVA data in Table 4 show that the sum of squares between and within groups respectively of:

Table 4. ANOVA table of mean achievement scores by use/non-use of the various language learning strategies.

Types of LLS	Sources of variations	Sum of squares	Df	Mean square	Sig. of F	Sig. @ 0.05 level
Cognitive	Between groups within groups	85990.6022 599658.2814	1 1399	85990.6022 428.6335	0.00	Significant
Linguistic	Between groups within groups	88348.86065 97300.0230	1 1399	88348.8606 426.9478	0.00	Significant
Meta-cognitive	Between groups within groups	546.8134 685102.0702	1 1399	546.8134 489.7084	0.00	Significant
Affective	Between groups within groups	90117.2748 595531.6089	1 1399	90117.2748 425.6838	0.00	Significant
Compensation	Between groups within groups	60318.6811 625330.2026	1 1399	60318.6811 446.9837	0.00	Significant
Socio-affective	Between groups within groups	6100.7641 679548.1195	1 1399	6100.7641 485.7385	0.00	Significant

1) 85990.6022 (df. 1) and 599658.2814(df. 1399) in respect of the difference in mean achievement scores of the students who use cognitive LLS and those who do not is significant at 0.00 level. For cognitive language learning strategy, this value is significant at 0.05 levels. This then implies that the observed difference in the mean achievement scores of students who use cognitive LLS and those who do not use it is actual difference not attributed to chance error(s).

2) 88348.8606 (df. 1) and 597300.0230 (df. 1399) in respect of the difference in mean achievement scores of the students who use linguistic LLS and those who do not is significant at 0.00. For linguistic LLS, this value is significant at 0.05 levels. This implies that the earlier observed difference in the mean achievement scores of students who use linguistic LLS and those who do not use it is actual difference not attributed to chance error(s).

3) 546.8134 (df. 1) and 685102.0702 (df. 1399) in respect of the difference in the mean achievement scores of the students who use meta-cognitive LLS and those who do not is significant at 0.00. For meta-cognitive LLS, this value is significant at 0.05 levels. This then implies that the observed difference in the mean achievement scores of students who make use of meta-cognitive LLS and those who do not use it is actual difference not attributed to chance error(s).

4) 90117.2748 (df. 1) and 595531.6089 (df. 1399) in respect of the difference in the mean achievement scores of the students who use affective LLS and those who do not is significant at 0.00. For affective LLS, this value is significant at 0.05 levels. This then implies that the observed difference in the mean achievement scores of students who use affective LLS and those who do not use it is actual difference not attributed to chance error(s).

5) 60318.6811 (df. 1) and 625330.2026 (df. 1399) in respect of the difference in the mean achievement scores of the students who use compensation LLS and those who do not is significant at 0.00. For compensation LLS, this value is significant at 0.05 levels. This then implies that the observed difference in the mean achievement scores of students who use compensation LLS and those who do not use it is actual difference not attributed to chance error(s).

6) 6100.7641 (df. 1) and 679548.1195 (df. 1399) in respect of the difference in the mean achievement scores of the students who use socio-affective LLS and those who do not is significant at 0.00. For socio-affective LLS, this value is significant at 0.05 levels. This then implies that the observed difference in the mean achievement scores of students who use socio-affective LLS and those who do not use it is actual difference not attributed to chance error(s).

From the foregoing, it has been shown that there is a significant difference between study subjects who use each of the language learning strategies—cognitive, linguistic, meta-cognitive, affective, compensation and socio-linguistic—and those who do not use them. This therefore invalidates the hypothesis which says that there is no significant difference between the mean achievement scores in the English language of the Igbo learners of English who use the various language learning strategies and those who do not.

DISCUSSION OF FINDINGS

The results from research question 1, and hypothesis 1 show that whereas there is no significant difference between those who use both cognitive and compensation strategies, there is significant difference between those who use the other four language learning strategies—linguistic, meta-cognitive, affective and socio-affective. The researcher is not utterly surprised at the above result, because in the words of Rivera-Mills and Plonsky, "... even students at low levels of L2 proficiency are meta-linguistically aware of second language acquisition processes to some degree" (4). The results in Table 4 which confirm those in Table 1 that the lowest percentage (50.9%) of the study population makes use of the cognitive language learning strategy, and that meta-cognitive language learning strategy is the second highest used (79.8%) contradict the study results ofO'Malley and Chamot's (1990) that beginning and intermediate-level ESL students use cognitive strategies more frequently than meta-cognitive ones.

Part of the implications of the above results is that a little above the average number of the study population makes use of the skills involved in the language learning strategies such as functional planning, extensive reading, selective attention and listening, question for clarification, note-taking, self-management and monitoring/ self-evaluation, classification, practising, summarizing, predicting, using context, reflecting, guessing, among others.

The results of the chi square test failed to validate the first hypothesis. This has led me to conclude that there is significant difference between the proportion of the Igbo learners of English who use the various language learning strategies and those who do not use them. It is also apparent that linguistic strategies are minimally used. This is a dangerous trend especially when one recalls that the greatest source of information about any language is the language itself: the tenets of linguistic strategies are, in the main, akin to language skills of listening, speaking, reading and writing.

Experience of the researcher shows that many students in Nigeria believe in what one would like to describe as language myth: believing—erroneously—that English is a subject that one does not need to read. The researcher had, on several occasions especially when examinations were approaching, overheard students say/ask: "English cannot be read/How can you read English?" These highlight the fact that students' strategies usage reflects their underlying beliefs about how the English language is learned.

The least proportion of the study population recorded for the use of cognitive strategy (50.9) suggests that the students have low aptitude.

Research question 2 intended to uncover the extent to which the mean achievement scores in English of the Igbo learners of English in SSS II depended on their use of the various language learning strategies. It is discovered that the mean achievement scores of the study population who use cognitive, linguistic, meta-cognitive, affective, compensation, and socio-affective language learning strategies stand at 46.49, 45.62, 39.10, 45.65, 45.11, and 39.69 respectively, as against the mean achievement scores for the students who do not use the same strategies which are 30.81, 29.56, 37.55, 29.41, 31.98, and 33.95 in that order. It is evident from the above results that those who use the language learning strategies perform better than those who do not. This implies that good performance in English depends on the use of the various language learning strategies. Cohen and Shively's comment corroborates this result: "Research on the immigrant students in the study-abroad context/programme support the notion that strategy use can promote second language learning" (193). The results of the ANOVA which was used to test hypothesis 2 show that there is also a consistent difference, in performance in the English language, between the users and non-users of the various language learning strategies. The results entail that the null hypothesis (i.e., Ho2) could not be sustained.

These findings are not totally strange. My expectation that the study sample should have high mean achievement scores is premised on the contention by earlier researchers that "meta-cognitive strategies," which received the second highest percentage usage score (Table 1), "are more predictive of high academic performance..." (Garcia & Pintrich cited in Woodrow, 229). Results of previous research have not also disputed the fact that learners who use language learning strategies perform better than those who do not. If those who used the various language learning strategies, in this study, did not perform better, one would question the efficacy of the characteristics of the language learning strategies discussed in the introduction of this work. The results of this study, therefore, do not contradict those of Rodgers (2006) whose research results reveal that those who know and use language learning strategies exhibit improved functional linguistic abilities, as measured by his study's cloze test passage, than those who neither know nor use the strategies (381).

Although those who use, or claim to use, the learner strategies in this study have better achievement mean scores than those who do not, the general low mean achievement scores they recorded is worrisome: Whereas the passing grades recorded by those who made use of the various language learning strategies do not reach average marks (46.49, 45.62, 45.65, and 45.11), others in this group failed to get passing grades (39.10 and 39.69). Intuitively, these results which indicate general poor mean achievement scores, in the English language, are unexpected. It was expected that the study subjects' achievement scores should be higher since they claimed that they make use of the various learning strategies, which are said to facilitate and promote language learning and language proficiency. Their low mean achievement scores might have resulted from their not using the language learning strategies appropriately, or they were using what Otagburuagu calls "bad strategies" which he says lead learners to handle tasks erroneously and block the acquisition of proper linguistic data for the development of language skills (English as a Second 1). Scholars in the field believe that learners who fail to do well in language learning have been known to adopt bad language learning strategies. I hypothesize that the low mean achievement scores could also be due to low IQ (aptitude) level of the sampled study subjects. It could again be attributed to their earlier stated unwholesome attitude to second language learning.

The findings here are consistent with those of the studies conducted by Cohen and Shively (2007) ,Woodrow (2006) and Vandergrift (2003) . The study population of each of these researchers comprised subjects who were in the native language environment. By using a sample population who were in a second language environment, the present study has broken new grounds.

CONCLUSION

The results of this study add to and confirm the literature in second language learning concerning the central role of language learning strategies in learning process and language proficiency. In other words, they support the hypothesis that the use of learner strategies usually leads to language learning success, and that successful language learners constantly employ language learning strategies.

The results of the study also reveal that:

1) The greatest proportion of the Igbo learners of English in SSS II (1181, i.e., 84.3%) makes use of socio- affective language learning strategy; this may be due to the many social practices prevalent in the area of the study. Meta-cognitive learner strategy is the second highest in use with 1118 users representing 79.8%. Cognitive strategy has the least proportion of the study population that makes use of it (713, i.e., 50.9%). A little above the average number of the study subjects uses each of the other three language learning strategies— linguistic (805, 57.7%), affective (809, 57.7%), and compensation (727, 51.9%);
2) There is significant difference, in the English language performance, between the users and non-users of the various language learning strategies. The former group performed better than the latter group in the cloze test used for this study. Although this particular result confirmed the generally held view that those who make use of language learning strategies perform better in language learning and language performance than those who do not, it also revealed a perplexing phenomenon: the mean achievement scores recorded by those who used the various language learning strategies are abysmally low. The passing grades recorded by those who used cognitive, linguistic, affective, and compensation strategies stand at 46.49%, 45.62%, 45.65%, and 45.11%, while those who used meta-cognitive and socio-affective strategies failed to score passing grades as their mean scores stand at 39.10% and 39.69% respectively. This is, to say the least, below standard. Consequent on the above, I feel that this study has not only contributed significantly to the literature of Applied Linguistics, but has also carved a niche for itself in the world of scholarship by discovering that:

The inappropriate use of the various language learning strategies by the Igbo learners of English in south- eastern geo-political zone of Nigeria is a predictor and/or factor that gives rise to their poor performance in the English language.

From the foregoing, the study has helped me to conclude that:

1) There is converse use of strategies (CUS) by the study subjects;
2) There is converse relationship between performance and strategies usage by the study group; and
3) Aberration in strategies application (ASA) results in low language performance (LLP).

RECOMMENDATIONS

Predicated on the findings of this study, the following recommendations are offered:

First and foremost, it should be considered a matter of urgency to develop and use language learning strategies materials for colleges of education and university classes, since it is not certain that the English language teachers in secondary schools, in Nigeria, themselves know these strategies. Writers of textbooks should deliberately and copiously incorporate language learning strategies into their works.

In addition, teaching and learning of language learning strategies should be introduced into a variety of secondary school classes for the second language students. The results of Vandergrift's (2006) study suggest, among other things, that students may and do benefit from strategy instruction and that such training does reduce the gap in transfer of first language inferencing skills to second language inferencing tasks (15). The training will provide avenues for the students to begin to:

1) Learn how to learn English;
2) Appreciate the relevance of learner strategies for language learning tasks;
3) Understand:

- What language resources/tools are available to them,
- What specific language learning strategies they might use in order to improve their own vocabulary acquisition and use, grammar rules and use, and (second) language skills of listening, speaking, reading and writing, and
- Which learner strategies are most appropriate for which learning tasks.

Teachers of English should begin to:

- Look at what their students are doing in the process of learning the language,
- Look at how students deploy language resources in social situations,
- Be interested in their students' "social cognition", i.e., what the students do, think, demonstrate, manipulate, achieve, acquire, and learn during concerted social interactions,

- Study their teaching contexts, paying attention to their materials, and

- Be interested in knowing whether their students often ask questions for clarifications, or corrections, and whether they cooperate with their peers or seen to have much contact outside of class with proficient second language users.

There should be learner reflection; i.e., students themselves should form the habit of self-reflection on their language learning and language learning strategies usage both during and after the LLS training in the class. Graham emphasizes the importance of this when he writes: "For learners, a vital component of self-directed learning lies in the on-going evaluation of the methods they have employed on tasks and of their achievements within the... programme" (170). Learner reflection is important, because language learning strategies obviously involve individual's unique cognitive, social, linguistic, and affective learning styles and strategies.

As a result of the general belief that first language provides the platform for successful second language learning, development of the mother tongue should be encouraged, so that it can promote cognitive development and act as a base for learning the second language—English—in Nigeria. Onukaogu's views (2002) , as embodied in the following passage, underscore the point being made:

Literacy in English and other tongues would be richly enhanced if the foundations of our children's literacy are our children's mother tongues. Those of us, who underrate the role of the mother tongue in the literacy acquisition of the Nigerian child, clip the wings of the child and make the child unable to fly ("Reading for the Attainment..." 292).

REFERENCES

1. Akwanya, A. N. (2007). English Language Learning in Nigeria: In Search of an Enabling Principle. Inaugural Lecture, Uni- versity of Nigeria, Nsukka.
2. Cohen, A. D. (1998). Strategies in Learning and Using a Second Language. London: Longman. http://www.tesl-ej.org/ej12/r10.html
3. Cohen, A. D., & Shively, R. L. (2007). Acquisition of Requests and Apologies in Spanish and French: Impact of Study Abroad and Strategy-Building Intervention. Modern Language Journal, 91, 189-212. http://dx.doi.org/10.1111/j.1540-4781.2007.00540.x
4. Ellis, R. (2005). Measuring Implicit and Explicit Knowledge of a Second Language: A Psychometric Study. Studies in Sec- ond Language Acquisition, 27, 141-172.http://dx.doi.org/10.1017/S0272263105050096

5. Dike, V. W. (2003). Portable Libraries as Vehicle for Literacy Development: A Library Service to Pupils and Prisoners in Nigeria. In A. E. Arua (Ed.), Reading for All in Africa: Building Communities Where Literacy Thrives (pp. 17-22). USA: International Reading Association.
6. Ezeokoli, F. O. (2004). Voluntary Reading Interests and Achievement in Reading Comprehension among Senior Secondary Students in Ibadan Nigeria. Literacy and Reading in Nigeria, 10, 317-324.
7. Firth, A., & Wagner, J. (2007). Second/Foreign Language Learning as a Social Accomplishment: Elaborations on a Reconceptualized SLA. Modern Language Journal, 91, 800-818. http://dx.doi.org/10.1111/j.1540-4781.2007.00670.x
8. Graham, S. (1997). Effective Language Teaching. Clevedon: Multilingual Matters.
9. Grant, H., & Dweck, C. S. (2001). Cross Cultural Response to Failure: Considering Outcome Attributions with Different Goals. In F. Salili, C. Chiu, & Y. Y. Heng (Eds.), Student Motivation: The Culture and Context of Learning (pp. 203-219). New York: Plenum. http://dx.doi.org/10.1007/978-1-4615-1273-8_10
10. Gwete, W. B. (1987). Reading for Functional Literacy. In S. L. James (Ed.), Reading for Career Development (RAN Monograph Series C) (pp. 35-53). Ibadan: Reading Association of Nigeria.
11. Heaton, J. B. (1988). Writing English Language Tests: Longman Handbook for Language Teachers (New Edition). London: Longman Group UK Ltd.
12. Kolapo,Y.(2008).GettingRoundtheHalf-BakedGraduateSyndrome.http://www.punchontheweb.com/Article.apsx?theartic=Art2008110526245
13. Lessard-Clouston, M. (1997). Language Learning Strategies: An Overview for L2 Teachers. Internet TESL Journal. http://iteslj.org/Articles/Lessard-Clouston-Strategy
14. Macaro, E. (2006). Strategies for Language Learning and for Language Use: Revising the Theoretical Framework. Modern Language Journal, 90, 320-337.http://dx.doi.org/10.1111/j.1540-4781.2006.00425.x
15. Nunan, D. (1991). Methods in Second-Language Acquisition Classroom-Oriented Research: A Critical Review. Studies in Second Language Acquisition, 13, 249-174.http://dx.doi.org/10.1017/S0272263100009967
16. Nwosu-Izuwa, L. U. (2002). Balanced Literacy Development in a Multilingual Environment: The Shared-Reading Teaching Approach. Literacy and Reading in Nigeria, 9, 225-235.

17. Ogenyi, L. C. (2008b). Reading Proficiency: The Touchstone for Success in Education Reform. Review of Education: Institute of Education Journal, University of Nigeria, Nsukka, 19, 132-143.

18. O'Malley, J. M., & Chamot, A. (1990). Learning Strategies in Second Language Acquisition. Cambridge: Cambridge University Press.http://dx.doi.org/10.1017/CBO9781139524490

19. Onukaogu, C. E. (2002). Reading for the Attainment of Sustainable Democracy. Literacy and Reading in Nigeria, 9, 287- 298.

20. Osakwe, N. N. (1998/99). The Nature of Students' Reading Problems at the Tertiary Level. Literacy and Reading in Nigeria, 8, 138-148.

21. Otagburuagu, E. J. (1999). English as a Second Language: A Perceptual Approach. Owerri: Intercontinental Educational Books & Publishers.

22. Otagburuagu, E. J. (1997). Teaching and Learning the Writing Skill in the English Language: Theories, Issues and Practice. Onitsha: Cape Publisher International Ltd.

23. Oxford, R. L., & Burry Stock, J. A. (2008). Strategy Inventory for Language Learning (SILL). http://homepage.wtuc.edu.tw/sill.php

24. Rivera-Mills, S. V., & Plonsky, L. (2007). Empowering Students with Language Learning Strategies: A Critical Review of Current Issues. Foreign Language Annals, 40, 535-548.http://ducantian.blog.163.com/blog/216549752007112511016466/

25. Rodgers, D. M. (2006). Developing Content and Form: Encouraging Evidence from Italian Content-Based Instruction. Modern Language Journal,90,373-386.http://dx.doi.org/10.1111/j.1540-4781.2006.00430.x

26. Steinberg, D. D., & Sciarini, N. V. (2006). An Introduction to Psycholinguistics (2nd ed.). Harlow: Pearson Longman.

27. Vandergrift, L. (2003). Orchestrating Strategy Use: Toward a Model of the Skilled Second Language Listener. Language Learning, 53, 463-496. http://dx.doi.org/10.1111/1467-9922.00232

28. Vandergrift, L. (2006). Second Language Listening: Listening Ability or Listening Proficiency? Modern Language Journal, 9, 6-18. http://dx.doi.org/10.1111/j.1540-4781.2006.00381.x

29. Woodrow, L. J. (2006). A Model of Adaptive Learning. Modern Language Journal, 90, 297-314. http://dx.doi.org/10.1111/j.1540-4781.2006.00424.x

30. World Bank (1995). Priorities and Strategies for Education. Washington DC: The International Bank for Reconstruction and Development.

Chapter 3

RECOGNITION VOCABULARY KNOWLEDGE AS A PREDICTOR OF ACADEMIC PERFORMANCE IN AN ENGLISH AS A FOREIGN LANGUAGE SETTING

Thomas Roche and Michael Harrington

Language Testing in Asia

ABSTRACT

This paper presents findings of a study of recognition vocabulary knowledge as a predictor of written Academic English Proficiency (AEP) and overall Academic Achievement in an English medium higher education program in an English-as-a-Foreign-Language (EFL) context. Vocabulary knowledge was measured using a Timed YES/NO (TYN) test. AEP was assessed using an academic writing test based on IELTS. Performance on these measures was correlated with Grade Point Average (GPA) as a measure of academic achievement for Arabic L1 users (N=70) at an English-medium College of Applied Sciences in the Sultanate of Oman. Vocabulary size and speed correlated with both academic writing and GPA measures. The combined vocabulary and writing measures were also examined as predictors of academic achievement. The TYN test is discussed as reliable, cost and time effective general measure of AEP and for showing if students have the necessary vocabulary knowledge to undertake study in a tertiary level English medium program.

BACKGROUND

English as a Medium of Instruction

English has become the dominant medium of instruction used in higher education internationally. In 2006 English was used as a medium of instruction in 103 countries, whereas the second most commonly used university classroom language was French in 42 countries (Ammon,2006)[a]. This growth is particularly noticeable in countries defined by Kachru (1985) as being in the outer- and expanding-circles of English use where English is traditionally considered a foreign language (Bashir, 2007).

In Kachru's notion of language circles, the national context of English use can be classified as situated within inner-, outer- or expanding-circles, according to a nation's historico-political relationship with Anglo-American hegemonic power. Inner-circle nations are those where English is the primary language of the state (e.g. New Zealand). Outer-circle nations consist of former British dominions where English is still widely used as a second language to communicate between different groups (e.g. India). The expanding-circle refers to those nations without direct experience of British rule, where English plays an important role, be that in commerce, education or elsewhere (e.g. Oman).

Research exploring the challenges facing L2 students in English medium programs primarily focus on L2 English users in Anglophone countries, such as Australia and USA (see, Murray, 2012; Read, 2008), rather than English L2 users at universities and colleges in countries where English is not the primary language outside the classroom[b]. Those studies concerned with L2 English users studying at English medium universities in expanding- and outer-circle contexts indicate that such students experience a number of language proficiency related difficulties. In one self-assessment questionnaire study of students' perceptions of their study experience in English medium faculties of Social Science, Humanities, Engineering and Business at Norwegian and German universities, 42% of the Norwegian sample and 72% of the German students reported substantial comprehension difficulties (Hellekjaer, 2010). In another self-report study of students in English medium higher education programs in China, students identified comprehending lectures, understanding specialist vocabulary and writing in an appropriate academic style, as the major difficulties associated with studying through English as an L2 (Evans & Morrison, 2011)[c]. Research by Kırkgöz (2005) in Turkey, similarly found among first and fourth year English L2 undergraduate students that the incomprehensibility of both lectures and reading material were amongst students' greatest concerns. Though little empirical research exists into the relationship between L2 comprehension and performance in these expanding- and outer-circle educational contexts, one study of 2000 bilingual Arab students in an English medium tertiary level science program, found that proficiency in pre-faculty study preparatory year English correlated significantly with academic performance in a Calculus course (Yushau & Omar, 2007). The current research aims to contribute to the literature by investigating the relationship between academic English proficiency and overall academic performance of students studying in English medium tertiary level programs in the Sultanate of Oman, a country on the Arabian Peninsula with no direct experience of British rule but where English plays a key role in education and commerce, and as such will be considered as being in the expanding-circle of English use for the purpose of this study.

Vocabulary and success at English medium universities

Research in the 1980s and 90s lead to the recognition that vocabulary knowledge is a precondition for most other language abilities, (see, Alderson & Banerjee, 2001, for a review of that research); and, the emergence of lexical approaches to language learning (Willis, 1990; Lewis,2002; McCarthy, 2003). Corpus linguistics studies reported that the most frequent 2,000 headwords used in English account for between 80-85% of the words of any spoken or written English text, depending on the text type (Nation, 1990; Nation & Waring, 1997; Nation & Newton,1997). The educational corollary of this research is that L2 learners should first master these 2000 most frequently occurring words before attempting to study content through English (Meara, Lightbown & Halter, 1997).

Unassisted comprehension of English texts requires vocabulary knowledge greater than the most 2,000 frequently occurring headwords. In this research the headword *build*, forms the core of a word-family including related words such as *builder*, *building*, and *built*. Between 95-98% of the word-families in a text must be comprehensible for unassisted comprehension of that text (Waring & Nation, 2004; Hsueh-Chao & Nation, 2000). Knowledge of only the 2000 most frequent word-families would typically mean that approximately one in every five words encountered in an academic English text will still be unknown and thereby render the text largely unintelligible (Nation & Waring, 1997). More recent studies suggest that learners need knowledge of 8,000 to 9,000 word-families for unassisted comprehension of written texts, and 6,000 to 7,000 for spoken texts (Nation, 2006). However, this figure of 8,000-9,000 word-families is not a gatekeeping figure for undertaking higher education studies in English medium environments. Although some researchers insist that a vocabulary of 10,000 word-families is necessary for successful study in linguistically demanding higher degree courses (Hazenberg & Hulstijn 1996 in Schmitt, Schmitt & Clapham,2001),there is general agreement in the literature (Nation, 1990, Schmitt, 2000, Meara et al., 1997) that an L2 learner's passive vocabulary should reach a minimum threshold of 5,000 word-families before L2 users undertake studies in English medium universities and colleges.

The greater the learner's vocabulary knowledge, the less cognitive demands are placed on a learner. More developed levels of vocabulary knowledge enable learners to read with less effort (Segalowitz & Segalowitz, 1993; Segalowitz,

Segalowitz & Wood, Segalowitz, Segalowitz & Wood, ; Segalowitz, Segalowitz & Wood,1998) and result in better performance on comprehension tests (Chen, 2011; Miller & Peleg, 2010; Nassaji, 2003; Qian, 1999). The preponderance of the evidence indicates that in order for an L2 to become a vehicle for learning, vocabulary knowledge must first be sufficiently developed. This in turn suggests that measures of vocabulary knowledge could predict written AEP proficiency and academic performance.

Learners' vocabulary size has been assessed using both traditional multiple-choice checklist formats involving yes/no judgments (Meara & Buxton, 1987; Mochida & Harrington, 2006. A widely used paper-based test of vocabulary size is the *Vocabulary Levels Test* (Nation, 1990). The test uses a multiple matching format in which items are banded by frequency levels, allowing size to be inferred from performance across decreasing frequency levels. An alternative measure of vocabulary size is the Yes/No test first introduced by (Meara & Buxton, 1987; Meara & Jones, 1988). The test presents a mix of frequency-banded words as well as phonologically-possible nonwords. The learner simply checks which words are known and which are not. The inclusion of nonwords is designed to control for guessing, with nonword errors subtracted from correct word performance for an overall score (Mochida & Harrington, 2006). Although the validity and usefulness of the correcting for guessing in educational testing has been questioned (Ebel, 1979), nonword performance provides an important control variable for the format, especially when guessing varies across participants. The use of non words does raise a number of issues for the validity and reliability of the format, and these have received significant attention from researchers (Beeckmans, et al., 2001; Cameron, 2002; Eyckmans, 2004; Huibregtse, Admiraal, & Meara Huibregtse, Admiraal, & Meara ; Huibregtse, Admiraal, & Meara 2002; Mochida& Harrington, 2006). Although the YN test does not directly elicit vocabulary knowledge, it has been shown to correlate highly with standard measures of vocabulary knowledge (Mochida & Harrington, 2006). The *Timed Yes/No* test used here differs from earlier versions in that it also collects participants' response time, thus providing an additional, implicit measure of L2 vocabulary knowledge.

The TYN test measures vocabulary knowledge as a discrete, context-free (trait) entity (Read & Chapelle, 2001). The use of both vocabulary size and speed of access provides, in principle, a measure of vocabulary ability that will be more valid than either dimension alone (Chapelle,2006). The instrument has been piloted with tertiary EFL learners in Singapore, and has also been tested extensively in Australia on students who were newly arrived in that country, and thus had EFL equivalent proficiency at the time of testing.

Test findings, including validity and reliability data have been reported (Harrington & Carey, 2009; Harrington, 2006; Harrington, 2007; Mochida & Harrington, 2006). The effectiveness of this timed Yes/No response test has never been established in an outer- or expanding circle EFL setting, and this is one of the reasons why this study is important.

A secondary aim of this study is to establish whether decontextualized word recognition tests are valid tools for assessing Arabic L1 users' English language proficiency. Schmitt, Schmitt& Clapham (2001, 64) point out that the linguistic, cognitive and cultural background of participants influences their response (time and/or accuracy) to vocabulary tests. Research by Fender (2003; 2008) and Ryan & Meara (1991) indicates that Arab L1 users experience greater difficulty than proficiency equivalent ESL learners generally in reading tasks and in isolated word recognition tasks. Fender (2008) suggests that nature of Arabic literacy and a difference in decoding skills used in English and Arabic may account for these difficulties. Across the Arab world online and print materials of the mass media are typically written in Modern Standard Arabic, an alphabet that does not encode short vowels thus requiring that readers not only utilize the explicit phonological information in the orthography, but also extra-lexical information such as morpho-syntactic knowledge and discourse context (Fender, 2008; 26; Abu Rabia & Seigel,, 26; Abu Rabia & Seigel, 26; Abu Rabia & Seigel,1995). In terms of culture, universal school education began in the Sultanate of Oman in the late sixties, prior to which there were only three schools and no universities in Oman (Roche, 2009), as a result of which the widespread illiteracy of the 1960's dropped to below 19% in the early twenty-first century (CIA, 2011). Al-Amrani (2009) found that current Omani EFL university students are reluctant readers who use less effective bottom-up reading strategies than proficiency equivalent non-Omani EFL student peers. Given this background the present study also attempts to establish whether word-recognition tasks can be used with Arabic L1 users to determine their Academic English Proficiency.

The study

This study explores the relationship between vocabulary knowledge, written Academic English proficiency and academic performance of EFL students in Oman. The first objective of the study, is to establish whether:

1) Academic performance by Arabic L1 users at an English medium institution in Oman can be predicted by two key measures of written academic English proficiency.

Academic Performance will be measured by Grade Point Average (GPA) taken from students' academic transcripts, and written Academic

English Proficiency (AEP) will be measured through scores on a mock IELTS academic writing test. The second hypothesis is a refinement of the first:

2) The TYN Test is an effective predictor of written academic English proficiency for the participants.

The motivation for this study is to examine the relationship between vocabulary recognition knowledge, written academic English proficiency, and student academic performance in an English medium institution in an expanding-circle context for Arabic L1 users. Of particular interest is the potential use of measures of vocabulary recognition knowledge as a tool for identifying learners who may lack the needed written English proficiency to undertake tertiary studies in English medium institutions in this context. To the extent the effectiveness of the tool can be established, it will provide these institutions an efficient and cost-effective method for identifying students who may require further academic English language support before attempting tertiary study in English.

METHODS

Participants

The participants from this study (n= 70) were students in an English language medium higher education institution in the Sultanate of Oman, Rustaq College of Applied Science. These students were from the first and fourth year of Faculty study and all reported their first language to be Arabic. The data collection period took place within one week with students in their 13th and 14th week of the second 15-week semester for that academic year. Participation was voluntary and the study, was carried out in accordance with the College's ethical guidelines.

Materials

Academic English written proficiency was assessed using a task adapted from practice IELTS materials (Cambridge University Press, 2005). Each paper was rated on a ten-point scale reflecting proficiency in grammar, vocabulary, coherence and response to the task.Each student was directed to write a 250 word short essay on the topic "Oman in the past, Oman in the future". Students were given 40 minutes to complete the task.

A discrete item computerized timed YES/NO response test was used to determine vocabulary knowledge. Two versions of 100 items each were used. Each test consisted of 72 words (18 each from four frequency levels) and 28 nonwords. The words are drawn from bands of the 1000 (1K), 2000 (2K), 3000 (3K), 5000 (5k) and 10,000 (10K) most frequently occurring words in the British National Corpus (Harrington & Carey, 2009). In the first set, Word Test A, less frequent words were used from the 2K, 3K, 5K, 10K bands; in Word Test B, more common words from the 1K-5K frequency bands were tested. Nonwords used are phonologically permissible English words (e.g. *blurge*) as opposed to non-permissible items (e.g. *rbgeul*). The TYN test measures participants' reaction time and accuracy, responding "YES" to words and "NO" to nonwords. "YES" responses to nonwords (false-alarms) resulted in a reduction in the participants' score. See Table 1 for the matrix of possible responses used to test vocabulary knowledge. For each set of words, each item appears for 5000 milliseconds (5 seconds), if a participant fails to respond within that time the word disappears to be replaced by a new word. Response time score is taken from the mean response of each participant to the presented items. The test was administered using *LMAP*, a web-based testing tool developed at the University of Queensland, Australia, http://www.languagemap.com.

Table 1. Matrix of possible responses, where UPPER CASE = correct responses

	Word	**Non-word**
Yes	HIT	False alarm
No	Miss	CORRECT REJECTION

The academic performance of the students was measured by the participants' Grade Point Average (GPA) in their studies for the current semester. The GPAs were provided with the students' permission, by the Dean's Office.

Procedure

Data collection took place during the 13th and 14th weeks of the 15-week second semester. The tests were administered by the first author and collaborating staff. All testing was done in a computer lab. Students first completed the writing tests, followed by the computer-based vocabulary tests. Instructions in Modern Standard Arabic were given in written form and were also read aloud by an Omani research assistant. The testing format was explained and students did a set of practice items for each test. In both tests they were encouraged to work as quickly and as accurately as possible, as both accuracy and response time measures were being collected.

For the Vocabulary test students were warned that clicking "YES" for nonwords would result in lower scores. They were also told that each item would appear on the screen for only 5000 milliseconds (5 seconds) and then disappear. If there was no response it was counted as incorrect. There were very few no responses, comprising less than 0.05% of the total response set. In addition to being an additional window on underlying proficiency, the inclusion of the response time condition discouraged strategic and reflective processing on the part of the students, thus providing a more direct measure of vocabulary knowledge.

RESULTS

The academic writing papers were marked by trained and practicing IELTS examiners, with a random sample of essays (20%)marked by both raters. Interrater reliability was assessed by using the intra-class coefficient (ICC) statistic, which measures the consistency between the raters' judgment (Field, 2009). ICC = .88, $p < .001$; 95% confidence interval, 67.00 - 96.10. This indicates a high level of consistency across the two raters.

Score reliability for the vocabulary measures was assessed using Cronbach's Alpha. Table 2 reports the reliability coefficients for accuracy and response time measures for the Advanced and Basic versions.

Table 2. Cronbach's Alpha reliability coefficients for advanced and basic word tests

	Words	**Nonwords**	**Combined**
	(72 items)	**(28 items)**	**(100 items)**
Advanced test			
Accuracy	.89	.89	.85
Response time	.96	.92	.97
Basic test			
Accuracy	.89	.88	.84
Response time	.95	.92	.94

Separate coefficients for the word and nonword items were calculated as the recognition of words and the rejection of nonwords arguably reflect different dimensions of underlying lexical knowledge (Mochida & Harrington, 2006). Combined reliability values were also calculated.

The descriptive statistics for the language measures and grade-point averages are presented in Table 3. Mean performance on the Basic test was better than on the Advanced tests, for both accuracy and response time, presumably reflecting the difficulty of the items in the respective tests.

Table 3. Descriptive statistics (means, standard deviations, range) for advanced and basic word tests, grade point average and IELTS writing scores, N = 70

	M[a]	SD	Range	
Advanced word				
Accuracy	35.96	12.05	8.93	58.93
Response time[b]	1590	371	946	3200
False alarm rate	23.70	13.46	3.57	60.71
Basic word				
Accuracy	53.23	15.83	8.33	80.95
Response time	1571	372	909	3120
False alarm rate	22.57	11.03	3.57	50.00
IELTS writing	5.18	.86	3.50	7.00
Grade point average	2.79	.55	1.00	3.70

[a] Corrected for guessing score, proportion of yes responses to words (hits) minus proportion of yes responses to nonwords (false alarms).

[b] Milliseconds (msc).

A pair wise t-test on the mean accuracy differences for Test A and B was significant, $t(69) = 12.43$, $p<.001$, Cohen's $d = 1.22$, the latter indicating a strong effect size. The mean response times were log-transformed for all statistical analyses reported here. The response time differences were not significant. False alarm rates for both word tests compare with pre-faculty English language students in Australia whose mean false alarm scores were 25% for beginners and 10% for advanced learners (Harrington & Carey, 2009). There were a small number of students with extremely high false alarm rates that could have arguably been removed as outliers. However, given that a motivation for the study is to assess the effectiveness of the TYN Test in an authentic testing context, these potentially distorting data points were not removed, as they might be in a typical psychology or laboratory setting study.

The strength of association among the word, writing and GPA measures are evaluated by first reporting on the bivariate correlations between the measures. See Table 4.Also reported is a composite word measure. This measure combines the individual participants z-scores for accuracy and response times into a single measure in an attempt to provide a more stable measure of underlying word skill (Ackerman & Cianciolo, 2000). The effectiveness of the composite score as a predictor of academic achievement will be assessed in both the bivariate correlations and a regression analysis that evaluates the relative contributions the word and writing measures make in predicting academic performance.

Table 4. Bivariate correlations for language measures and grade-point-average

	2. Adv RT	**3. Adv Comp**	**4. Basic Acc**	**5. Basic RT**	**Basic Comp**	**7. Acad Writ**	**8. GPA**
1. Advanced word accuracy	.02	.70**	.68**	-.06	.47**	.35*	.14
2. Advanced word response time	1	-.70**	-.16	-.17	.57**	-.20	-.27*
3. Advanced word composite		1	.60**	-.49**	.69**	.38*	.29*
4. Basic word ac-curacy			1	-.25*	.79**	.51**	.34**
5. Basic word response time				1	-.79**	-.11	-.38**
6. Basic Word composite					1	.36*	.43**
7. Academic writing						1	.40**
8. Grade-point-average							1

** Correlation is significant at the 0.01level (two-tailed).

* Correlation is significant at the 0.05level (two-tailed).

As is evident in Table 4 all the language measures, with the exception of the results for Advanced Word Accuracy, had a moderately strong correlation with GPA. The lack of correlation between accuracy and response time for the respective tests indicated there was no systematic speed-accuracy trade-off by the participants.

In general, faster and more accurate word recognition skill had a significant correlation with GPA, as did performance on the writing task. The composite scores had a stronger correlation with GPA than the accuracy and response time results for the respective tests. It was also evident that vocabulary skill was a moderately strong predictor of writing outcomes.

Regression analyses were also carried out to assess how well the vocabulary and writing measures predicted GPA when the two variables were considered in combination. Given the inter-correlations between vocabulary, writing and GPA, it is not clear if better vocabulary performance is due to being a better writer, or better vocabulary skills determine writing performance, the similar correlations ($r = .3$ and $-.4$) with GPA indicating that the two measures tap the same underlying knowledge. Alternatively, the vocabulary and writing scores may make relatively independent contributions to academic achievement. If the former, then the two measures would be interchangeable as tests of academic English skill, though with important practical differences between the two in terms of administration and scoring. Alternatively, if the vocabulary (accuracy and response time) and writing measures each account for a substantial amount of additional variance in GPA, this would indicate that two complement each other in indexing learner proficiency levels. The regression models assess how much overall variance the measures together account for, and the relative contribution of each measure to this amount.

Table 5 reports four analyses. The Advanced and Basic Word results are evaluated separately. For each word test two models were developed. The first assess the contribution of the word measures to predicting the criterion GPA after the writing measures are entered. The second model will enter the vocabulary measures first and then the writing measures. The composite scores, which were generated from the raw measures, will not be analysed.

Table 5. Hierarchical regression analyses of the advanced word and writing measures with GPA as criterion variable and writing and word measure as predictors

Advanced word models	R^2	**Adjusted** R^2	R^2**change**	**B**	**SEB**	**β**
Writing	.160	.147	.160***	.230	.077	.399
Advanced accuracy	.160	.135	.000	.001	.005	.021
Advanced response time	.198	.162	.028	-1.171	.659	-.200
Advanced accuracy	.02	.005	.02	.001	.005	.021
Advanced response time	.091	.063	.071*	-1.172	.659	-.2
Writing	.198	.162	.108**	.230	.077	.357
Basic word models						
Writing	.16	.147	.160***	.215	.079	.334
Basic accuracy	.184	.160	.024	.003	.004	.093
Basic response time	.267	.234	.083**	-1.708	.624	-.299
Basic accuracy	0.215	0.079	0.334	0.003	0.004	0.093
Basic response time	0.003	0.004	0.093	-1.708	0.624	-0.299
Writing	-1.708	0.624	-0.299	0.215	0.079	0.334

B, Unstandardized coefficient; SEB, Standard Error B; β, Standardized coefficient.

F significant at * $p < .05$, ** $p < .01$, *** $p < .001$.

$N = 70$.

To summarize the regression analyses, as expected from the bivariate correlations, the word measures and writing measures predicted significant variance in GPA differences. The model based on the Basic word measures accounted for nearly 25% of the GPA variance (total adjusted R^2 = .234) while the Advanced word model only accounted for 16% (.162). This is due to both the accuracy and response time results serving to discriminate between GPA differences. Although the word and writing measures have similar correlations with GPA in the bivariate comparisons, writing is a better predictor when the two variables are considered together.

DISCUSSION

The first objective of the study was to assess the ability of Arabic L1 users' written Academic English Proficiency (AEP) to predict academic performance at tertiary education institutions in an expanding-circle context. Results indicate that AEP, both academic writing skills and vocabulary knowledge are good predictors of overall academic performance in this context. The TYN Test is a less sensitive measure than the academic writing tests but nonetheless predicts academic performance. These results give support to research outlining the importance of English proficiency (Yushau & Omar, 2007), and in particular, vocabulary knowledge as a prerequisite for academic success in English medium programs (Meara, et al. 1997; Waring & Nation, 2004; Hsueh-Chao & Nation, 2000).

It is of note that the results gathered on the TYN Test present a high number of false alarms. As noted above, lower false alarm rates were evident in studies in Anglophone countries. The results of the regression analysis indicate that the TYN Test can be used as a screening tool with fairly comparable effectiveness to a writing task. However, the results here differed noticeably from those obtained from previous studies with English L2 university students in English speaking countries. As noted above, the mean false alarm rates were much higher and the group means (as a measure of vocabulary size) were also lower, with students in this study performing at the level of pre-tertiary students in Australia. It is possible that the results are influenced by the participants' L1 Arabic. Arab students have been shown to encounter greater difficulty with English spelling and word processing than proficiency equivalent ESL learners from other L1 backgrounds. This effect has been attributed to the influence of Arabic orthography and literacy practices (Fender, 2008; Ryan & Meara, 1991; Milton, 2009). Performance on the written TYN Test requires knowledge of spelling and word meaning, and it is not clear the extent to which the poorer performance on both the words and nonwords (the latter conforming to English spelling rules) can be reduced to spelling difficulties.

This is a question for future research. This overall higher false alarm rate might be because the instructions were not clear and participants were not aware that they were being penalized for incorrect guesses; or, that these were acquiescent responses (Dodorico-McDonald, 2008) - random clicks that brought the test to an un-taxing end rather than reflecting their knowledge or lack of knowledge of the items presented. For improved results the test results should be meaningful to the students, for example we would expect fewer false alarms if the test acted as gateway to further study or was integrated into courses and contributed towards students marks. Further research might also look at how test performance interacts with instructional variables such as time of semester. The comparatively slower response times may indicate that no tall students were aware that speed of response was also being measured, another recommendation of the study is that the instructions should be delivered online in a standardized format with a video demonstration on the computer to improve the clarity of the instructions.

The results also show that vocabulary recognition test scores serve as a predictor of written academic English language proficiency. There was a strong correlation between *Language MAP* test scores and academic writing scores, particularly with Word Test B, which represents words from the 1-5K most commonly occurring words, which authors such as Nation (1990), Schmitt (2000) and Meara et al., (1997)) claim are essential for reading English texts and are the minimum knowledge required to begin study in English medium programs. Once again, the findings here are not as strong as the correlations resulting from studies using *Language MAP* and placement tests for students studying in inner-circle settings, such as pre-Faculty courses in Australia (Harrington & Carey, 2009) but the results are nonetheless significant. The weaker the student's vocabulary knowledge the poorer they are likely to perform both in measures of their academic English proficiency, which is fundamental to success in their studies, and in overall academic performance. This highlights the TYN Test's potential for use as an English language proficiency placement tool, or for tracking and monitoring changes in written academic English proficiency among matriculated students for Post-Enrolment Language Assessment (PLA) purposes.

CONCLUSION

This study contributes to a growing body of research stressing the fundamental importance of L2 English proficiency for achieving success in English medium tertiary education programs (Murray, 2012; Read, 2008; Harrington & Roche, submitted). The results presented here recommend the TYN Test as a useful predictor of both overall academic achievement and written academic

English language proficiency for Arabic L1 users, despite concerns raised to the contrary in the literature concerning the written language processing strategies used by Arabic L1 users of English (Ryan & Meara, 1991; Fender, 2008; Abu Rabia & Seigel, 1995), and in particular their difficulties in reading English electronic texts (Al-Amrani, 2009). The results show that visual word recognition is a good of measure of L2 proficiency. The TYN Test is especially attractive given the limited resources needed to administer the test and generate results. As for future directions, research is underway that assesses the predictive power of the test as a diagnostic for readiness to take IELTS by learners in expanding-circle settings like the one examined here.

Endnotes

[a]Of approximately 6,000 living languages, 82 are used in tertiary education, 39 languages are used in 2 or more countries' universities and only 13 are used in three or more (Ammon, 2006, 557).

[b]For example, research shows that non-English speaking background (NESB) students' English language proficiency correlates positively with academic success in Australian Universities (Feast, 2002).

[c]The students' perceptions fit well with Lin & Morrison's (2010) vocabulary levels research which reported that the majority (76.1%) of Hong Kong students at English medium universities do not have sufficient vocabulary to comprehend lectures in English or undertake tertiary study.

Authors information

Thomas Roche is the Director of Studies of the English Language Centre at Southern Cross University, Australia, an Associate Professor at Sohar University, Sultanate of Oman, and an Associate Research Fellow in the School of Languages & Comparative Cultural Studies at the University of Queensland, Australia. His research interests include individual difference in foreign language learning and language testing.

Michael Harrington is a Senior Lecturer in Second Language Acquisition in the School of Languages & Comparative Cultural Studies at the University of Queensland, Australia. He has published in areas including lexical processing and the measurement of L2 vocabulary skills.

Declarations

Acknowledgements

This research was supported by a grant from the Omani Research Council

[Grant number ORG SU HER 10 003]. The authors would like to thank the anonymous reviewer for useful comments and suggestions.

Competing interest

The authors declare that they have no competing interest.

Authors' contribution

Both authors read and approved the final manuscript.

REFERENCES

1. Abu Rabia S, Seigel LS: Different orthographies, different context effects: The effects of Arabic sentence context in skilled and poor readers. Reading Psychology 1995, 16: 1–19. 10.1080/0270271950160101**View Article**
2. Ackerman PL, Cianciolo AT: Cognitive, perceptual-speed, and psychomotor determinants of individual skill acquisition. Journal of Experimental Psychology: Applied 2000, 6: 259–290.
3. Alderson JC, Banerjee J: Language testing and assessment (Part 1) "State of the art review". Language Testing 2001, 18: 213–236.
4. Al-Amrani S: Strategies for reading on-line and printed texts by Omani EAP students. In Orientations in language learning and translation. Edited by: Roche T. Muscat, Oman: Al Falaj Press; 2009:41–60.
5. Ammon U: The language of tertiary education. In Encyclopaedia of languages & linguistics. Edited by: Brown EK. Amsterdam: Elsevier; 2006:556–559.**View Article**
6. Bashir S: Trends in international trade in higher education: implications and options for developing countries education working papers series. Washington: World Bank; 2007.
7. Beeckmans R, Eyckmans J, Janssens V, Dufranne M, Van de Velde H: Examining the yes-no vocabulary test: Some methodological issues in theory and practice. Language Testing 2001, 18: 235–274.
8. Cambridge University Press: Cambridge IELTS 4. Examination papers from University of Cambridge ESOL Examinations. Cambridge, UK: Cambridge University Press; 2005.
9. Cameron L: Measuring vocabulary size in English as an additional language. Language Teaching Research 2002, 6: 145–173. 10.1191/1362168802lr103oa**View Article**

10. Chapelle C: L2 vocabulary acquisition theory: The role of inference, dependability and generalizability in assessment. In Inference and generalizability in applied linguistics: multiple perspectives. Edited by: Chalhoub-Deville M, Chapelle CA, Duff P. Amsterdam: John Benjamins; 2006:47–64.**View Article**
11. Chen KY: The impact of EFL students'vocabulary breadth of knowledge on literal reading comprehension. Asian EFL Journal 2011., 51: Retrieved from http://www.academia.edu/2346635/The_Impact_of_Vocabulary_Knowledge_Level_on_EFL_Reading_Comprehension
12. CIA: World factbook: Middle East: Oman. 2011. Retrieved from https://www.cia.gov/library/publications/the-world-factbook/geos/mu.html
13. Dodorico-McDonald J: Measuring personality constructs: The advantages and disadvantages of self-reports, informant reports and behavioural assessments. Enquire 2008., 1(1): Retrieved from http://www.nottingham.ac.uk/shared/shared_enquire/PDFs/Dodorico_J.pdf
14. Ebel RL (Ed): Essentials of educational measurement. Englewood Cliffs, NJ: Prentice-Hall; 1979.
15. Evans S, Morrison B: Meeting the challenges of English-medium higher education: The first-year experience in Hong Kong. English for Specific Purposes 2011, 30(3):198–208. 10.1016/j.esp.2011.01.001**View Article**
16. Eyckmans J: Measuring receptive vocabulary size. Utrecht: LOT; 2004.
17. Feast V: The impact of IELTS scores on performance at University. International Education Journal 2002, 3(4):70–85.
18. Fender M: English word recognition and word integration skills of native Arabic- and Japanese-speaking learners of English as a second language. Applied Psycholinguistics 2003, 24: 289–315.**View Article**
19. Fender M: Spelling knowledge and reading development: Insights from Arab ESL learners. Reading in a Foreign Language 2008, 20(1):19–42.
20. Field A: Discovering statistics using SPSS. London, UK: SAGE Publications; 2009.
21. Harrington M: The lexical decision task as a measure of L2 lexical proficiency. EUROSLA Yearbook 2006, 6: 147–168. 10.1075/eurosla.6.10har**View Article**
22. Harrington M: The coefficient of variation as an index of L2 lexical processing skill. University of Queensland working papers in linguistics. Brisbane, Australia: School of English, Media Studies and Art History, The University of Queensland; 2007.
23. Harrington M, Carey M: The on-line Yes/No test as a placement tool.

System: An International Journal of Educational Technology and Applied Linguistics 2009, 37: 614–626. 10.1016/j.system.2009.09.006**View Article**

24. Harrington M, Roche T: Identifying academically at-risk students at an English-medium university in Oman: Post-enrolment language assessment in an English-as-a-foreign language setting. submitted
25. Hellekjaer GO: Lecture comprehension in English-medium higher education. Hermes 2010, 45: 11–34.
26. Hsueh-Chao MH, Nation P: Unknown vocabulary density and reading comprehension. Reading in a Foreign Language 2000, 13: 403–30.
27. Huibregtse I, Admiraal W, Meara P: Scores on a yes-no vocabulary test: correction for guessing and response style. Language Testing 2002, 19: 227–245. 10.1191/0265532202lt229oa**View Article**
28. Kachru BB: Standards, codification and sociolinguistic realism: The English language in the outer circle. In English in the world: Teaching and learning the language and literatures. Edited by: Widdowson RQAH. Cambridge, UK: Cambridge University Press; 1985:11–36.
29. Kırkgöz Y: Motivation and student perception of studying in an English-medium university. Journal of Language and Linguistic Studies 2005, 1(1):101–123.
30. Lewis M: Implementing the lexical approach. Boston: Thomson and Heinle; 2002.
31. Lin LHF, Morrison B: The impact of the medium of instruction in Hong Kong secondary schools on tertiary students' vocabulary. Journal of English for Academic Purposes 2010, 9(4):255–266. 10.1016/j.jeap.2010.09.002**View Article**
32. McCarthy M: Vocabulary. Oxford: Oxford University Press; 2003.
33. Meara P, Buxton B: An alternative multiple-choice vocabulary test. Language Testing 1987, 4: 142–145. 10.1177/026553228700400202**View Article**
34. Meara P, Jones G: Vocabulary size as a placement indicator. In Applied Linguistics in Society. Edited by: Grunwell P. London, UK: CILT; 1988.
35. Miller P, Peleg O: Doomed to read in a second language: Implications for learning. Journal of Psycholinguistic Research 2010, 39(1):51–65. 10.1007/s10936-009-9125-3**View Article**
36. Milton J: Measuring second language vocabulary acquisition. Bristol, England: Multilingual Matters; 2009.
37. Mochida A, Harrington M: The Yes-No test as a measure of

receptive vocabulary knowledge. Language Testing 2006, 23: 73–98. 10.1191/0265532206lt321oa**View Article**

38. Meara P, Lightbown P, Halter R: Classrooms as lexical environments. Language Teaching Research 1997, 1: 28–47. 10.1177/136216889700100103**View Article**
39. Murray N: Ten "Good Practice Principles" ten key questions: considerations in addressing the English language needs of higher education students. Higher Education Research & Development 2012, 31(2):233–246. 10.1080/07294360.2011.555389**View Article**
40. Nassaji H: Higher-level and lower-level text processing skills in advanced ESL reading comprehension. The Modern Language Journal 2003, 87: 261–276. 10.1111/1540-4781.00189**View Article**
41. Nation P: Teaching and learning vocabulary. Boston: Heinle & Heinle; 1990.
42. Nation P: The Canadian Modern Language Review /La revue canadienne des langues vivantes. 2006, 63(1):59–81. September/septembre 2006**View Article**
43. Nation P, Newton J: Teaching vocabulary. In Second language vocabulary acquisition. Edited by: Coady J, Huckin T. Cambridge, UK: Cambridge University Press; 1997.
44. Nation P, Waring R: Vocabulary size text coverage. In Vocabulary: description, acquisition and pedagogy. Edited by: Schmitt NA. Cambridge, UK: Cambridge University Press; 1997.
45. Qian DD: Assessing the roles of depth and breadth of vocabulary knowledge in reading comprehension. Canadian Modern Language Review/La Revue canadienne des languesvivantes 1999, 56(2):282–308. 10.3138/cmlr.56.2.282**View Article**
46. Read J: Identifying academic language needs through diagnostic assessment. Journal of English for Academic Purposes 2008, 7(3):180–190. 10.1016/j.jeap.2008.02.001**View Article**
47. Read J, Chapelle CA: A framework for second language vocabulary assessment. Language Testing 2001, 18(1):1–32.**View Article**
48. Roche T: Introduction. In Orientations in language learning and translation. Edited by: Roche T. Muscat, Oman: Al Falaj Press; 2009:7–8.
49. Ryan A, Meara P: The case of the invisible vowels: Arabic speakers reading English words. Reading in a Foreign Language 1991, 7: 531–540.
50. Schmitt N: Vocabulary in language teaching. Cambridge, UK: Cambridge University Press; 2000.

51. Schmitt N, Schmitt D, Clapham C: Developing and exploring the behaviour of two new versions of the vocabulary levels test. Language Testing 2001, 18: 55–88.

52. Segalowitz N, Segalowitz S: Skilled performance, practice, and the differentiation of speed-up from automatization effects: Evidence from second language word. Applied Psycholinguistics 1993, 14: 369–385. 10.1017/S0142716400010845**View Article**

53. Segalowitz SJ, Segalowitz NS, Wood AG: Assessing the development of automaticity in second language word recognition. Applied Psycholinguistics 1998, 19: 53–67. 10.1017/S0142716400010572**View Article**

54. Waring R, Nation ISP: Second language reading and incidental vocabulary learning. Angles on the English Speaking World 2004, 4: 97–110.

55. Willis D: The lexical syllabus: A new approach to language teaching. London, UK: Collins COBUILD; 1990.

56. Yushau B, Omar MH: Preparatory year program courses as predictors of first calculus course grade. Mathematics and Computer Education 2007, 41(2):92–108.

Chapter 4

MULTILINGUALISM AND THE LANGUAGE EDUCATION LANDSCAPE: CHALLENGES FOR TEACHER TRAINING IN EUROPE

Gudrun Ziegler

DICA-lab, University of Luxembourg, Luxembourg L-2721, Luxembourg

ABSTRACT

Europe is at the forefront of the development of policies that promote multilingualism in its member states, both on the social and the institutional level, as well as plurilingualism on the individual level. As Europe faces the challenge of multilingual education and diversity on various and exceedingly heterogeneous levels with regard to plurilinguals' realities, stakeholders and key decision-makers have developed visions of the situation of language teacher education and its structures. This paper presents these visions and provides insights from a recent critical evaluation of the policy instrument "European profile for language teacher education" (first published in 2004). Based on the study results obtained from a hundred decision-makers and language teacher trainers who participated in a European study on language teacher education, we discuss their perspectives relative to the current training infrastructure available in Europe. This study highlights key problematic issues, especially in light of the increasingly diverse student bodies, and highlights potential solutions for the European language context.

INTRODUCTION

Multilingualism and multiculturalism are functional realities in today's European societies. These realities challenge traditional visions of language education, where each language is taught one after another as first and successive foreign languages. However, advances to promote multilingualism in and through this one-language teaching paradigm face resistance due to contradictions at different levels, which this paper discusses in detail below. One important contradiction concerns the individual language-teaching professional who supposedly works in favour of multilingualism, yet, has usually been trained as a specialist in one language.

Drawing both on socio-cultural (Lave & Wenger 1991, Vygotsky 1978) as well as socio-educational perspectives, the present paper discusses a study that was conducted with language teaching specialists and stakeholders in the area of language teacher training across Europe. The results highlight a need for the development of a framework by defining the grounds, implications, and aims of a language teacher (education) in and for an advocated multilingual Europe.

The results of the study also show an imminent need for identifying the changing identities of the language teacher in multilingual realities (Singh & Richards 2006) and review the said necessity to create consistency throughout Europe in developing and professionalizing teachers of languages as agents of multilingualism. This paper builds on the concept of "professionalizing" as attempting to gain a sense of "self" when developing as a professional language teacher. Multilingualism is shown to have a key influence on the language teaching professional though the practice of it often contradicts established practices. Specifically, the case of young professionals and language teacher trainees, who have been facing established "one-language-one-teacher" paradigms during their school experience in a particular national or generational setting, highlights the on-going need for change in the field of training language professionals as agents of multilingualism.

Based on the results of the study, this paper suggests that the construction of a methodological and conceptual foundation, with multilingualism at its center, is necessary in order to identify the field to which a language teacher will need to assimilate to as a professional. The development of practices that will guide the creation of a community of language teaching professionals who go beyond monolingual language training and educational structures is an important issue, especially with the goal of defining a complementary pedagogical approach for a multilingual Europe. The distinction made by the Council of Europe between a collective or social dimension of "multilingualism" and the individual's dimension of "plurilingualism" as "plurilingual repertoire" is particularly challenging when it comes to educational implications for teacher education and the varying realities of languages and diversity of population in the different European contexts (cf. http://www.coe.int/t/dg4/linguistic/division_fr.asp).

Background of the study: multilingualism as a critical issue in language teacher education of the 21st century

Language teachers have been given a special position relative to teachers of other subjects. A language is presented as being the reified object of teaching (e.g., vocabulary or grammar). Moreover, language practices especially in classrooms, raise intercultural and power issues, which often appear when human artefacts or symbolic tools such as language are put to use (Blyth 1997, Faraco 2006, de Haan and Elbers2009).

Arguing that teachers of language and their working contexts in the classroom are different from that of other subjects, we consider their global role along two axes. Firstly, the language teacher represents the language under study as well as other related elements. For instance, the French language teacher in certain contexts might be associated not only with the language but also with specific elements related with current political or historical issues of France. Secondly, the language teacher is interacting in a particular, situated, classroom setting that might evoke his/her age, hobbies and other dimensions that come up in classroom communication and interaction. The language teacher is thus also approaching language as a mediating tool for communication and acting in the language, which is then no longer, and not exclusively, an object of teaching but a means of interaction.

Multilingualism represents a challenging issue for current schooling contexts and language teachers are often considered to be intuitive main actors in this area, promoting and integrating multilingualism. Accordingly, the two aforementioned role-domains of the language teachers are critical when assessing how they will carry out their intuitively or politically defined roles as agents of multilingualism in Europe. Firstly, the professional identity of language teachers generally emerges from training as a language teaching professional, but in one language only. A potential professional identity of the one-language teacher evolving into one of multilingualism (i.e. to represent not only the one language of teaching but several languages and their interaction in general) is currently a challenge for him or her. A second challenge of multilingualism arises in interaction with learners who are both learners of the language classroom and also plurilingual individuals with their respective linguistic biographies and practices from their language communities.

At the beginning of the 21st century, these issues, which are situated at the intersection between Europe's proclaimed societal multilingualism and its plurilingual individuals, have been addressed in the report on the "European Profile for Language Teacher Education" (EPLTE) (Kelly and Grenfell 2004). The report responds to a call for a synoptic outline of the challenges of language teacher education in an increasingly multilingual, mobile, and technology-driven society, both within and beyond European borders. While the EPLTE has been largely disseminated, little information is available on the interpretation and understanding of the EPLTE, as regards to multilingualism and diversity of plurilingual repertoires in classrooms. We especially lack feedback from Europe's language teachers, relevant political stakeholders, and teacher educators. To address this issue, Ziegler et al. (2009a) conducted a study which brought together language teaching professionals, political stakeholders and players in the area of language teacher education around the EPLTE. Based on the findings and recommendations of this study, the current paper discusses core issues, focusing in particular on the importance of language teacher identities in professional, educational, and related policies in the face of multilingualism.

Methods and participants of study: challenges of a common framework for language teacher education in multilingual Europe

Europe's policies on plurilingual repertoires focus on the individual learners and their linguistic biographies through language portfolios, intercultural (auto-) biographies, and media literacies for gaining access to various languages (Byram 1997, Council of Europe 1997, Cope & Kalantzis 2000, Zarate et al. 2008). However, language teachers, as major facilitators of language learning, are rarely in focus in the development of plurilingualism on a European scale. The European portfolio for language teacher education (Kelly and Grenfell 2004, Kelly2009) points to the pivotal role of language teachers in this process in Europe. Specifically, the EPLTE (2004) stresses the fact that language teachers are in direct contact with the plurilingual learners and have to manage local contexts of multilingualism, diversity, and the relevance of a specific language in the local educational context. Therefore, the EPLTE provides a set of elements, which is meant to help individual European countries to act towards a more common language-teacher educational framework. Specifically, the EPLTE highlights the importance of a sustainable dissemination of a multilingual perspective of language teacher education across Europe and gives indications on how to strive for suitable implementations of a common multilingual framework of language-teacher education. However, suggested syllabi for language-teacher education show little awareness for this issue in terms of professionalization, specific preparation, and training of candidates across Europe. Furthermore, the pan-European concern of suitable language-teacher education in and for multilingualism needs to be concerned with context-sensitive implementations in a given national or regional environment. Hence, potential pitfalls of a common European perspective on syllabi of language teacher education have to be addressed, especially as the individual language teacher faces a training scheme geared towards the development of a professional vision of a teacher education in the light of multilingualism and plurilingual repertoires.

A group of stakeholders and language teacher educators (N=106) discussed the challenges of a common framework of language teacher education in Europe. 96% (102) of the participants were from the EU, while 4% (4) represented non-European institutions that deal with European languages. As depicted in Figure 1, 15% (16) of the participants were policy makers at ministries or European institutions in the area of teacher education planning, 37.5% (40) were syllabi/curriculum planners or teacher trainers and 47.5% (50) were managers, directors of institutions for teacher training, language pedagogy including teacher unions. Identifying a group of stakeholders and teacher educators as regards language teacher education in Europe requires careful assessment, given the heterogeneity of educational issues across Europe. Decisions are taken on different levels: certain groups of stakeholders play an important role in one national context and are barely visible in a neighbouring country. Therefore, the study identified a maximum of three participants per European country from three relevant areas of intervention in language teacher education; policy makers, language teacher educators, and directors of teacher training institutions. Other stakeholders (e.g., non language teaching areas which are also concerned by multilingualism such as general education or subject matters) were not included. The participants declared their interest and availability to participate in the study. The selection as well as the limited size of the sample of stakeholders shows the limitations of the study. Yet, given the complex situation of language teacher education across Europe (ethical approuval was provided by the project, http://semlang.eu), this study marked a first step in providing comprehensive, yet limited insights into the area.

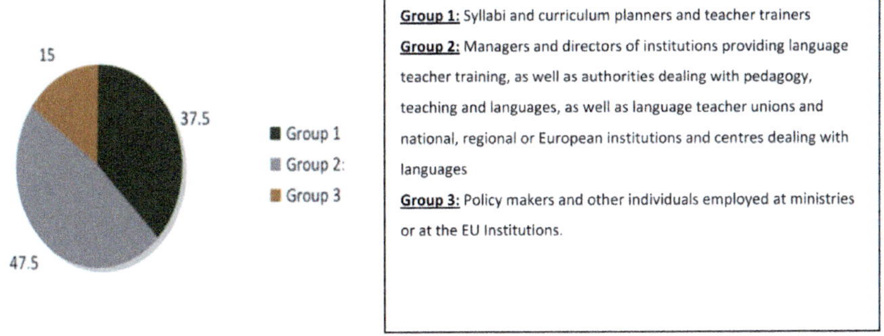

Figure 1. Participants in the study (adapted from Ziegler et al. 2009a).

In order to explore the visions and perspectives of participants relative to the current state of a common framework of language-teacher education in each participant's local context, the study (conducted in 2009) applied a mixed method approach, bringing together i) a first exploratory survey, ii) a second thematic survey and iii) focus-group interviews. The two surveys were open to all participants and were conducted anonymously by means of online questionnaires. The questionnaires were mainly composed of multiple-choice questions, providing free writing space for comments, insights from experience, and suggestions. Additionally, and in order to assess the often complex local situations of language-teacher education of the participants, four focus-group discussions were conducted. In line with the exploratory participant-bound perspective (Ziegler et al., 2009b, 6), the study was interested in the rating as done by the participants with regard to key topics and critical issues in a common framework for language teacher education (ii, second survey). A first survey allowed for stating if and to which extent participant stakeholders rank the issue of multilingualism in their context of language-teacher education. The focus group discussions centred around questions that arose from the survey (see Appendix) in order to better grasp the visions of the participants as expressed in the ranking according to relevance of a topic. The points raised and discussed in the focus group interviews help to put into perspective the quantified ranking of most critical issues in the context of a common framework of language teacher education in Europe.

Finding 1: relevance of multilingualism in a common framework of language teacher education

Participants indicate multilingualism as being a core element in language-teacher education, and in the life and work of a language teacher in Europe. In survey 1, when asked about the participants' awareness of multilingualism, 95% (101) indicate that multilingualism is familiar to them as a concept and as a European effort, and that it therefore should ultimately be seen as an integral part of language teacher education (see Figure 2).

Interestingly, only 47% (50) of the respondents have actual experience in working with multilingual groups in their educational contexts. In the focus group interviews, participants raise four major concerns as regards multilingualism and a common framework of language-teacher education in Europe.

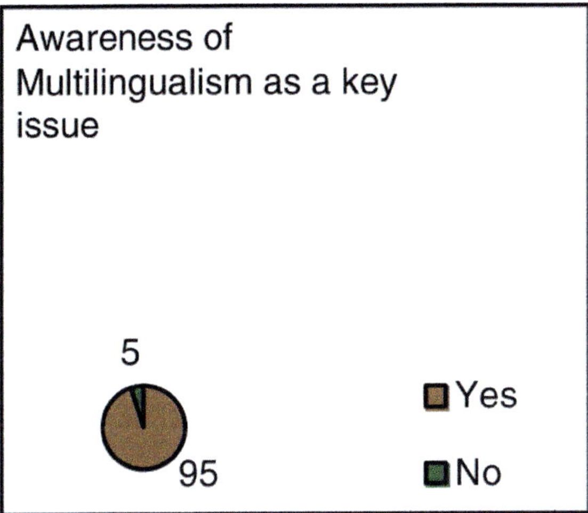

Figure 2. Multilingualism as a key element in language teacher education (adapted from Ziegler et. al. 2009a).

Firstly, they indicate that within their contexts (e.g., syllabi of language teacher education on a national level) the multilingual and multicultural aspect in language teacher training is given too little attention. The impact of multilingualism as experienced by pre- and in-service teacher trainees was raised as language teachers face various kinds of multilingualism and language varieties on the one hand and are in charge of the foreign language of the local syllabus on the other hand. Participants particularly pointed to the pre-service and in-service trainee contexts. In these contexts, the European vision of multilingualism meets local expectations, which trainee-teachers (and others) have as regards outcomes in a given foreign language. Yet, trainee-teachers face the reality of the challenges in line with plurilingual repertoires, which the heterogeneous student populations bring along. Current language teacher education across Europe does not address possibilities for integrating multilingualism in pre- and in-service education of language teachers.

Secondly, stakeholders identified two pedagogical areas, which according to their visions are in line with the aims and issues of multilingualism in language-teacher education. Early foreign language teaching, as well as the ever more generalized use of Content and Language Integrated Learning (CLIL), are well known schemes amongst language teachers and language teacher education frameworks. However, these well known pedagogical approaches currently remain largely below their potential to work for the proclaimed European multilingualism. Teacher education frameworks seem to fail to embed these promoted approaches or to present the practical knowledge from these approaches in language-teacher education. Participants of the study highlight that a common framework of language teacher education should draw from such flagship approaches and experiences.

Thirdly, stakeholders in the area of language-teacher education point out that models and concepts of teaching languages from a multilingual perspective still lack concepts and theoretical underpinnings. Models, pedagogical instruments, and tools for evaluation in language teaching often contain visions of monolingual learning and idealisations, such as considering the "native" speaker of a language as the norm (cf. European language portfolio). Language teachers in particular are sensitive to these issues and their concerns of being a professional in a language need to be taken seriously, especially in light of the theoretical and practical implications of multilingualism. In the perspective of the participants of the study, many efforts on the European level are concerned with political visions and practical instruments but fail to address multilingualism as an individual reality of plurilingual repertoires and lifelong learning (e.g., language identities, transversal competences).

Finally, the issue of how a common framework of language teacher education can be applied to diverse contexts as a frame of reference is identified as a problematic domain. Participants argue that, content-wise, such a framework (e.g., EPLTE) runs the risk of being considered too general or even vague when addressing overall issues. Participants suggest a closer focus on transversal language competences and ways of conveying such integrated competences. Other areas under discussion include a focus on curricula integrated multiple languages, contrastive grammar, or devices for the learning of languages in a multilingual context.

In sum, perspectives of the stakeholders participating in this study show a need for better understanding the implications of multilingualism and plurilingual repertoires at a general level, but also to embed existing structures and practices in a larger, but locally valid picture, which recognizes the expertise - linguistic and pedagogical - of a language teacher within a given educational setting (Toohey and Waterstone2004).

Finding 2: core issues for language-teacher education facing diversity

Following the various dimensions relevant for the conception of a common framework for language teacher education (Kelly and Grenfell2004), participants of the study ranked a set of themes and topics according to their priority for the advancement of language teacher education facing multilingualism and related challenges.

Participants' perspectives on the importance and the relevance of the topics were assessed by means of a thematic questionnaire in Survey 2 (see list of items below, Figure 3) and these provide interesting insights into the participants' lived reality of conceptual elements, institutional practices and hands-on implications of language teacher education according to their contexts. Therefore, it is of interest to state and to further investigate the ratings of importance of the topics as they show the perceived needs and pitfalls of a common framework for language teacher education and an instrument such as EPLTE (Kelly and Grenfell 2004). In fact, the participants' perspectives clearly identify the major issues in their reality impact.

Rating of themes, relevant for language teacher education
(6,0 highest rank, 1,0 lowest rank)

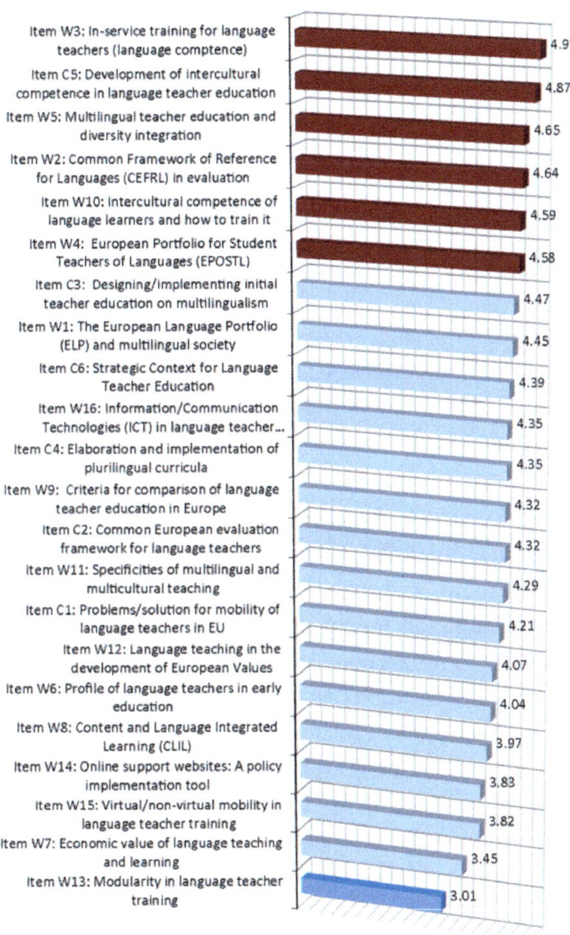

Figure 3. Rating of given topics for current situation of language teacher education (based on Ziegler et al. 2009a).

Participants were asked to rate the themes according to their perceived importance, value 6 being very important, value 1 being of little importance. The following six themes scored highest (above rating 4,5) in the thematic survey. Figure 3 provides an overview:

1. The role of in-service training for language teachers in the domain of language competence (average rating: 4.97)

2. Incorporating the development of intercultural competence in language teacher education (average rating: 4.87)

3. Multilingual teacher education and diversity integration (average rating: 4.65)

4. Using the Common European Framework of Reference for Languages (CEFRL) in evaluation - challenges and opportunities (average rating: 4.64)

5. Intercultural competence of language learners and how to train it (average rating: 4.59)

6. The use of the European Portfolio for student teachers of languages (average rating: 4.58)

The results of this ranking were presented to the European agencies as regards the potential of a common framework for language teacher education (see Ziegler et al. 2009a). In this section, we critically discuss these results in the light of a suitable concept for the professional identity of a language-teaching expert facing multilingualism and plurilingual repertoires alike, both as a challenge and as an opportunity.

Firstly, the results illustrate that the highest rated topics concern major domains of improvement and areas of actions with regard to the ongoing development of the language teaching professional. Specifically, participants rank highest the key area in language-teacher education, which is the language taught in its larger implementation (rank 1). Similarly, they rank second the need felt for ongoing development in terms of cultural awareness and intercultural competence (rank 2) as well as its integration in core education and training. Both domains address the need for lifelong learning issues and intergenerational work as a major element in language teachers' professionalization and suitable adaption to the challenges of today. Moreover, these ratings point to the fact that these dimensions are relevant in the heterogeneous reality of language-teacher education and require attention from all key actors in this field. In line with these results, participants raise, in the focus group discussions, the issue that the development of teachers is often neglected: the actual multilingual practices of language teachers are not taken into account. Yet, the participants highlight that the assurance of their language teacher identity and professionalization consist in areas such as intercultural understanding and language competences at large.

Secondly, stakeholders are aware of the challenges and opportunities of today's educational landscape. In fact, the relevance of concepts and practices of multilingual education are highly rated which clearly shows its importance with regard to society's diversities and the management thereof (rank 3). Practices and the suitable integration of such into a non-fractured, European-bound language and general teacher education is a key concern. Moreover, opportunities of generalized frameworks are clearly welcomed by the participating stakeholders. They also state the problematic issue of knowledge evaluation. According to them, evaluation schemes are often inconsistent and go against a context-sensitive implementation of profile-bound tools for the evaluation of development. Specifically, participants point to the potential of the CEFRL, as it is exploited for suitable, lifelong learning-bound evaluation beyond profile-unspecific grids (rank 4). This dimension is closely related to the socio-economic value of language learning and therefore to the profession of language teaching.

Thirdly, the participants are concerned with language teaching using schemes with language learners of all ages in relation to cultural and intercultural issues. In fact, participants identify this need within the professionalizing structures, focusing on the impact of intercultural professional development (rank 5). This priority, then, together with the higher ranked priorities (ranks 1–4), show the importance of an adequate and integrated education in these respects for future professionals and student teachers. Participants also ranked available tools for integrated teacher education schemes, such as the European Portfolio for Student Teachers of Languages at the European level accordingly (rank 6).

In sum, the closely ranked issues (above value 4.8 for rank 1 and 2, above value 4.6 for rank 3 and 4, above value 4.5 for rank 5 and 6) show, however, a core domain (above value 4.8 > above value 4.6, 4.5.) with regard to the actual identity and relevant professional development of a language teaching professional within the larger educational landscape and the professional development, as continued across structural limitations and areas.

This is also supported by the focus group interviews, where the identity of language teachers was discussed with regard to their intercultural competences, cultural awareness and their ability to include all students in class activities and the classroom community. Moreover, the participants indicated a need for a wholehearted recognition of the language teacher's occupation in order to ensure that a skilled individual undertakes language teaching. Interestingly, this trend resonates with the need for an increased focus on intercultural competences, diversity, and integration in a multilingual society as well as more context-sensitive, European-bound, frameworks aiding the continued development of language teaching professionals. In sum, participants point to the necessity to insure the recognition of the language-teaching professional as a skilled and lifelong-trained professional. This fact is reflected in the high rating of issues such as intercultural competence and general cultural awareness, an increased and timely focus on multilingualism, as well as digital literacy as primary issues needing increased attention in language-teacher education.

Finding 3: language-teacher education: identity building for professionals of multilingualism

The perspectives on multilingualism for language teacher education and the ranking of issues at stake in this respect (see above) and the topics developed in the focus group interviews provide further insights into the main weaknesses in current training and the needs identified by the participants. Areas highlighting interrelations relevant for the development of the language teaching professional in the era of multilingualism and everyday issues of diversity and technology were also identified (Ziegler et al. 2009a, 46). The domains as given below read as complementary polarities - such as identity building on the one hand and professionalization on the other hand - which language teachers and their educational schemes currently struggle to integrate. Several domains address structural issues which stakeholders deem necessary to be in place on the local as well as on the European level as a basis for further developing a common framework of language teacher education (e.g., in-service training in another country, cf. Ziegler et al. 2009a, 52). With regard to a coherent vision of the identity of language teacher in the face of multilingualism and diversity, the current paper discusses the following areas in more detail:

- Identity vs. profession: Identifying the language-teaching professional
- Knowledge vs. values: Multilingual language education across borders and grids
- Multilingualism vs. Languages: Conceptual and practical needs

These complementary polarities (domains 1–3) are synthesized in line with the issues raised in the focus group interviews. The synthesis indicates the interconnectedness as well as hierarchical and structural overlaps and contradictions, which the individual language-teacher-actor is facing in general at any given point in his/her career today.

Identity vs. profession: Identifying the language-teaching professional

Instruments like the European Profile of Language Teacher Education and concepts of a common framework of language teacher education entail discussing the identity of a language teacher. The profession and professionalization of a language teaching professional is not only linked to the knowledge and understanding, strategies or skills or even values that such an individual possesses or displays in action (House and Rehbein 2004; Maulini and Montandon 2005). Rather, participating stakeholders discuss what characterizes such an individual and how this can be instigated through institutional support and evaluated in a suitable, context-relevant fashion.

"…was mir wichtig scheint ist zu überlegen was ist denn das was das Fremdsprachenlehrerdasein, ob Französisch, ob Deutsch als Fremdsprache, ob Englisch, ob Russisch auszeichnet, was müssen die sozusagen über diese allgemeindidaktischen pädagogischen Dinge hinaus können, was ist das Profil von den Leuten …" (Focus group, D-1)

(Translation author: What seems important to consider, from my perspective, is what constitutes the being-a-language-teacher, be that in French, German as a foreign language, English or even Russian. What do these individuals need to master beyond the general didactical pedagogical techniques…. what is their profile?)

Participants stated that a language teacher is marked by a desire or "… a certain charisma, perhaps" (Focus group, E-1) to be able to motivate students, create a learning environment as well as an ability to adapt teaching approaches to the educational context and individual needs of the learner (cf., Kelly and Grenfell 2004, point 22). The identity of a language teacher is different from that of another teacher, though participants highlighted the fact that every teacher is in a way a language teacher (Byram 2003; Byram and Feng 2004). The teacher needs structural support, training towards knowledge in specific areas, to be taught how to master skills and strategies and realize the importance of certain values; but he/she also needs to have a willingness to do so, to engage in professional development, to want to learn from the learners, and to consistently undergo an evaluation of his or her own approach towards the students.

"Sometimes [as] teachers, we do not consider that [we] are part of an interaction which is an asymmetric interaction and that [we behave according to patterns of interaction that are part of their culture. Sometimes these patterns are correct […] but most often they are not, which is why it's important

to be the student at times. I'm sure a period of going back to the classroom as students is also important for us." (Focus group, E-2)

Also, the language teacher is - with regard to the recent European past and also as regards the continuing integration of new member states - seen as a major actor in bringing about change and managing the diversity of today's societies.

	Focus group interview conducted in		
	German (translation GZ)	English	French (translation GZ)
Issues raised in discussing the identity of language teachers	• Identity Question is a question of professionalism • It appears that the (academic) requirements for becoming a language teacher are different than those of becoming e.g. a physics teacher • Today, anyone native in a language can become a langue teacher. One needs a system of sorts to prevent that and ensure quality • One needs to develop a common basis with other language teachers in the department, in the country from where one can share and exchange best practises and experiences	• Open mind • Flexibility and adaptability • Creativity • Charisma • Willingness to explore together with students	• There's lots of research currently being done in the field, complexity of identity because of the cultural dimension • How language teacher envisage themselves in relation to other teachers • Publication on the matter, dealing with that exact issue • I think, one is asking too much of the language teacher, maybe even too much for her to manage in the time allocated (in relation to other teachers) • A langue teacher is like a door, a window, to the outside, a different world, a different society

Figure 4. Overview of issues raised in focus groups on the discussion of the identity of the language teacher (developed from Ziegler et al. 2009a , 2009b).

The participants in the focus groups as presented in Figure 4 highlighted the fact that a more tangible definition of the language teacher was needed. The analysis of the focus group interviews reveals the use of more descriptive adjectives in trying to characterize the individual language teacher. Other contributions try to explain their understanding in more structure-system oriented ways, and yet other comments offer metaphors. What is interesting to note is that the three focus group set-ups (French-speaking, German-speaking and English-speaking) refer differently to the issues raised throughout the focus groups, which can serve as an indicator for the need of the development of a shared vision and, as a first step, a common language on the matter (Allen & Negueruela-Azarola, 2010; Byram and Feng 2004). For instance, the general adjectives came from the English-speaking focus group, the structural system-oriented from the German-speaking, and the metaphorical from the French-speaking focus group. Although there were several nationalities in the groups, mostly using the language at hand as a foreign language, the similarities in the wording of the issues as regards language-teacher identity were surprising. The summarized table (Figure 4) provides an overview of the items used in each one of the focus groups.

Knowledge vs. Values: multilingual language education across borders and grids

"I think there are several ways of collaboration... we can have projects, international projects...where...groups or groups of teachers form different contexts...they gather around a problem a common situation ... and then they devise solutions for their different context but within common principles..." (Focus group, E-3)

In Survey 1, it was found that 60% (64) of the participants acknowledged they had some experience with intercultural learning, while 65% (69) had an understanding of intercultural teaching. 95% (101) were familiar with multilingualism (as a concept) and 68% (72) of those were also familiar with the concept of European citizenship. Nevertheless, only 47% (50) had experience in teaching multilingual groups. In terms of changes needed to language teacher education in their home countries, 19% (20) argued that the most important were aspects such as teaching respecting plurilingual repertoires, intercultural awareness or even European citizenship. Specifically, 29% (31) of the participants argued that multilingual and multicultural aspects need to be integrated, either as an element during teacher education, or as a value that the trainee teachers should know how to promote and teach themselves. This is in line with a European vision of citizenship as promoted by the European Profile of Language Teacher Education (Kelly and Grenfell 2004, 42): "European citizenship corresponds to a set of shared values and beliefs in democracy, the rule of law, the free press and a shared cultural heritage". Despite these statements and identified needs in this area of European language teaching, participants agree that little is available about the content of these European values.

Given this highlighted and identified necessity, the enormous efforts in evaluation along grids of "knowledge" and not of values is perceived as a major challenge for language teaching professionals, as they wish to provide sustainable work in line with the European aims. Yet, these initiatives (e.g., actual work on the creation of European-bound perspectives and values) are poorly rewarded by otherwise content-driven evaluation-only schemes. One group of participants framed this as a paradox, which they summarized as "getting rid of the grids", as these seldom allow for including both contents and values in the teacher's work. At the same time, the wish for standards and common goals for the profession and suitable outcomes (e.g., multilingual learning) is clearly stated.

Multilingualism vs. Languages: conceptual and practical needs

In regards to the pressing contradiction between plurilingualism as a mode of living on the one hand (cf. Grosjean 1984; Grosjean 2010) and languages as separately taught entities in educational contexts, participants illustrate the fact that multilingualism is highly available in discourses but is still in its infancy from a methodological and applied viewpoint. For instance, language teachers have to be ready to develop practices that aim at dealing with multilingualism and plurilingualism on multiple levels (e.g., syllabi policies, individual learners) and to various degrees (e.g., develop a general understanding, develop specific techniques for dealing with multilingual literacies). Language teachers faced with the challenge of multilingualism and plurilingual repertoires can no longer draw on single resources like bringing in materials in a given language or from experienced multilingual practices (e.g., Erasmus exchange) (Goodman 2009). More than in the past, language teachers have to integrate language resources of multiple kinds, often available from the learners themselves – on site (e.g., classroom community), in parallel (e.g., videogames, music videos) and in a continued active form (e.g., languages used in play).

In fact, the participating stakeholders state that multilingualism has become a core topic in many contexts of policy making and the planning of teacher education (see above, survey 1). However, the focus group interviews address the need for empirically grounded, rather than model driven or policy driven, approaches towards multilingualism as a reality in today's societies. Specifically, multilingualism has, up until now, largely been dealt with in terms of different languages and how to master or teach them. Discussions have been focusing to a lesser extent on how to deal with multilingualism, plurilingual individuals, and languages in their cultural realities per se. That is, multilingualism has often been used in the context of immigrant issues or minority languages, where the individual speaker is expected to assimilate other languages in order to fulfill some societal, or even social, expectations. More recently however, the terms multilingualism and plurilingualism have become denominators in EU language policies, as the EU strives to become a multilingual community with the aim to reap the benefits of such rich linguistic and cultural resources (Group of intellectuals for intercultural dialogue, 2008).

Participants point out that plurilingual people (here, learners) often attribute different functions to their languages. These functional attributes however have little to do with linguistic diversity, or being able to speak many languages. Plurilingualism rather often involves identity issues, social perspectives on professional development and success. In this respect, there is pressing need to enable professionals to implement, exploit and foster multilingualism and plurilingualism at both the conceptual and practical levels (Byrnes 2009; Crookes 1997, Jessner 2008). Concomitantly, when a language teacher deals with individuals, who face multilingualism at different levels – something that has become common even beyond the European context – he or she does not only have to teach the language for the learner to be able to use the language, but needs to pay increasingly close attention to the various dimensions (e.g. functional, identity, social). The language will resonate differently for any given individual and at different moments across the lifespan (e.g., one out of two or more family languages, languages of higher educational success, languages of tourism). Regarding pre- and in-service teacher training, a multilingual environment will challenge the trainee teacher and require him or her to develop a certain stance towards multilingualism in its most tangible forms. He or she will train to teach one language as an entity and to teach within a framework with multifaceted plurilingualism. Participants highlight the need for the construction of a methodological and conceptual basis for dealing with multilingualism at its core. Otherwise, debates on how to make teacher education in Europe more multilingual, in any one of the two perspectives of multilingualism and plurilingualism, will fail to respect the fact that the language teacher is to act as a primary agent and placed at the centre of multilingualism and education.

Strikingly, these issues - such as the value of language teaching – have still not found their way as key values or topics in the European educational landscape, let alone in language teacher education, which functions as a magnifying glass for the issue at hand. This is – as the following compilation shows – a major concern for the profession of language teaching, the training of young researchers and potential language students. Specifically, participants state "not to know enough about multilingualism and diversity" and to "lack examples of good practices" that show how to "handle multilingual contexts not only as problem" but to see "intercultural education as an advantage" (data Ch-1). Moreover, they highlight the fact that the "integration of diversity in various fields of work, research, and teaching should be promoted" on the level of "group work and the management of learning processes" by working in line with the value of diversity, multilingualism and plurilingualism (data Ch-2).

The results show that some initiatives that attempt to deal with languages as having a functional effect are beginning to appear, delineating a move away from language teaching for the sole purpose of interpersonal communication. From a language teaching perspective, CLIL (Content and Language Integrated Learning) was highlighted by many participants in the focus groups as a method that ensures that languages were not taught just for the sake of the language, but rather as tools for serving functional purposes (e.g., learning science in French, or learning maths in German) and thereby promoting the language from an early age. The identity of the language teacher as the language expert, however, was considered to be jeopardized in regards to CLIL practices. However, methods such as CLIL are currently not an integral part of a potential common framework of language teacher education.

Finally, the issue of ICT and the digital divide between learners and language teachers is an issue that sheds light on multilingualism in the literacy and language practices of today (Max 2011). Participants pointed out that learners often are active beyond the one-language entity, acting within a multilingual digital mode on an often daily and/or community basis (e.g., social media) to which language teachers have only limited access.

A summary of the issues put forth by the participants provides the following picture of the discussion of the professional teacher's identity and the values related to language education and multilingualism as an encompassing reality. As indicated in Figure 5, the issue of the nature of the identity of language teacher (1) in terms of expertise in a language, related pedagogical issues, societal multilingualism and individuals' plurilingualism is embedded in the definition of values defined for education today. In fact, the issue of decontextualised standards per individual language (2) is crucial as they are poorly responding to (3) multilingualism as a reality of biographies, communities, and various levels of literacies.

The findings highlight three issues that concern a potential common framework of language teacher education (Ziegler et al. 2009a, 58–59): the issue of being a professional European language teacher at the individual identity level; the ever growing need for more coherent professionalization at the individual's professional level, and the growing concentration on multilingualism and languages which poses needs for clarification in any given socio-cultural and socio-educational context at a societal as well as institutional level.

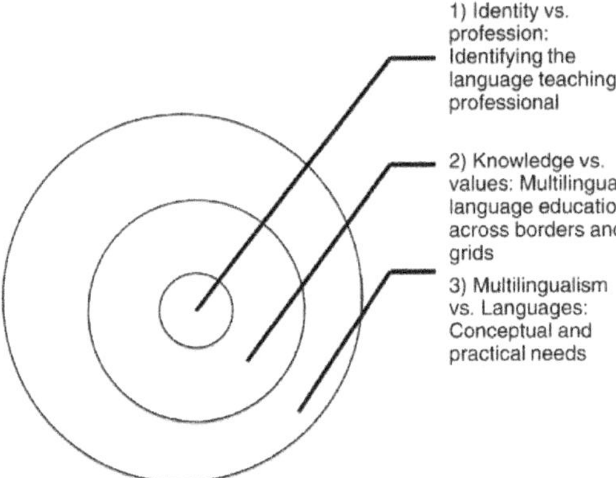

Figure 5. Language teacher identity at the centre of language teacher education facing multilingualism.

Discussion: building language teacher identities in face of multilingualism

The results of the participating stakeholders' views on challenges of language teacher education in the face of multilingualism and plurilingualism point to the larger area of roles and values, critical for language teaching professionals. The importance of self-representation among professionals in education, as opposed to other professions, has been discussed as regards choice of professions (Antonek et al.1997; Crookes 1997; Daniels et al. 2010). For instance, previous studies highlight the reasons for choosing a language as a teaching subject over other schooling subjects (Markee 1997; Singh & Richards 2006). The findings of the current study however addresses the issue of what the profession of a "language teacher" means in the educational as well as societal landscape today by focusing on two issues in particular:

- The ongoing development of common frameworks for education in general and language-teacher education in light of diversities of societies in particular (cf. Kelly and Grenfell 2004).

- More importantly, as revealed by the current findings, the multifaceted realities of multilingualism as an aim (e.g., language to be taught) and as a challenge (e.g., language resources by the learners to be integrated) in the language-teaching profession today.

This study then points to the bi-focused underpinning of the language teaching profession which addresses the language teacher as the subject teacher in the schooling framework on the one hand and as an agent to bring about change and managing the multilingual and multicultural diversity of the classroom on the other hand. The gap between these tasks of the language teacher, which has been voiced by the participants of this study in terms of a call for reconsidering the very definition of the professional identities of the language teaching professional, shows the need for a deeper focus on "how language teaching professionals think about and perform language teaching" (Markee 1997, 80) in the face of changing societal realities. These changes challenge and often contradict the methodological guidelines currently in place. This is of particular relevance for language-teacher education schemes on the local and national levels, and more importantly, as regards initiatives for common frameworks, which ideally should act as a resource for dealing with societal realities beyond the local context (e.g., migration, professional mobility).

Participants in this study, who as stakeholders in the area of language teacher education assess and plan the teacher education schemes of the future both in the light of common frameworks as well as local needs, bring up the missing element in the current debates. This element is the identity of the profession of the language teacher to which in-service and pre-service teachers would comply. The results highlight the lack of a thorough analysis of the meaning of language teaching in the current educational arena. Available matrices of professional identity constructions address various domains (Kumaravadivelu 2009). For instance, language teaching methods and general methodological orientations serve as identity matrices when professionals comply with or reject specific methodological elements for their professional self-representation (Kumaravadivelu 2009). Participants in this study specifically highlight popular definitions of the past, which orient towards the language teacher as an applied linguist, a literature-person, or a person driven by the motivation to promote foreign cultures. Also, the very definition of language and the language selected by the professional to be taught often implies elements of professional identity by an individual teacher (e.g., teaching a language for the purpose of promoting cultural awareness). A specific, and voiced, understanding of grammar and acquisitional processes, which entail related teaching schemes, has served the purpose of indicating professional identity (Klein & Perdue1992). Moreover, a certain vision of language learners, their identities and the constructions of such inside and outside the classroom, inside or outside of testing schemes work as relevant planes for defining professional identities (Kasper 2004; Seedhouse 2004; Ziegler 2008). The present study then points out that little, if any, matrices are available which would allow for identity-building of the language teacher in the multilingual scene today, especially in Europe. More precisely, the participants of this study labelled this gap and the missing planes for identification by opposing "languages" (Cuq 2009, 27) which refers to a somewhat insufficient ideal of a language-and-culture-expert and "multilingualism" which refers to a somewhat unspecific vision of encompassing languages within education at large, across the life-span and across the various domains of living.

Following the indications given by the stakeholders participating in this study, the findings allow for the following - open - conclusions, which address indications of language teacher education and the definition of this very educational process, labelled here as "professionalization" in terms of professional identity starting with pre-service training in a lifelong learning perspective.

CONCLUSIONS

Plurilingual education perspectives in multilingual Europe

Firstly, language-teacher education acting to build professional identities should address tensions with regard to multilingualism and plurilingual repertoires as discussed above. Specifically, the struggle for building language teachers' identities should be framed as a consequence of the two ways conceiving of the "the language teacher". Pre-service and in-service teachers alike should be aware of the idealisations of not solely linguistic "homogeneity" within an individual European country, which often limits training to the "one-language-teacher". These idealisations, which take for granted a "prototypical communicative exchange" of "two or three interlocutors, who all conduct the interaction in the same standard target language, all agree on what the purpose of the exchange is and what constitutes a culturally appropriate topic of conversation, all have equal speaking rights and opportunities" (Kramsch & Whiteside 2008, 645), need to be reframed. Bi-, tri-, and multilingualism, as enacted in school, require the individual teacher to construct interaction through a multilingual perspective. This however, raises the issue of "multilingual competence" with regard to "plurilingual repertoires" within and beyond linguistic competence in a language. In fact, the findings of this study of the European context highlight the worrisome gap between the politically advocated multilingualism on the one hand and the still poorly managed realities of plurilingual repertoires which often lead to a poorly monitored "English only" practice despite available linguistic resources. The findings, therefore, point to the need to model, analyse, and develop schemes for plurilingual education with a specific focus on language teacher education, responding to the shortcomings discussed. A concept of plurilingual education with regard to teacher education should therefore highlight the importance of developing multilingual competences considering that "le plurilinguisme n'est pas, comme le bilinguisme, conçu comme une adition de monolinguismes mais comme une compétence particulière" (Cuq 2009, 15). This competence has been present in the research literature with different labels: communicative competence (Hymes 1972), interactional competence (Kramsch 1986), or symbolic competence (Kramsch & Whiteside 2008, 664). Symbolic competence includes linguistic competences and follows a definition, which puts the creation of a plurilingual in language teaching at the centre. Specifically, the language teacher within such a symbolic competence promotes "the ability not only to approximate or appropriate for oneself someone else's language, but to shape the very context in which the language is learned and used" (Kramsch & Whiteside 2008, 664). A specific feature of a language teacher would then be to have a specific understanding of the various resources, which one speaker refers to when engaging in talk and interaction. The teacher would have a special lens for being sensible to issues of identity (cf. reference to a specific community or context of speaking) as enacted through language in a multilingual interaction. School, then, "as a social event" and "language as a social event" (Andrews 2006, 53), would take into account the way learners' identities are expressed through plurilingual resources and languages. In that respect, participants in language teaching are addressed as agents who resituate, "inhabit" (Durus 2009), and "rehistorizise" (Kramsch & Whiteside 2008, 667) the resources, which are available to them at any given moment in time.

Language-teacher education as acting for change

Language-teacher education supporting the building of language-teacher identities beyond the "one language" tradition addresses language teachers in particular as agents of change in the societies of the 21st century. Whereas teachers were previously conceived of as external agents in a linear and hierarchical track, moving from educational policies down to the classroom and the individual learner via the teacher, a more suitable framework takes into account the individuals and the contexts as agents. Specifically, language teachers and their education as professionals would focus on the factors, which "influence how change actually occurs in language education" (Markee 1997, 90). The syllabi of language teacher education would then move away from contents and methods but focus on the context-bound question of "Who adopts what, where, when, why, and how?" (Markee 1997, 82).

On the level of the "individual," we therefore speak about language teachers who "may act as change agents, clients, adopters (or resisters), implementers, or suppliers of innovations" ultimately acting as agents of change within their classroom setting or school, but also externally with regard to home contexts and the integration of various resources, even including contradictions (cf.

Markee 1997). This conception of language teachers as agents of change not only understand and integrate the dynamics and complexity of social identities and roles within interaction but they also sustain interests and, specifically, the interest of the teaching of a language with and for the learners. From the perspective of the individual, we are able to separate the elements of a process that was previously in a limited vision of "teaching" and to see both the top-down and the bottom-up infrastructural movements in terms of individual actors that are able to situate themselves in a multi-party process. In this line, we should consider "moving from a training perspective to a professional development perspective and substantiating this change with new practices that address foreign language graduate students' long-term needs as teachers and scholars" (Allen & Negueruela-Azarola 2010, 377). Following the findings of this study, then, a language teacher "not only needs structural support and possibilities, training toward acquiring understanding or knowledge in specific areas, being taught to master skills and strategies to realize the importance of certain values, but also willingness to engage in professional development, to learn from the learners" (Ziegler et al. 2009a, 8) and to undergo a constant assessment of his or her approaches in the light of the actual situation constructed with the learners. Instead of conceiving of the language teacher as a second order agent, language-teacher education would address the issue of change and innovation as a matter of fact in language education, done on a moment by moment basis induced by the teacher on awareness of his/her professional identity as a language teacher working towards plurilingual education rather than merely facing diversity and multilingualism.

Language teaching and plurilingual education

Language-teacher education largely fails to integrate in a sustainable and tangible way, for trainers and trainees, the issue of language teaching as plurilingual education in general. This has massive implications for the professional identity of language teachers, because disciplinary delimitations (e.g. the delimitations between two languages) are a heavy burden. Working towards an understanding of language teacher education as building a professional identity that encompasses language and plurilingual repertoires as a general (i.e., essential) educational feature, which integrate various subjects and elements (e.g., media) beyond disciplinary fractions. In fact, realities of the lives of the learners may serve as a guidebook for developing such an integrated or plurilingual vision of language education and the professional identity for the language teacher in line with this attempt. Various research efforts point in this direction, involving school-level initiatives developed to support language teacher education from an educationally integrated perspective. Most of these initiatives address the "across-discipline" or "language-transversal" perspective despite the fact that - interestingly - plurilingual initiatives on the level of language teacher education are still an exception (see for instance: The Teacher Development Model for Sustainable Education Reform (TDMSER) (Wilhelm1997, 520), Career in Teaching program (CIT), Peer Assistance and Review (Crookes 1997, 71), Languages Across the Curriculum (Byrnes2009), Student teacher portfolio (Antonek et al. 1997, 15) or CALL (Computer assisted language learning) (Zapata 2004, 339). Language teacher education then allows professionals to become participants in the construction of knowledge in line with local contexts, workplaces, and individual repertoires. Specifically, such an initiative would address the issue of building professional identities for the language teacher being educated with a perspective of multilingualism and larger and common frameworks for plurilingual education across Europe. With regards to previous education schemes, such a vision of language teacher education beyond disciplinary and medial divides would mark a step forward. This vision would then overcome many of the rather conservative factors in the currently existing trainings of language teachers in place at educational institutions. These institutions would then act as actual learning institutions and be "less like the static, time-defying forms" of education (Crookes 1997, 75).

The gaps in terms of disciplinary anchorage, generational segregation (cf. former points of reference in terms of being a language teacher), and also media divides in terms of media literacy are overcome by working towards suitable constructions of professional identities for language teachers. Such constructions operate across and beyond a one-language vision of the language teacher and bring about a multi-faceted but coherent vision of language teaching, which has multilingualism not only as an aim and a challenge but plurilingualism as a catalyst in and for education - of the learners and the teachers.

Appendix

Stimulus questions of focus group discussions, English version. One question per area (1, 2, 3, 4, 5, 6, 7) was presented for discussion to the group.

1

- Is there an identity problem of "the language teacher"?
- Is s/he an expert of grammar, language, culture…?
- Is any teacher a language teacher?

- How about CLIL? Is CLIL in this respect a "danger" or an "open door" for "the language teacher"?
- What are the specificities of "the language professional"?
- How can s/he be trained with regard to these specificities?

2

- What is Europe's obligation in language teacher education?
- In which area do you think money is needed to do more investigation/research?

3

- What do you think about organizing meetings of stakeholders across Europe?
- Who should be invited with regard to your local/national context?

4

- Do you feel overwhelmed, frustrated by all these elements language teacher have to be aware of / take care of? Multilingualism, Information technologies … and other element as mentioned in the European framework for language teacher education?

5

- What does "Learning to learn" (as stated in the EPLTE) mean to you? Is this the business of a language teacher?
- What do you think about the "research attitude" as stated in the EPLTE?
- How do you rate/judge/understand the European Profile for language teacher education in general?

6

- Which are the biggest challenges/problems in language teacher education?
- Which are the biggest needs in language teacher education regarding your country and/or a particular level of schooling you are concerned with?

7

- Do you think it is possible to build a friendly relationship with trainee teachers and mentors today?
- How important is networking/collaboration/team teaching today, in your country? In Europe?

Authors' information

Gudrun Ziegler is an Associate Professor of Learning, Interaction and Multilingualism at the trilingual University of Luxembourg where she created and directed the Research Master – Learning and Development in Multilingual and Multicultural Contexts (2007–2011), a programme which figures on the list of innovative approaches for multilingual education by UNESCO, Institute for Lifelong Learning (Ziegler 2011a,2011b). She received her PhDs from Sorbonne Nouvelle and Saarland University, specialising in language learning and interaction. Her international research projects focus on interaction, multilingual language development, teacher education in multilingual contexts, professional development in lingua franca contexts and the construction of disciplinary knowledge in multicultural and multimodal learning environments. She served as editor of ForumSprache, a multilingual journal on language learning and teaching (2008–2011), and has edited special issues on the construction of literacy in diverse contexts, language acquisition and professionalization of language professionals.

Acknowledgments

The findings discussed in this paper draw from results of the SEMLANG project, funded by the European Commission (http://www.semlang.eu/). The paper is presented with the support of multi-LEARN Institute for Interaction and Development in Diversity, Luxembourg and the DICA-lab research group, University of Luxembourg (http://dica-lab.org). We thank two anonymous reviewers for their insightful comments on earlier versions of this paper.

Competing interests

The authors declare that they have no competing interests.

REFERENCES

1. Allen HW, Negueruela-Azarola E: **The professional development of future professors of foreign languages: looking back, looking forward.** *Mod Lang J* 2010, **94:**337–395.**View Article**
2. Andrews L: *Language exploration and awareness. A resource book for*

teachers. New Jersey: Lawrence Erlbaum; 2006.

3. Antonek JL, McCormick DE, Donato R: **The student teacher portfolio as autobiography: developing a professional identity source.***Mod Lang J* 1997, **81:**15–27.**View Article**
4. Blyth C: **A constructivist approach to grammar: teaching teachers to teach.** *Mod Lang J* 1997, **81:**50–66.**View Article**
5. Byram M: *Teaching and Assessing Intercultural Communicative Competence*. Clevedon: Multilingual Matters; 1997.
6. Byram M: **Teacher education – visions from/in Europe.** *Babylonia* 2003, **3–4:**7–10.
7. Byram M, Feng A: **Culture and language learning: review article.** *Lang Teach* 2004, **37:**149–168.**View Article**
8. Byrnes H: **The role of foreign language departments in internationalizing the curriculum.** *Mod Lang J* 2009, **93:**607–627. **View Article**
9. Cope B, Kalantzis M (Eds): *Multiliteracies: literacy learning and the design of social futures*. London: Routledge; 2000.
10. Council of Europe: *Plurilingual and pluricultural competence*. Strasbourg: Council of Europe; 1997.
11. Crookes G: **What influences what and how second and foreign language teachers teach?** *Mod Lang J* 1997, **81:**67–79.**View Article**
12. Cuq JP: **Diversité culturelle, diversité linguistique ... vers une diversité métodologique pour les professeurs de langue?** In*Approches comparées de l'enseignement des langues et de la formation des enseignants*. Edited by: Gonçalves C, Groux D. Paris: L'Harmattan; 2009:99–11.
13. Daniels H, Edwards A, Engeström Y, Gallagher T, Ludbigsen SR (Eds): *Activity theory in practice. Promoting learning across boundaries and agencies*. London: Routledge; 2010.
14. de Haan M, Elbers E: **From research to practice. What the study of multiethnic classrooms has to offer.** In *Social interactions in multicultural settings*. Edited by: César M, Kumpulainen K. Rotterdam: Sense; 2009:171–202.
15. Durus N: *Discourse strategies in learner inhabited talk. Scientific Master thesis, unpublished.* : University of Luxembourg; 2009.
16. Faraco M (Ed): *La classe de langue: Théorie, méthodes et pratiques*. Aix-en-Provence: Presses universitaires de Provence; 2006.

17. Goodman AE: **Language learning and study abroad: the path to global citizenship.** *Mod Lang J* 2009, **93:**607–627.**View Article**

18. Grosjean F: *Life with two languages. An introduction to bilingualism.* Harvard: Harvard University Press; 1984.

19. Grosjean F: *Bilingual. Life and reality*. Harvard: Harvard University Press; 2010.

20. Group of intellectuals for intercultural dialogue: *A rewarding challenge. How the multiplicity of languages could strengthen Europe*. Brussels: European Commission; 2008. http://europa.eu/languages/en/document/106/5. Accessed 15 March 2012

21. House J, Rehbein J: **What is 'multilingual communication'?** In *Multilingual communication*. Edited by: House J, Rehbein J. Amsterdam: Benjamins; 2004:89–102.

22. Hymes DH: **On communicative competence.** In *Sociolinguistics: Selected Readings*. Edited by: Pride JB, Holmes J. Harmondsworth: Penguin; 1972:269–293.

23. Jessner U: **Multicompetence approaches to language proficiency development in multilingual education.** In *Encyclopedia of Language and Education, Volume 5: Bilingual Education*. Edited by: Cummins J. Amsterdam: Springer; 2008:91–103.

24. Kasper G: **Orientations in German conversation-for-learning.** *Mod Lang J* 2004, **88:**551–567.**View Article**

25. Kelly M: *Strategic contexts for the education of language teachers*. 2009. http://europa.eu/languages/en/document/106/5. Accessed 15 March 2012

26. Kelly M, Grenfell M: *European Profile for Language Teacher Education (EPLTE). A frame of reference*. Southampton: University of Southampton; 2004. http://ec.europa.eu/education/languages/pdf/doc477_en.pdf. Accessed 15 March 2012

27. Klein W, Perdue C: *Utterance structure. Developing grammars again*. Amsterdam: Benjamins; 1992.

28. Kramsch C: **From language proficiency to interactional competence.** *Mod Lang J* 1986, **70:**366–372.**View Article**

29. Kramsch C, Whiteside A: **Language ecology in multilingual settings. Towards a theory of symbolic competence.** *Appl Linguist* 2008, **29:**645–671.**View Article**

30. Kumaravadivelu B: *Understanding language teaching. From method to postmethod*. New York: Routledge; 2009.

31. Lave J, Wenger E: *Situated Learning. Legitimate peripheral participation*. Cambridge: University of Cambridge Press; 1991.**View Article**

32. Markee N: **Second language acquisition research: a resource for changing teachers' professional cultures?** *Mod Lang J* 1997,**81**:80–93. **View Article**

33. Maulini O, Montandon C (Eds): *Les formes de l'éducation: variété et variation*. Brussels: De Boeck; 2005.

34. Max C: **The development of initial teacher education focusing on multilingualisms: the innovative approach of Luxembourg.** *ForumSprache* 2011, **5**:59–78. http://www.ingentaconnect.com/content/hueber/forum. Accessed 15 March 2012

35. Seedhouse P: *The interactional architecture of the language classroom: A conversation analysis perspective*. Oxford: Blackwell; 2004.

36. Singh G, Richards J: **Teaching and learning in the language teacher education course room.** *Reg Lang Cent J* 2006, **37**:37–46.

37. Toohey K, Waterstone B: **Negotiating expertise in an action research community.** In *Critical pedagogies and language learning*. Edited by: Norton B, Toohey K. Cambridge: Cambridge University Press; 2004:111–123.

38. Vygotsky LS: *Mind in society. Development of higher psychological processes*. Harvard: Harvard University Press; 1978.

39. Wilhelm KH: **Sometimes kicking and screaming: language teachers-in-training react to a collaborative training model.** *Mod Lang J*1997, **81**:527–542.**View Article**

40. Zapata G: **Second language instructors and CALL: a multidisciplinary research framework.** *Comput Assist Lang Learn* 2004,**17**:339–356. **View Article**

41. Zarate G, Lévy D, Kramsch C (Eds): *Précis du plurilinguisme et du pluriculturalisme*. Paris: Editions des archives contemporaines; 2008.

42. Ziegler G: **De l'apprenant à l'acteur: les catégorisations dans l'interaction comme lieu d'acquisition.** In *Précis du plurilinguisme et du pluriculturalisme*. Edited by: Zarate G. Paris: Editions des archives contemporaines; 2008:39–42.

43. Ziegler G (Ed): In *Language teacher education in Europe. ForumSprache 5*. 2011. http://www.ingentaconnect.com/content/hueber/forum. Accessed 15 March 2012

44. Ziegler G: **Innovation in learning and development in multilingual and multicultural contexts: principles learned from a higher educational**

study programme in Luxembourg. *Int Rev Educ* 2011, **57:**685–703. doi:10.1007/s11159-011-9252-6.**View Article**

45. Ziegler G, Eskildsen L, Bottin C, Coonan CM, Ludbrook G: *Training teachers of languages in Europe. Analytical report.* Sèvres: CIEP; 2009.
46. Ziegler G, Eskildsen L, Bottin C, Coonan CM, Ludbrook G: *Recommendations for optimising language teacher training in Europe.* Sèvres: CIEP; 2009. http://www.semlang.eu/. Accessed 15 March 2012

Chapter 5

AN EMPIRICAL STUDY OF CONTENT-BASED INSTRUCTION APPLIED IN NON-ENGLISH-MAJORED GRADUATE ENGLISH TEACHING IN THE POST-MASSIFICATION

Yougen Lou

School of Foreign Studies, Yangtze University, Jingzhou, China

ABSTRACT

In the post-massification period, it is a beneficial attempt to the reform of English Teaching based on subject content for non-English-majored graduate students. Content-Based Instruction (CBI) has been defined as "the teaching of content information in the language being learned with little or no direct or explicit effort to teach the language itself separately from the content being taught", which can make non-English-majored graduate students not only learn subject knowledge but also improve their foreign language (English) ability in learning content. Results in this study showed that: in the post-massification period, content-based English teaching could improve the level of motivation and English language ability of students in their English learning, but CBI was not suitable for poor English learners with no good foreign language (English) basis.

INTRODUCTION

Content-Based Instruction (CBI) has been defined as "the teaching of content or information in the language being learned with little or no direct or explicit effort to teach the language itself separately from the content being taught" (Krahnke, as cited in Richards & Rodgers, 2001). This teaching approach is considered by many researchers as an effective and realistic teaching method in terms of combining language and content learning. According to Crandall (1999) , CBI can be used in various ways depending on the skills being taught and includes not only traditional teaching methods such as grammar-based instruction or vocabulary development but also contemporary approaches such as communicative language teaching and humanistic methods. CBI is related to Krashen's "Monitor Model". Krashen (1982) emphasized ways of decreasing learner anxiety, such as providing interesting texts as well as meaningful activities, which were comprehensible to learners, and CBI had the following essential features: "learning a language through academic content, engaging in activities, developing proficiency in academic discourse and fostering the development of effective learning strategies" (Crandall, 1999) . Content-Based Instruction is based on three main theories of language and four teaching models. Three main theories of language are: "language is text and discourse-based," "language use draws on integrated skills," and "language is purposeful"(Crandall, 1999) . Four teaching models are "theme-based approach", "sheltered-content courses", "adjunct courses" and "language for special purposes".

CBI in foreign language teaching has been used to improve students' subject knowledge and cognitive ability and promote the improvement of its language (Mohan, 1986) . CBI was born in immersion program teaching experiment in Montreal, Canada in 1960s. CBI in foreign language teaching in foreign countries had many successful examples (Benesch, 1988; Brinton et al., 1989; Kasper, 1994, 1997; Chumpavan, 2001) . Some scholars (Lv, 2001; Li, 2002) in China suggested that foreign (English) language teaching form should be combined foreign (English) language with content. There were teaching researches (Yu & Han, 2003) based on the combination of foreign language and the subject content in the college English teaching environment in China, but CBI in non-English-majored graduate students' English teaching research was still at groping stage in the post-massification period in China.

RESEARCH METHODS

Research Design

In order to make clear that, in the post-massification period, 1) Does content-based instruction (CBI) help non- English-majored graduate students improve their motivation to learn English? 2) Does content-based instruction help non-English-majored graduate students improve their English language proficiency? 3) Is CBI beneficial to all graduate students in the study in English learning? A comparative research method was used in this study. The subjects were divided into the control group (CG) and the experimental group (EG). And the conventional English teaching method was used in CG, which focused on learning the form of the language and on teachers' teaching the knowledge of the language in the text, while EG was taught by a new English teaching method, namely English teaching based on subject content.

Subjects

In September 2014, 115 first-year non-English-majored graduates in 3 classes from Yangtze University participated in this study. Among the 115 subjects, 60 were females and 55 males, average age 22 with Chinese as the main language. Their majors are chemistry, agriculture, plant protection, finance, biological technology. All 115 students who had learned graduate English first semester and had passed CET4 were divided into CG (57 students) and EG (58 students) randomly. Their level of education, family background, age, personality and life experiences and other factors were same, that was to say, their overall learning and cognitive abilities were almost equal. The second semester, EG were taught with the subject content course Experimental Design the English original material as the course materials in English teaching. CG were continued to learn conventional English course material Graduate English. The survey found that before the experiment, EG and CG showed no significant difference in learning motivation level ($t = .139$, $p = .446$) (Table 1). Meanwhile, two groups of students in English language ability were not significantly different ($t = .163$, $p = .968$) (Table 3). Therefore, we can say that EG and CG are homogeneous before the experiment.

Instruments

The instruments used in the study were the English Learning Motivation Questionnaire, English Language Applied Ability and interviews

English Learning Motivation Gardner & Lamber's language learning motivation, attitude/motivation test Scale AMTB (Attitude/Motivation Test Battery), as the survey tool in the study was used to measure students' English language learning motivation, and desire that the three-point Likert scale for scale, a total of 20 questions, which related to the motivation and desire 10 questions respectively. Prediction of internal reliability was .90, meaning that the scale display was reliable.

English Language Applied Ability. The National College English Test band 6 (2013 New Style) (full score of 710) and the National CET Oral Test (full score of 15) as the English language tools were used in this study to test the ability of students to use English. Content of CET 6 were showed inTable 2.

Interviews There were interviews with all 58 students in EG about the course experimental design and the harvest of learning English through the subject content. The teacher wrote down all interviews with all 58 students in

EG about the course experimental design and the harvest of learning English through the subject content.

Data Collection and Analyses

Before the research experiment (September 2013) and after the experiment (February 2014) two surveys on English learning motivation and two tests on English language applied ability were conducted to compare changes between the two groups of students in English learning motivation and the ability to use English. In this study, social scientific software SPSS 17.0 was used for statistical analysis to the collected data, the results showed that, the internal consistency reliability of the use of questionnaires and survey papers reached more than .77, indicating that the test results were reliable. In order to find out CBI proved superior to the conventional teaching (such as grammar-translation) method, comparison of Means was adopted to compare two groups of

Table 1. Test of English learning motivation between CG and EG.

		CG (N = 57)		EG (N = 58)			
		M	S	M	S	t	p
Pretest	MS	2.21	.42	2.19	.50	.374	.182
	DL	2.24	.43	2.26	.49	−.235	.264
	Total	4.35	.80	4.45	.91	.139	.446
After the experiment	MS	2.19	.45	2.28	.46	−1.62	.053
	DL	2.24	.43	2.35	.48	−1.17	.022*
	Total	4.43	.85	4.63	.86	−2.79	.025*

*Means $p \leq .05$; CG for Control Group; EG for Experimental Group; MS for Motivation Strength; DL for Desire of Learning.

Table 2. Comparison of teaching content and teaching process between CG and EG.

Items \ Groups	CG	EG
Teaching Content	Priority to English language knowledge, interpretation of the text content for students acquiring language knowledge	Priority to experimental design knowledge and linguistic knowledge as complementary
Schedules	2 hours for the teacher's teaching reading and writing (the teacher explaining language points, students answering a few questions); 2 hours for non-English-majored graduate students listening to listening material from textbooks and College English Test (CET) Level 6	2 hours for the teacher's teaching reading and writing (the teacher explaining related chapters, at the same time, students exploring chapters content and design of experiment in English); 2 hours for listening (via Internet to download audio and video data to discuss design of experiment)
Language Material	Domestic non-English-majored graduate students textbooks and College English Test (CET) Level 6 papers	Original English textbooks, English audio and video materials, and English programs on the network
Teaching Language	Combination of Chinese and English	English
Teaching Activities	Priority to the explanation, and little interaction between teachers and students	Teacher's explanation as complementary; more presentations and discussions between students; Interaction between teachers and students; Communication between students
Teaching Means	Reading and writing lessons in regular classrooms; listening lessons in language-learning lab	All the lessons in classrooms with network and multimedia equipment

graduate students' average scores of their pretest and after the experiment on the basis of two samples. And the independent sample T-test was adopted to exanimate if there were significances between CG and EG before the experiment and after the experiment.

COURSE CONTENT AND TEACHING ORGANIZATION PROCESS

This experiment was carried out a semester, the implementation details were shown in Table 2. English classroom teaching time for CG and EG was, respectively, 4 hours per week, reading, and writing listening and speaking lessons taught by the same English teacher. EG was taught with teaching mode CBI, Experimental Design used as subject material, and the experimental accuracy, the experiment results of statistical analysis, random design, and factor experiment design involved as the subject content. Students in EG read the content of the relevant chapters before class, teaching activities for EG in class were teachers answering questions from students or solving problems from students who did not understand the subject content they read, a topic presentation made by students from EG, group discussion and question answering between students in EG and so on.

In class, the teacher's explanation for subject content and student's statements for subject content were conducted in multimedia network classroom, with broadcast audio and video materials to help students understand the course content knowledge. In EG, English used as the teaching language in teaching activities, students in EG were encouraged by the teacher to communicate freely about the subject content in English, and to interpreter, induce and analyze the facts and opinions in the subject content. Contemporary Graduate English (intensive reading) used as the teaching material for CG, teachers mainly adopted the combination of teaching methods for CG: grammar-translation and listening, and explained language knowledge and the text content, students answered the questions from the teacher on the text.

RESULTS

In this study, social sciences software SPSS17.0 was used for statistical analysis to collected data to obtain relevant results, and the results were discussed and analyzed.

English Learning Motivation

After the half-year experiment, students' English learning motivation were improved between CG and EG. At the end of the experiment, CG was lower than EG in the overall level of learning motivation ($t = -1.62$, $p = .053$), while CG was less strong desire than EG to learn English ($t = -1.17$, $p = .022$) (Table 1).

English Applied Ability

As showed in Table 3, after half-year experiments, the ability to use the English language in CG and EG were improved, but the ability to use English of the students in CG was, in general, lower than EG, which showed a significant difference ($t = -6.237$, $p = .034$). Specifically, CG was significantly inferior to EG compared to the increase in the output of the skills, such as composition ($t = -2.082$, $p = .042$) and oral ($t = -2.107$, $p = .0348$), indicating that students in EG in English writing skills and spoken English skills had been significantly improved. CG was significantly inferior to EG on the skills of reception, such as hearing ($t = -2.121$, $p = .037$) and reading ($t = -.585$, $p = .047$), which showed that EG in English Listening comprehension and reading comprehension had improved significantly. While there was no significant difference ($t = .656$, $p = .513$) in the integrated skills (translation) between CG and the experimental group.

Interview

After the experiment, the teacher had interviews with EG of 58 students about the course experimental design and the harvest of learning English through the subject content. 49 students from EG said that their English ability (composition, listening, reading, translation and oral English) was improved a lot. 9 students from EG said that their English ability (composition, listening, reading, translation and oral English) was improved a little.

DISCUSSION

Needs to promote the development of learning motivation, and learning motivation was an important factor in the development of language learning. Seen in Table 1, we know that, after half-year experiment CG was lower than EG in the overall level of learning motivation, especially the desire to learn English.

The main reasons are:

First, English courses teachers were required by non-English-majored graduate students. When teaching content related to the interest of learners, students would have a strong desire to learn subject content, this correlation was a prerequisite for maintaining long-term motivation to learn. Some of students in EG already had a strong interest in learning English, the teachers chose English language as a medium to teach curriculum content and design of experiments to help students learn needed academic subject knowledge. After the experiment, talked with the students in EG we knew that they thought learning English as a medium to gain academic subject knowledge, which promoted the development of their English learning motivation.

Table 3. Test of English applied ability between CG and EG.

		CG (N = 57)		EG (N = 58)			
		M	S	M	S	t	p
Pretest	Composition	87.17	9.04	86.60	9.86	.277	.837
	Listening	141.19	12.39	139.55	10.23	.663	.175
	Reading	147.12	11.82	148.60	11.28	−.585	.657
	Translation	44.55	4.46	44.64	4.97	−.092	.658
	Oral English	9.40	1.06	9.42	1.12	−.100	.958
	Total	429.43	38.77	428.81	37.46	0.163	.968
After the experiment	Composition	85.21	8.24	89.12	8.32	−2.082	.042*
	Listening	143.1	9.45	145.2	9.12	−2.121	.037*
	Reading	149.02	10.82	151.210	9.28	−.585	.047*
	Translation	45.93	5.75	45.14	5.21	.656	.513
	Oral English	9.46	1.32	9.57	1.38	−2.107	.038*
	Total	432.72	35.58	440.24	33.31	−6.237	.034*

*Means $p \leq .05$; CG stands for Control Group; EG stands for Experimental Group.

Second, the course content was from the real experimental content and language content. In this study, original content-based English teaching materials were used for English textbooks, which was helpful for students to develop their own experimental design. Students' learning motivation changed gradually from the instrumental motivation to integrative motivation.

Therefore, the combined effect of the differences on overall academic achievement between the two groups of students was contributed to the internal and external factors from two groups of learners in the experiment. Students in the experimental listened to teachers explain the subject content knowledge in English, after class they listening to and watching English programs related to the course, so that they were in English listening environment to enhance their listening ability of a great help. After the experiment, the researcher in this study, after the conversation with students in EG, knew that some graduate students with poor basic English foundation in this study said that they felt English learning pressure increased and their ability to use the English language to be improved was not obvious in CBI. This indicated that the course content was limited to help students with poor English basis.

LIMITATIONS AND SUGGESTIONS

Though the present study has provided a comparatively detailed description of CBI applied among some first- year non-English-majored graduate students, there are still some limitations of the study. Having the limitations in mind, suggestions for further research, therefore, can be put forward at the same time in order to achieve a lot thorough understanding of CBI

Firstly, being time limitation (only half year) and other practical restrictions such as the subjects in the study consisted of only 115 non-English-majored graduate students in one university need to be broadened in further research.

Secondly, the instruments used to investigate non-English-majored graduate English teaching with CBI involve structured questionnaire, tests and interviews. The study would be much better, if it were combined with other instruments such as observation, verbal report. More instruments should be used in investigation in further research.

Finally, CBI applied in non-English-majored graduate English teaching can improve non-English-majored graduate students' English learning and their course learning, but CBI also works for other subjects such as undergraduate students, we need further research.

Despite of the restraints of the study, it is hoped that it can offer some guidelines for further research on CBI applied in English teaching.

CONCLUSION

This study was designed to explore CBI in English teaching in the post-massification period. Results in this study showed that: in the post massification period, content-based English teaching could improve the level of motivation and English language ability of students in their English learning, but CBI was not suitable for poor English learners with no good foreign language (English) basis.

REFERENCES

1. Benesch, S. (1988). Linking Content and Language Teachers: Collaboration across the Curriculum. In S. Benesch, (Ed.), Ending Remediation: Linking ESL and Content in Higher Education. Washington DC: Teachers of English to Speakers of Other Languages.
2. Brinton, D. M., Snow, M. A., & Wesche, M. B. (1989). Content-Based Second Language Instruction. New York: Harper & Row.
3. Chumpavan, S. A (2001). Comparative Study of Two English as a Foreign Language (EFL) Programs: Non-Content-Based and Content-

Based at the University Level in Thailand. PhD Dissertation, Normal: Illinois State University.

4. Crandall, J. (1999). Content-Based Instruction (CBI). Concise Encyclopedia of Educational Linguistics (pp. 208-604). Oxford, UK: Cambridge University Press.
5. Kasper, L. F. (1994). Improved Reading Performance for ESL Students through Academic Course Pairing. Journal of Reading, 5, 376-384.
6. Kasper, L. F. (1997). The Impact of Content-Based Instructional Programs on the Academic Progress of ESL Students. English f or Specific Purposes, 4, 309-320. http://dx.doi.org/10.1016/S0889-4906(97)00035-5
7. Li, L. S. (2002). Sustained-Content Language Teaching Mode and Its Enlightenment to College English Teaching Reform in China. Foreign Language World, 4, 36-40.
8. Lv, L. H. (2001). The Integration of Language and Content—Trend of Foreign Language Teaching Reform. Global Education, 8, 52-56.
9. Mohan, B. A. (1986). Language and Content. Reading, MA: Addison-Wesley.
10. Richards, J., & Rodgers, T. (2001). Approaches and Methods in Language Teaching (p. 204). New York: Cambridge University Press. http://dx.doi.org/10.1017/CBO9780511667305.021
11. Yu, L. M., & Han, J. X. (2003). Based on Course Teaching in Ottawa and Its Enlightenment. Foreign Language Teaching and Research, 3, 465-468.

Chapter 6

INTRODUCTION TO THE LINGUISTIC STUDY OF LANGUAGE

INTRODUCTION

Linguistics encompasses many fields related to language in general, but my major concentrations are in second language acquisition (SLA) and language pedagogy. I received my Bachelor's degree in French & Linguistics in 2004 and my Master's degree in Linguistics & Teaching English as a Second Language in 2007. I was officially awarded my PhD in Applied Linguistics in December 2015.

My major research interests are related to the role textbooks play in language teaching and learning, including the use of (or lack of) realia and informal language, as well as the teaching of vocabulary with regards to frequency and corpora and the importance of listening comprehension for learning vocabulary. I'm also interested in the role technology plays in language learning, especially computer-assisted language learning (CALL) that allows for more audio-visual input than the regular classroom.

I will be updating this section with more information on Applied Linguistics, Second Language Acquisition, and Language Pedagogy in the future. Also make sure to check out the Teaching English articles for information on teaching English as a second language as well as English grammar and the history of English.

WHO THESE BOOKS ARE FOR

This is the first of two books for teachers about the English language. We believe that all teachers, not just English teachers, share the responsibility for helping students develop their abilities to speak, read, and write. Students must learn to communicate appropriately about math, chemistry, history, and every other school subject. Teaching students these skills necessarily extends across the curriculum. Thus, while one part of our intended audience is English K-12 teachers, we have prepared this book and its companion with teachers (and student teachers) from all disciplines in mind.

How to Use These Books

In these books, we use certain typographical marks to help you focus on key points. Important terms are bolded. You can find their definitions in the text and in the glossary. Examples are noted in italics or are separated from the text.

What These Books Are About

These books are about language, but specifically about the English language and its uses. The first book is about the grammar of English; the second is about related topics, including language variation (e.g., dialects), language learning, English spelling, and the history of the English language. Generally, when people hear the word "grammar," they immediately think of "correct" or "incorrect" and "good" or "bad" language. Thinking about language in this way is said to be prescriptive. English has a long tradition of judging some expressions as "correct" and others as "incorrect." For example, expressions such as We was are viewed as "incorrect," even though a great many people use them. The "correct" version is said to be We were. Counter-posed to the prescriptive tradition is the descriptive one, which developed in linguistics, anthropology, and sociology. This approach is concerned with describing and understanding the linguistic behavior of a community, without judging it. From a descriptive point of view, We was is unobjectionable when used by a member of a community of speakers who characteristically use this expression. However, it is unacceptable to the wider English speaking community in, for example, formal speaking and writing. The point of view presented in these books is essentially descriptive. However, except where the topic is explicitly about linguistic variation, we describe the form of English used in relatively formal public speaking and writing. We recognize that language changes, and that consequently even the prescriptive rules have to change. We believe that these rules should be descriptions of the best accepted practices of the day rather than impositions (often irrelevant) on the language and its use.

Communication

Communication occurs when one person acts with the intention of influencing the mind of another, for example, by getting him/her to entertain some idea, and when that other person recognizes the first person's intention to influence his/her mind. Clearly, it is possible to influence another person's mind unintentionally; for instance, if I (unintentionally) sneeze, I might prompt you to think that I might have a cold. However, this is a rather different kind of event than one in which I intentionally sneeze and you recognize that my sneeze was intentional. From my first (unintentional) sneeze, you cannot infer that I am trying to get you to think I have a cold; from my second (intentional) sneeze, you can infer that I am trying to get you to think something or another, perhaps that I have a cold. Imagine that we have gone to a party together and that we want to coordinate our leaving. So, before we get to the party I say to you, "I'll pretend to sneeze when I'm ready to go home," and you agree to interpret my sneeze in this way. When I sneeze at the party you can infer that I sneezed intentionally and interpret my sneeze as indicating my desire to leave. For this communication to succeed two elements must be in place: first, the assumption that I intend to influence you in some way, and second, our agreement about the meaning of my intentional sneeze. There is nothing in the nature of a sneeze that requires it to mean "Let's go home." We could have agreed that it was to mean, "It's safe to slip upstairs to steal the host's jewelry." By specifying a meaning for a sneeze, we have created a little code, a sort of miniscule language.

Language

Fortunately, we cannot read each others' minds. So, if we want to allow someone access to what we are thinking, we must provide them with clues that they can perceive. Language is a system that connects thoughts, which can not be heard, seen, or touched, with sounds, letters, manual signs, or tactile symbols (e.g., Braille) which can. In this way, one person's private ideas may be communicated to another person. For example, imagine that I want to communicate to you my idea that my study needs to be tidied up. You can't see, hear, touch, taste, or otherwise perceive that idea; it's locked away in my mind. To communicate it to you I have to cast it in a form that you can perceive—typically in spoken, visual, or tactile form—that is systematically connected to the idea, for example, the sentence, My study needs to be tidied up. Without this perceivable expression, you cannot know that I have an idea to communicate; without the systematic connection between the idea and the form of the expression, you cannot know which idea I want to communicate. So, language is a code that systematically connects private thoughts with public expressions. These books are about the systems we use to connect private ideas to public activities. Language has been a major topic of research for well over two centuries. Linguistic research intersects with anthropology, biology, computer science, history, human development, literature, philosophy, politics, psychology, as well as reading and writing

Discourse

When we communicate we engage in discourse; that is, we deploy language with the purpose of providing our audiences with clues about how we want to influence them. All discourse takes place in context; that is, the producer of a piece of discourse (speaker/writer) purposefully deploys, at some time and in some place, clues about his or her intention which are to be interpreted by their intended recipient(s) (audience). The clues have, generally, been selected with that audience, in that time and place, and with those purposes in mind. Some scholars argue that because different discourse situations require different patterns of communicative practice, we must speak of discourses rather than of discourse (Gee 1992, 1996).

We have, for instance, the discourse in which we are currently engaged—the discourse of linguistics, which differs from the discourse of literary study, which differs from the discourse of chemical engineering, which differs from the discourse of history, and so on. A student who aims to be a practitioner in a field must master the ways in which practitioners in that field communicate with each other about topics in the field. Recognizing these specialized communicative practices has given rise to the Writing Across the Curriculum (WAC) movement.

Text

When people communicate, they produce texts. Texts always occur in some medium, which may be auditory, visual, tactile, or some combination of these. Texts also always occur in some channel, that is, the environment through which the medium travels from the text's producer(s) to its receiver(s). For ordinary face-to-face conversation, the medium is the air, which is set in motion by the producer and whose motions affect the ears of the receiver(s). Communication by telephone involves at least two channels—the air between the speaker's mouth and the phone, the mechanical and electronic devices that connect the speaker's and receiver's phones, and the air between the receiver's phone and his/her ear. Texts may incorporate non-linguistic elements such as pictures, diagrams, music, and the like.

Genre

A genre is a communicative category. Genres differ from each other in participants, forms, and purposes. Texts come in genres; for example, a Shakespearean sonnet is a different type of text from a business letter, which is a different type of text from a casual conversation. Communicative acts come in genres, too. The sales pitch of a car salesman differs from an end-of-term class presentation, which differs from texting a party invitation to a friend. The various discourses require their own specific genres. For example, the discourse of creative writing in English includes the genres of the short story, the novel, and poetry (which includes such sub-genres as the lyric and the dramatic monologue). The discourse of business includes the annual report, various kinds of advertisements, and business letters.

Ideology

Many scholars stress the power of discourse and language to influence speakers' perceptions and conceptualizations of their worlds, and to create and maintain the structures of their societies. Educators interested in language emphasize its power to create and maintain ideologies, i.e., beliefs about the ways in which goods are distributed in society. Goods are "anything that the people in the society generally believe are beneficial to have or harmful not to have, whether this be life, space, time, 'good' schools, 'good' jobs, wealth, status, power, control, or whatever" (Gee, 1996: 21).

Language in Education

Language is central to education: it is the means by which educational content is communicated; it is an object of study; it is an object of beliefs that are important in education; it is a key element of students' identities; it poses potential problems in education, largely because of the beliefs we have about it; and it is a valuable resource for those who know how to make use of it. Language is a means of education in that it is the primary medium of communication between students and teachers and between students and textbooks. Language is an object of education because it is the material out of which texts are woven, and because language itself is the object of study in writing and speaking courses. We focus on language as we learn to edit our essays and speeches. We develop our vocabularies and learn the meanings, uses, and conventional spellings of words. We learn to control the genres required for various disciplines and the specific characteristics expected in those genres, for example, personal essays, academic papers of various sorts, business letters, reports, and magazine articles. Language is also an object of study in so far as we develop our skills in using it to communicate, to acquire knowledge from lectures and books, to integrate new information with old, to replace false beliefs with new true ones, and to increase or decrease our estimates of the likelihood that some belief we hold is true. It is important to note here that students who are learning English as a second language labor under a double burden, because English is simultaneously both the means and an object of their education.

ExerciseWhen asked what she thought was the most important aspect of learning English as a second language, a Japanese student replied: "Knowing many vocabularies." What do you think she meant? Is her expression an acceptable piece of English? How would you change it so it retains her apparent meaning and is acceptable? Why would you make that particular change? Is (your understanding of) her assertion true?

Language is also an object of our beliefs. Many people believe that some forms of English are good and others bad; that some languages are beautiful and others ugly; that some languages are limited in what they can express when compared to languages such as English; that people who speak certain varieties are uneducated, perhaps stupid, and unworthy of certain types of work. Beliefs like these constitute ideologies about language. Some ideologies are liberating and others quite oppressive. Whether liberating or oppressive, they must become objects of critical awareness for teachers and of critical discussion for students (Kress 1985; Fairclough 1989, 1992). Language also represents one of the key elements of our students' social, cultural, and personal identities. Writing explores values our students may not be able to explore otherwise. As their writing improves, the range and sophistication of these identities increases. Teachers have potentially powerful effects on students' lives. Our response to our students' language will influence their attitudes. Young children have a fascination with language and almost no inhibitions about it. Adults, in contrast, typically display considerable anxiety about their language. They often have "strongly negative attitudes towards their native speech pattern" (Labov 1972: 117). This anxiety is known as linguistic insecurity. This insecurity does not develop naturally; it is the consequence of repeated experiences in which their native speech patterns are disparaged, often by teachers (who should know better). This problem is particularly acute for students who are not native speakers of English, or who do not speak the variety of the language regarded as "correct."

Exercise 1. How do you feel about your ability as a singer? Would you be willing to sing Madonna's "Love Profusion" in front of your class? (It's on her American Life album, if you want to practice beforehand.) What experiences with singing have formed your attitude? What attitudes about singing do children have? What light does this shed on linguistic insecurity?

2. How many words do you have in your vocabulary? Consider first your active vocabulary, i.e., words you use regularly in speaking and writing, such as often. Then estimate your passive vocabulary, i.e., words that you recognize and understand, but which don't come readily to mind when you want them, for example, prestidigitation. Estimates based on objective study appear at the end of this chapter.

Language is a potential problem to the extent that it—or our beliefs about it—impedes students' learning. If we believe that students who speak English with a Latino accent, or who speak Black English (a.k.a. "Ebonics"), will be unable to keep up in our classes, then very likely they will not, because teachers' expectations strongly affect students' success in school. Because teachers respond to students' language on many levels, they must develop a critical awareness of their own linguistic preferences, prejudices, and beliefs—everyone has these beliefs, even linguists. They must also be able to critically evaluate textbooks, dictionaries, style manuals, computerized style analyzers, and newspaper articles on language, because these also embody assumptions about language, many of them just plain wrong, often destructively so. Language is a potential resource for teaching critical thinking. We can evaluate our attitudes about other languages and other dialects and their speakers; we can collect linguistic data, observe its patterns, and articulate those patterns as hypotheses which we can then test; we can evaluate the ways we talk about language for their precision, and come to appreciate the value of precision in language use generally. Language data for analysis is very readily available. Students can collect their own data from bumper stickers, license plates, ads, poems—whatever. Schools (or the internet) can provide computerized collections of authentic spoken and written texts (corpora) along with computer programs to analyze them (concordancers). Because the linguistic study of language is fundamentally scientific, studying language in this way can provide us and our students with an understanding and appreciation of scientific methods.

Exercise 1. Write a brief essay on at least two of the ways in which language is an element in education. 2. In your college library, consult the journals Linguistics and Literature, Style, and Linguistics and Education. Report back to the class on (a) the types of topics covered in each journal and (b) one article that interested you. 3. What do you understand by the term "grammar"?

Thinking Critically About Language

Clearly, teachers must know about reading and writing, as well as about teaching their disciplines. But why should they learn about language? One answer is that teachers should have a well-developed critical understanding of at least some modern thinking about the nature of language and its roles in education because reading, writing, and all subject matters crucially depend on language. Good craftspeople always understand their materials, and as language is the raw material of the discourses of all disciplines, teachers should understand its nature. Second, all modern approaches to reading and writing—cultural, feminist, Marxist, post-modernist, psychological—accord language a central place. Third, because the linguistic study of language is quite different in its approaches, goals, and methods from the approaches to the study of reading or writing, it complements those approaches. Fourth, societal attitudes to language (teachers', students', and parents') can profoundly affect students' learning and performance. One of our goals is to enable you to think critically about language and the claims of those who write about it (including ours). Critical thinking has many facets, including creating and evaluating arguments, reasoning from premises to conclusions, and detecting covert claims in arguments. In language study, we think critically when we determine whether a grammar, style manual, or dictionary is appropriate for our students, or whether a linguistic claim (e.g., "double negatives make a positive") has any validity. Critical thinking is important in any discipline, but it is of particular importance in reading and writing. To be able to read in any discipline, students must know how to accurately interpret the language of texts in that discipline and to be able to recreate their authors' meanings. Both of these tasks require, at a minimum, knowing the discipline's technical terms. Some disciplines may require readers to be knowledgeable about further aspects of the language. Literature students, for instance, must be able to understand language made difficult by archaisms, rhetorical figures, complex grammar, and willful grammatical and semantic violations (Dillon, 1978). When writing, students think critically when they analyze their personal preconceptions and biases, when they assess the relevance and effectiveness of their ideas, and when they decide on the best linguistic formulation of those ideas for their intended audiences. The ability to think critically about language is particularly needed now, because the school grammar tradition has generally become quite uninformed about research into current English discourse practices. The responsibility for this situation lies partly with linguists themselves. We have not been successful in our efforts to educate the public about language. However, the greatest share of the responsibility lies with institutions, journalists, and teachers who have vigorously defended an ultra-conservative status quo, who know little if anything about language, and who often misconstrue what linguists have to say about it. Many believe, for instance, that linguists claim that "anything goes in English these days." Nothing could be farther from the truth, as we will show in our chapter on Conceptions of Language.

Standard English

Learning to read and write is partly a matter of linguistic development, i.e., the growth in a student's ability to communicate appropriately in an increasingly broad range of circumstances. Teachers who concern themselves with the linguistic development of their students typically view their role as twofold: (a) to promote their students' ability to speak, read, and write in their disciplines, and (b) to develop their students' ability to write in Standard English (SE), the variety of English generally expected in formal communication in various disciplines.

Grammar

You probably answered exercise 3 on page 10 by saying that "grammar" tells us which expressions are correct. You would, of course, have meant "prescriptive grammar." However, linguists add at least two other interpretations to the word. First, they use it to refer to the knowledge that a speaker or writer of a language must have in order to be able to use the language at all. Second, they use it to refer to any attempt to describe that knowledge. We will return to these issues in the next chapter when we discuss prescriptive and descriptive approaches to language study more thoroughly. It is important, when we speak about "grammar," that we are clear, to ourselves and our audiences, which meaning of "grammar" we intend. This first book is about the grammar of English. Some of our readers will be required to teach grammar classes per se; others will use information about English grammar while teaching composition; and still others will use it while teaching writing-intensive classes across the curriculum. It is important to note that grammar refers only to a part of language, and that these books deal with language, not just grammar. We believe that a teacher's knowledge of language is far more broadly relevant than just knowledge of "grammar." It is also important to recognize that teaching "grammar" is highly controversial. To get a sense of the arguments, we recommend that you read the relevant articles in English Journal 1996: 85.7 and 2003: 92.3, as well as other NCTE publications such as Grammar Alive: A Guide for Teachers (Haussamen et al 2003) and Code Switching: Teaching Standard English in Urban Classrooms (Wheeler and Swords 2006). You might also browse Freeman and Freeman (2004) and Honegger (2005). Neither you nor we can predict what you will believe about language, grammar, and the teaching of either by the time you have read these books. However, we do know that in discussions about how to teach writing, you will hear arguments that teaching grammar "out of context" does not improve students' writing. (Generally what is meant by "grammar" in those discussions is the set of prescriptive conventions for speaking and writing Standard English.) Certainly there is a large body of research going back more than a century purporting to support this position. However, we repeat, these books are not just about grammar; they are about language, including how grammar fits into language. It is as important for teachers to know about language as it is to know about their subject matter. A teacher who knows nothing about language is a cyclist without wheels. Worse, a teacher who knows nothing about language is a chemist who knows (and cares) nothing about the environmental consequences of the substances he or she creates. Our approach to the study of language is heavily influenced by the results of recent linguistic research and methods. This allows us to tie our discussion to critical thinking, literature, Writing Across the Curriculum, and composition studies, as well as to philosophy and the social, psychological, neurological, and computer sciences (see Traugott and Pratt 1980 as well as journals like English Journal and Style). Most of this book deals with English grammar. Aside from the fact that the general public expects teachers to have a mastery of grammar (by which is usually meant prescriptive grammar), you will probably be expected to teach the subject in one way or another. We do not suggest that you use this book as a syllabus. It contains too much material and is not geared to a junior or senior high-school audience. Nonetheless, in spite of the amount of material it covers, it's merely a good basis for continuing your study of language. We hope that you will find the analytic and critical methods of exploring language used in the books to be more productive and interesting than the more conventional handbook approach—exposition plus drill-and-practice. More importantly, we hope that you will present to your students the broader conceptions about language that are expressed in these books. These conceptions are presented initially in our chapter on Conceptions of Language, but are developed in various ways in other chapters.

Other Reasons for Studying and Teaching About Language

Besides its importance in the development of critical thinking skills, there are many other reasons for studying language. You might want to know about language variation ("dialects" of various sorts), about how languages change over time, about the history of English, about the standardization of languages, about how languages are learned, about language disorders, about the relationships between language and culture or society, or about how computers are programmed to understand or produce language. These are all to one degree or another relevant to teachers and we deal with many of them in these books. Deciding what should be included in books like these is remarkably difficult. We have followed the guidelines of the National Council of Teachers of English (NCTE) and the National Council for Accreditation for Teacher Education (NCATE) about what English teachers should know, and we depended on the research on Writing Across the Curriculum (WAC). Nonetheless, because such a huge amount is known about language generally, and about English in particular, and because (as in any area of vigorous intellectual activity) there are many competing approaches to these topics, it would be impossible to synopsize them all here. In the first book, we present a grammar of English which addresses traditional topics and concerns, but which is influenced considerably by current grammatical and discourse research. In the second book we present a range of topics that we hope will be of interest and value to teachers across the disciplines. Fulfilling the goals of instruction becomes particularly important in a world growing in technological complexity, social diversity, and multiple "Englishes." (See the essays in Kachru 1992 and Kachru and Nelson 1996, as well as Crystal 2003; Jenkins 2003; McArthur 1998; Melchers and Shaw 2003.) Many students are passionate about their studies in literature, the physical and social sciences, business, or in other intellectual pursuits; unfortunately, however, many students and teachers see the study of language as merely the study of "correct grammar." We have already begun to sift through the various meanings of "grammar" and will develop this discussion in later chapters. Teachers face a complex set of responsibilities. Parents, boards of education, and legislators look increasingly to school systems to prepare students for the demands of the future. Worries that American students lag behind those of other developed countries translate directly into concerns about public funding (i.e., taxes) and accountability in education, as the No Child Left Behind Act requires. These pressures appear in the form of demands for success on standardized tests, for "getting back to basics," for public funding of private education ("vouchers" and "charter schools"), for longer school years, for ongoing competency testing for teachers, and for the assessment and ranking of schools. From our perspective, teachers' responsibility is to their students. We must meet the needs of the learner rather than simply present material on a take-it-or-leave-it basis. As a result, the learnability of classroom material becomes more important than its teachability (how easily it can be taught), or its assessability (how easily it can be assessed). Moreover, in the coming generation, the diversity of its students in US classrooms will change dramatically. The 2008 US Census Bureau projected percentages for the major racial/ethnic groups are displayed in the following chart:

	2008	2050
White	66	46
Hispanic	15	30
Black	14	15
Asian	5.1	9.2

(See U.S. Census Bureau National Population Projections.) In 2005 the percentage of the US population born abroad was 12.4. These projections suggest that in addition to knowing their disciplines and how to teach them (ideally by incorporating lots of writing), teachers will also have to know about how to teach ESL (English as a Second Language). In the rest of this introduction we will explain the organization of these books and provide some hints for working successfully with them.

The Organization of These Books

The next chapter of this book (Conceptions of Language) is on the nature of language. The remaining chapters are on various aspects of the English language, including its sound system, its vocabulary, its parts of speech, word meanings, and the ways in which words are combined into phrases, clauses, and sentences—essentially the grammar of English. Book I gives you some basic information about English grammar, about how to do simple linguistic analyses, and about thinking critically about language. Because it is impossible to remember the analysis of every expression you might be asked about by a student (there are far too many), our main concern is to help you become independent by providing you with the means to do linguistic analysis as you need it.

We regularly use an analytic method, in which we formulate criteria for determining how to categorize words, phrases, or sentences. For example, whenever we want to know the part of speech of a particular word, we use these criteria to test a hypothesis about the word's part of speech. We will ask you to do similar activities in the exercises, sometimes by gathering data, sometimes by analyzing material that lies just a step beyond what is covered in the text. Book II deals with selected topics of particular importance to teachers: spoken and written language; spelling; variation in language; usage; punctuation; history of the English language; and language acquisition. Our presentation brings together current studies in each of these areas and prepares you to read applied studies that you will encounter in your career. These chapters can be read independently of Book I, though on occasion you will find some crossreferences to chapters in Book I, along with some phonetic notation that may send you back to our chapter on Phonetics and Phonology. In many instances we will mention a topic, briefly discuss it, and return to it in greater depth later. Our hope is that this cycling will provide you with an opportunity to get an initial familiarity with a topic and then build on that familiarity later. These books are far from covering the wealth of information on topics that you might be interested in as a teacher. To survey all of these would require several more books. We encourage you to consult your instructor for further references and bibliographical resources, for example on linguistics and literature, composition, or reading.

Hints for Success

The study of the English language is demanding. First, you will find yourself confronting challenges to linguistic assumptions (and even prejudices) that have become ingrained in you through your education and that are widely accepted without critical examination by the majority of educated English speakers.

Second, you may find yourself in a mode of analysis quite different from that of your own studies. Third, you will confront considerable linguistic detail and the large number of new terms required to conceptualize and describe it. While we cannot guarantee that these new ideas will be easy to master (although many people do find them so), we believe that they are worth your effort and will serve you well in your career. Because what you will learn in these pages is as much skill as information, do not expect to master this material in a single reading. The best strategy for most people is to do a preliminary reading, do the exercises, and then reread (and reread again). Research on learning and remembering shows what is perhaps obvious—the more frequently and deeply you review material the better you will remember and understand it. If you are a student, attend class and ask questions; if you are having difficulties, the chances are good that many of your classmates are too and will benefit from the instructor's answers to your questions. Exercises are scattered throughout the book. We encourage you to tackle as many as possible. This need not involve working them out in full detail (unless your instructor requires it); you might just work out the outline of a solution. However, you cannot learn the analytic skills required to study linguistics or grammar without doing lots of hands-on work. If you have difficulties with a problem, try to identify them as specifically as possible. If you get an incorrect answer, make sure also to get an explanation of the correct one. Try to retrace the thinking that led you to miss the question. Sometimes you can learn more from mistakes than from perfection. One of our goals is to help you develop your skills in independent language analysis. Teachers are regularly called upon to answer questions whose answers cannot be found in textbooks or reference works. Doing exercises is essential for independence. Terminology is plentiful in linguistics, just as in every other discipline. Remember that technical terms usually have specific meanings so you may not be able to substitute ordinary words for them. We have provided glossaries to help you identify definitions; you should consult them often. Be particularly careful with terms (e.g., semantics) that may have a familiar meaning in ordinary language, but a significantly different one in technical usage. Definitions should be supplemented with explanations, elaborations of the minimal statements in the glossary. Remember, though, to use precise language in defining terms. Linguists like to think of themselves as scientists and so value precision and accuracy. Explanations may be taken from the text (or from class notes, if you are a student). Try to have a specific, prototypical example of each term. Select an example that is clear to you and is uncontroversial, and be sure to understand just why your example exemplifies the concept. Memorization has had a bad press, but it is necessary more often than we think (and not only for exams). We do not encourage memorization for its own sake, but rather to make your passive knowledge more active.

The best time to memorize is after you have become familiar with a concept through exposure. For long lists (e.g., the prepositions of English), do not try to remember every item; select a small number, and then only to illustrate a concept, and use the criteria given in the book for deciding which other items belong to the list. As you gain experience, try to add gradually to that short list. We do not recommend that you require your students to learn lists of items, unless they are learning English as a second or foreign language (and even then only sparingly). Second opinions aren't just good for your health. Reading other authors on the topics of these books will greatly help you to learn and remember what you study. We encourage you to seek out other books on these topics, beginning with those we've listed in the References and Resources at the end of each chapter. At the head of each chapter, we list the chapter's key concepts. For teachers, we hope these will help you find topics you want to read about. For students, we imagine these topics serving as the focus for essays that might form a part of your course work. The internal parts of the chapters are clearly indicated by headings to allow for easy access.

REFERENCES

1. Atchison, Jean. 1994. Words in the Mind: An Introduction to the Mental Lexicon. (2nd ed.) Oxford, UK: Basil Blackwell.
2. Cowrie, Bernard. (ed.) 1990. The World's Major Languages. Oxford, UK: Oxford University Press.
3. Crystal, David. 1987. The Cambridge Encyclopedia of Language. Cambridge, UK: Cambridge University Press.
4. _____ 1995. The Cambridge Encyclopedia of the English Language. Cambridge, UK: Cambridge University Press.
5. _____ 2003. English as a Global Language. (2nd ed.) Cambridge, UK: Cambridge University Press.
6. Dillon, George. 1978. Language Processing and the Reading of Literature. Bloomington: Indiana University Press.
7. Fairclough, Norman. 1989. Language and Power. London: Longman.
8. _____ 1992. Critical Language Awareness. London: Longman.
9. Freeman, David E. and Yvonne E. Freeman. 2004. Essential Linguistics: What you Need to Know to Teach Reading, ESL, Spelling, Phonics, Grammar. Portsmouth, NH: Heinemann.
10. Gee, James Paul. 1992. The Social Mind: Language, Ideology, and Social Practice. New York: Bergin and Garvey.
11. _____ 1996. Social Linguistics and Literacies. London UK: Taylor and

Francis.

12. Haussamen, Brock, Amy Benjamin, Martha Kolln, and Rebecca S. Wheeler.
13. 2003. Grammar Alive! A Guide for Teachers. Urbana, IL: NCTE.
14. Honegger, Mark. 2005. English Grammar for Writing. Boston: Houghton Mifflin.
15. Jenkins, Jennifer. 2003. World Englishes: A Resource Book for Students. London, UK: Routledge.
16. Kachru, Braj B. (ed.) 1992. The Other Tongue: English Across Cultures. (2nd ed.) Urbana, IL: University of Illinois Press.
17. Kachru, Braj B. and Cecil L. Nelson. 1996: 71-102. World Englishes. In Sandra L. McKay and N. H. Hornberger. (eds.) Sociolinguistics and Language Teaching. Cambridge, UK: Cambridge University Press.
18. Kress, Gunther. 1985. Linguistic Processes in Sociocultural Practice. Oxford: Oxford University Press.
19. Labov, William. 1972. Sociolinguistic Patterns. Philadelphia: University of Pennsylvania Press.
20. McArthur, Tom. 1998. The English Languages. Cambridge, UK: Cambridge University Press.
21. _____ (ed.) 1992. The Oxford Companion to the English Language. Oxford, UK: Oxford University Press.
22. Melchers, Gunnel, and Philip Shaw. 2003. World Englishes. London, UK: Arnold.
23. Traugott, Elizabeth, and Mary Louise Pratt. 1980. Linguistics for Students of Literature. New York: Harcourt Brace Jovanovich, Inc.
24. Trudgill, Peter and Jean Hannah. 1994. International English: A Guide to the Varieties of Standard English. London: Arnold.
25. U.S. Census Bureau National Population Projections website: http://www.census.gov/population/www/projections/
26. Wheeler, Rebecca S. and Rachel Swords. 2006. Code Switching: Teaching Standard English in Urban Classrooms. Urbana, IL: NCTE.

Chapter 7

THE STUDY OF LANGUAGE AND LANGUAGE ACQUISITION

THE NATURALISTIC APPROACH TO LANGUAGE

Fundamental to modern linguistics is the view that human language is a natural object: our species-specific ability to acquire a language, our tacit knowledge of the enormous complexity of language, and our capacity to use language in free, appropriate, and infinite ways are attributed to a property of the natural world, our brain. This position needs no defense, if one considers the study of language is an empirical inquiry. It follows, then, as in the study of biological sciences, linguistics aims to identify the abstract properties of the biological object under study—human language—and the mechanisms that govern its organization. This has the goal set in the earliest statements on modern linguistics, Chomsky's The Logical Structure of Linguistic Theory (1955). Consider the famous duo: (1) a. Colorless green ideas sleep furiously. b. Furiously sleep ideas green colorless. Neither sentence has even a remote chance of being encountered in natural discourse, yet every speaker of English can perceive their differences: while they are both meaningless, (1a) is grammatically well formed, whereas (1b) is not. To understand what precisely this difference is is to give 'a rational account of this behavior, i.e., a theory of the speaker's linguistic intuition the goal of linguistic theory' (Chomsky 1955/1975: 95)· —in other words, a psychology, and ultimately, biology of human language. Once this position—lately dubbed the biolinguistic approach (Jenkins 1999, Chomsky 2000)· —is accepted, it follows that language, just like all other biological objects, ought to be studied following the standard methodology in natural sciences (Chomsky 1975, 1980, 1986, 1995a).). The postulation of innate linguistic knowledge, the Universal Grammar (UG), is a case in point. One of the major motivations for innateness of linguistic knowledge comes from the Argument from the Poverty of Stimulus (APS) (Chomsky, 1980: 35). A well-known example concerns the structure dependency in language syntax and children's knowledge of it in the absence of learning experience (Chomsky 1975, Crain & Nakayama 1987). Forming an interrogative question in English involves inversion of the auxiliary verb and the subject:

(2) a. Is Alex *e* singing a song?
b. Has Robin *e* finished reading?

It is important to realize that exposure to such sentences underdetermines the correct operation for question formation. There are many possible hypotheses compatible with the language acquisition data in (2):

(3) a. front the first auxiliary verb in the sentence
b. front the auxiliary verb that most closely follows a noun
c. front the last auxiliary verb
d. front the auxiliary verb whose position in the sentence is a prime number
e. . . .

The correct operation for question formation is, of course, structure-dependent: it involves parsing the sentence into structurally organized phrases, and fronting the auxiliary that follows the first noun phrase, which can be arbitrarily long:

(4) a. Is [$_{NP}$ the woman who is sing] *e* happy?
b. Has [$_{NP}$ the man that is reading a book] *e* had supper?

Hypothesis (3a), which arguably involves simpler mental computation than the correct generalization, yields erroneous predictions:

(5) a. *Is [the woman who *e* singing] is happy?
b. *Has [the man that *e* finished reading] has finished supper?

But children don't go astray like the creative inductive learner in (3). They stick to the correct operation from very early on, as Crain & Nakayama (1987) showed using elicitation tasks. The children were instructed, 'Ask Jabba if the boy who is watching Mickey Mouse is happy', and no error of the form in (5) was found.

Though sentences like those in (4) may serve to disconfirm hypothesis (3a), they are very rarely if ever encountered by children in normal discourse, not to mention the fact that each of the other incorrect hypotheses in (3) will need to be ruled out by disconfirming evidence. Here lies the logic of the APS:[2] if we know X, and X is underdetermined by learning experience, then X must be innate. The conclusion is then Chomsky's (1975: 33): 'the child's mind . . . contains the instruction: Construct a structure-dependent rule, ignoring all structure-independent rules. The principle of structure-dependence is not learned, but forms part of the conditions for language learning.' The naturalistic approach can also be seen in the evolution of linguistic theories through successive refinement and revision of ideas as their conceptual and empirical flaws are revealed. For example, the 1960s language-particular and construction-specific transformational rules, while descriptively powerful, are inadequate when viewed in a biological context. The complexity and restrictiveness of rules made the acquisition of language wildly difficult: the learner had a vast (and perhaps an infinite) space of hypotheses to entertain. The search for a plausible theory of language acquisition, coupled with comparative linguistic studies, led to the Principles and Parameters (P&P) framework (Chomsky 1981), which suggests that all languages obey a universal (and putatively innate) set of tightly constrained principles, whereas variations across constructions and particular languages—the choices that a child learner has to make during language acquisition—are attributed to a small number of parametric choices. The present book is a study of language development in children. From a biological perspective, the development of language, like the development of other organic systems, is an interaction between internal and external factors; specifically, between the child's internal knowledge of linguistic structures and the external linguistic experience he receives. Drawing insights from the study of biological evolution, we will put forth a model that make this interaction precise, by embedding a theory of knowledge, the Universal Grammar (UG), into a theory of learning from data. In particular, we propose that language acquisition be modeled as a population of 'grammars', competing to match the external linguistic experiences, much in the manner of natural selection. The justification of this approach will take the naturalistic approach just as in the justification of innate linguistic knowledge: we will provide evidence—conceptual, mathematical, and empirical, and from a number of independent areas of linguistic research, including the acquisition of syntax, the acquisition of phonology, and historical language change—to show that without the postulated model, an adequate explanation of these empirical cases is not possible. But before we dive into details, some methodological remarks on the study of language acquisition

The Structure of Language Acquisition

At the most abstract level, language acquisition can be modeled as below:

(6) $\mathcal{L}: (S_0, E) \rightarrow S_T$

A learning function or algorithm L maps the initial state of the learner, S_0, to the terminal state S_T, on the basis of experience E in the environment. Language acquisition research attempts to give an explicit account of this process.

Formal Sufficiency

The acquisition model must be causal and concrete. Explanation of language acquisition is not complete with a mere description of child language, no matter how accurate or insightful, without an explicit account of the mechanism responsible for how language develops over time, the learning function L. It is often claimed in the literature that children just 'pick up' their language, or that children's linguistic competence is identical to adults. Such statements, if devoid of a serious effort at some learning-theoretic account of how this is achieved, reveal irresponsibility rather than ignorance. The model must also be correct. Given reasonable assumptions about the linguistic data, the duration of learning, the learner's cognitive and computational capacities, and so on, the model must be able to attain the terminal state of linguistic knowledge S_T comparable to that of a normal human learner. The correctness of the model must be confirmed by mathematical proof, computer simulation, or other forms of rigorous demonstration. This requirement has traditionally been referred to as the learnability condition, which unfortunately carries some misleading connotations. For example, the influential Gold (1967) paradigm of identification in the limit requires that the learner converge onto the 'target' grammar in the linguistic environment. However, this position has little empirical content. First, language acquisition is the process in which the learner forms an internalized knowledge (in his mind), an I-language (Chomsky 1986). Language does not exist in the world (in any scientific sense), but resides in the heads of individual users. Hence there is no external target of learning, and hence no 'learnability' in the traditional sense. Second, section 1.2.2 below documents evidence that child language and adult language appear to be sufficiently different that language acquisition cannot be viewed as recapitulation or approximation of the linguistic expressions produced by adults, or of any external target. And third, in order for language to change, the terminal state attained by children must be different from that of their ancestors. This requires that the learnability condition (in the conventional sense) must fail under certain conditions—in particular (as we shall see in Chapter 3) empirical cases where learners do not converge onto any unique 'language' in the informal and E-language sense of 'English' or 'German', but rather a combination of multiple (I-language) grammars. Language change is a result of changes in this kind of grammar combinations.

Developmental Compatibility

A model of language acquisition is, after all, a model of reality: it must be compatible with what is known about children's language. Essential to this requirement is the quantitativeness of the model. No matter how much innate linguistic knowledge (S_0) children are endowed with, language still must be acquired from experience (E). And, as we document extensively in this book, not all languages, and not all aspects of a single language, are learned uniformly. As long as this is the case, there remains a possibility that there is something in the input, E, that causes such variations. An adequate model of language acquisition must thus consist of an explicit description of the learning mechanisms, L, that quantify the relation between E, what the learner receives, and S_T , what is acquired. Only then can the respective contribution from S_0 and E—nature vs. nurture, in a cliché—to language acquisition be understood with any precision. This urges us to be serious about quantitative comparisons between the input and the attained product of learning: in our case, quantitative measures of child language and those of adult language. Here, many intriguing and revealing disparities surface. A few examples illustrate this observation and the challenge it poses to an acquisition model. It is now known that some aspects of the grammar are acquired successfully at a remarkably early age. The placement of finite verbs in French matrix clauses is such an example.

(7) Jean voit *souvent/pas* Marie.
Jean sees *often/not* Marie.
'John *often* sees/does *not* see Marie.'

French, in contrast to English, places finite verbs in a position preceding sentential adverbs and negations. Although sentences like (7), indicative of this property of French, are quite rare in adult-tochild speech (7%; estimate based on CHILDES—see MacWhinney & Snow 1985), French children, from as early as can be tested (1;8: Pierce 1989), almost never deviate from the correct form. This discovery has been duplicated in a number of languages with similar properties; see Wexler (1994) and much related work for a survey. In contrast, some very robustly attested patterns in adult language emerge much later in children. The best-known example is perhaps the phenomenon of subject drop. Children learning English, and other languages that require the presence of a grammatical subject often produce sentences as in (8):

(8) a. (I) help Daddy.
b. (He) dropped the candy.

Subject drop appears in up to 30% of all sentences around 2;0, and it is not until around 3;0 that they start using subjects at adult level (Valian 1991), in striking contrast to adult language, where subject is used in almost all sentences. Perhaps more interestingly, children often produce utterances that are virtually absent in adult speech. One such example that has attracted considerable attention is what is known as the Optional Infinitive (OI) stage (e.g. Weverink 1989, Rizzi 1994, Wexler 1984): children acquiring some languages that morphologically express tense nevertheless produce a significant number of sentences where matrix verbs are non-finite. (9) is an example from child Dutch (Weverink 1989):

(9) pappa schoenen wassen
daddy shoes to-wash
'Daddy washes shoes.'

Non-finite root sentences like (9) are ungrammatical in adult Dutch and thus appear very infrequently in acquisition data. Yet OI sentences are robustly used by children for an extended period of time, before they gradually disappear by 2;6 or later. These quantitative disparities between child and adult language represent a considerable difficulty for empiricist learning models such as neural networks. The problem is, as pointed out by Fodor & Pylyshyn (1988), that learning models without prior knowledge (e.g. UG) can do no more than recapitulate the statistical distribution of the input data. It is therefore unclear how a statistical learning model can duplicate the developmental patterns in child language. That is, during the course of learning,

(10) a. The model must not produce certain patterns that are in principle compatible with the input but never attested (the argument from the poverty of stimulus).
b. The model must not produce certain patterns abundant in the input (the subject drop phenomenon).
c. The model must produce certain patterns that are never attested in the input (the Optional Infinitive phenomenon).

Even with the assumption of innate UG, which can be viewed as a kind of prior knowledge from a learning-theoretic perspective, it is not clear how such quantitative disparities can be explained. As will be discussed in Chapter 2, previous formal models of acquisition in the UG tradition in general have not begun to address these questions.

The model developed in this study intends to fill this gap. Finally, quantitative modeling is important to the development of linguistics at large. At the foundation of every 'hard' science is a formal model with which quantitative data can be explained and quantitative predictions can be made and checked. Biology did not come of age until the twin pillars of biological sciences, Mendelian genetics and Darwinian evolution, were successfully integrated into the mathematical theory of population genetics— part of the Modern Synthesis (Mayr & Provine 1980)—where evolutionary change can be explicitly and quantitatively expressed by its internal genetic basis and external environmental conditions. If language development is a biological process, it would certainly be desirable for the interplay between internal linguistic knowledge and external linguistic experience to be quantitatively modeled with formalization.

Explanatory Continuity

Because child language apparently differs from adult language, it is thus essential for an acquisition model to make some choices on explaining such differences. The condition of explanatory continuity proposed here imposes some restrictions, or, to be more precise, heuristics, on making these choices. Explanatory Continuity is an instantiation of the well-known Continuity Hypothesis (Macnamara 1982, Pinker 1984), with roots dating back to Jakobson (1941), Halle (1962), and Chomsky (1965). The Continuity Hypothesis says that, without evidence to the contrary, children's cognitive system is assumed to be identical to that of adults. Since child and adult languages differ, there are two possibilities:

(11) a. Children and adults differ in linguistic performance.
 b. Children and adults differ in grammatical competence.

An influential view holds that child competence (e.g. grammar) is identical to adult competence (Pinker 1984). This necessarily leads to a performance-based explanation for child acquisition. There is no question that (11a) is, at some level, true: children are more prone to performance errors than adults, as their memory, processing, and articulation capacities are still underdeveloped. To be sure, adult linguistic performance is affected by these factors as well. However, if and when both approaches are descriptively adequate, there are reasons to prefer competence-based explanations. Parsimony is the obvious, and primary, reason. By definition, performance involves the interaction between the competence system and other cognitive/perceptual systems. In addition, competence is one of the few components in linguistic performance of which our theoretical understanding has some depth. This is partially because grammatical competence is to a large degree isolated from other cognitive systems—the so-called autonomy of syntax—and is thus more directly accessible to investigation. The tests used for competence studies, often in the form of native speakers' grammatical intuition, can be carefully controlled and evaluated. Finally, and empirically, child language differs from adult language in very specific ways, which do not seem to follow from any general kind of deficit in children's performance.□ For example, it has been shown that there is much data in child subject drop that does not follow from performance limitation explanations; see e.g. Hyams & Wexler (1993), Roeper & Rohrbacher (1994), Bromberg & Wexler (1995). In Chapter , we will show that a theory of English past tense learning based on memory lapses (Pinker

1999) fails to explain much of the developmental data reported in Marcus et al. (1992). Phonological rules and structures in irregular verbs must be taken into account to obtain a fuller explanation. And in Chapter □, we will see additional developmental data from several studies of children's syntax, including the subject drop phenomenon, to show the empirical problems with the performance-based approach. If we tentatively reject (11a) as, at least, a less favorable research strategy, we must rely on (11b) to explain child language. But exactly how is child competence different from adult competence? Here again are two possibilities:

(12) a. Child competence and adult competence are qualitatively different.
b. Child competence and adult competence are quantitatively different.

(12a) says that child language is subject to different rules and constraints from adult language. For example, it could be that some linguistic principle operates differently in children from adults, or a piece of grammatical knowledge is absent in younger children but becomes available as a matter of biological maturation (Gleitman 1981, Felix 1987, Borer & Wexler 1987). It is important to realize that there is nothing unprincipled in postulating a discontinuous competence system to explain child language. If children systematically produce linguistic expressions that defy UG (as understood via adult competence analysis), we can only conclude that their language is governed by different laws. However, in the absence of a concrete theory of how linguistic competence matures (12a) runs the risk of 'anything goes'. It must therefore remain a last resort only when (12a)—the approach that relies on adult competence, for which we do have concrete theories—is shown to be false. More specifically, we must not confuse the difference between child language and adult language with the difference between child language and Universal Grammar. That is, while (part of) child language may not fall under the grammatical system the child eventually attains, it is possible that it falls under some other, equally principled grammatical system allowed by UG. (Indeed, this is the approach taken in the present study.) This leaves us with (12b), which, in combination with (11b), gives the strongest realization of the Continuity Hypothesis: that child language is subject to the same principles and constraints in adult language, and that every utterance in child language is potentially an utterance in adult language. The difference between child and adult languages is due to differences in the organization of a continuous grammatical system. This position further splits into two directions:

(13) a. Child language reflects a *unique* potential adult language.
b. Child grammar consists of a *collection* of potential adult languages.

(13a), the dominant view ('triggering') in theoretical language acquisition will be rejected in Chapter. Our proposal takes the position of (13b): child language in development reflects a statistical combination of possible grammars allowed by UG, only some of which are eventually retained when language acquisition ends. This perspective will be elaborated in the rest of this book, where we examine how it measures up against the criteria of formal sufficiency, developmental compatibility, and explanatory continuity

A Road Map

This book is organized as follows. Chapter first gives a short but critical review of previous approaches to language acquisition. After an encounter with the populational and variational thinking in biological evolution that inspired this work, we propose to model language acquisition as a population of competing grammars, whose distribution changes in response to the linguistic evidence presented to the learner. We will give a precise formulation of this idea, and study its formal/computational properties with respect to the condition of formal sufficiency. Chapter applies the model to one of the biggest developmental problems in language, the learning of English past tense. It will be shown that irregular verbs are organized into classes, each of which is defined by special phonological rules, and that learning an irregular verb involves the competition between the designated special rule and the default -ed rule. Again, quantitative predictions are made and checked against children's performance on irregular verbs. Along the way we will develop a critique of Pinker and his colleagues' Words and Rules model (Pinker 1999), which holds that irregular verbs are individually and directly memorized as associated pairs of root and past tense forms. Chapter continues to subject the model to the developmental compatibility test by looking at the acquisition of syntax. First, crosslinguistic evidence will be presented to highlight the model's ability to make quantitative predictions based on adult-to-child corpus statistics. In addition, a number of major empirical cases in child language will be examined, including the acquisition of word order in a number of languages, the subject drop phenomenon, and Verb Second.

Chapter extends the acquisition model to the study of language change. The quantitativeness of the acquisition model allows one to view language change as the change in the distribution of grammars in successive generations of learners. This can again incorporate the statistical properties of historical texts in an evolving, dynamic system. We apply the model of language change to explain the loss of Verb Second in Old French and Old English. Chapter concludes with a discussion on the implications of the acquisition model in a broad context of linguistic and cognitive science research.

A VARIATIONAL MODEL OF LANGUAGE ACQUISITION

It is a simple observation that young children's language is different from that of adults. However, this simple observation raises profound questions: What results in the differences between child language and adult language, and how does the child eventually resolve such differences through exposure to linguistic evidence? These questions are fundamental to language acquisition research. (6) in Chapter , repeated below as (14), provides a useful framework within to characterize approaches to language acquisition:

(14) $\mathcal{L}: (S_0, E) \rightarrow S_T$

Language acquisition can be viewed as a function or algorithm, L, which maps the initial and hence putatively innate state (S_0) of the learner to the terminal state (S_T), the adult-form language, on the basis of experience, E, in the environment. Two leading approaches to L can be distinguished in this formulation according to the degree of focus on S_0 and L. An empiricist approach minimizes the role of S_0, the learner's initial (innate) and domain-specific knowledge of natural language. Rather, emphasis is given to L, which is claimed to be a generalized learning mechanism cross-cutting cognitive domains. Models in this approach can broadly be labeled generalized statistical learning (GSL): learning is the approximation of the terminal state (S_T) based on the statistical distribution of the input data. In contrast, a rationalist approach, often rooted in the tradition of generative grammar, attributes the success of language acquisition to a richly endowed S_0, while relegating L to a background role. Specifically, S_0 is assumed to be a delimited space, a Universal Grammar (UG), which consists of a finite number of hypotheses that a child can in principle entertain. Almost all theories of acquisition in the UG-based approach can called transformational learning models, borrowing a term from evolutionary biology (Lewontin 1987): the learner's linguistic hypothesis undergoes direct transformations (changes), by moving from one hypothesis to another, driven by linguistic evidence. This study introduces a new approach to language acquisition in which both S_0 and L are given prominent roles in explaining child language. We will show that once the domain-specific and innate knowledge of language (S_0) is assumed, the mechanism language acquisition (L) can be related harmoniously to the learning theories from traditional psychology, and possibly, the development of neural systems.

Against Transformational Learning

Recall from Chapter the three conditions on an adequate acquisition model:

(15) a. formal sufficiency
b. developmental compatibility
c. explanatory continuity

If one accepts these as guidelines for acquisition research, we can put the empiricist GSL models and the UG-based transformational learning models to the test. In recent years, the GSL approach to language acquisition has (re) gained popularity in cognitive sciences and computational linguistics (see e.g. Bates & Elman 1996, Seidenberg 1997). The GSL approach claims to assume little about the learner's initial knowledge of language. The child learner is viewed as a generalized data processor, such as an artificial neural network, which approximates the adult language based on the statistical distribution of the input data. The GSL approach claims support (Bates & Elman 1996) from experiments showing that infants are capable of extracting statistical regularities in (quasi)linguistic information (e.g. Saffran et al. 1996). Despite this renewed enthusiasm, it is regrettable that the GSL approach has not tackled the problem of language acquisition in a broad empirical context. For example, a main line of work (e.g. Elman 1990, 1991) is dedicated to showing that certain neural network models are able to capture some limited aspects of syntactic structures—a most rudimentary form of the formal sufficiency condition—although there is still debate on whether this project has been successful (e.g. Marcus 1998). Much more effort has gone into the learning of irregular verbs, starting with Rumelhart & McClelland (1996) and followed by numerous others, which prompted a review of the connectionist manifesto, Rethinking Innateness (Elman et al. 1996), to remark that connectionist modeling makes one feel as if developmental psycholinguistics is only about 'development of the lexicon and past tense verb morphology'(Rispoli 1999: 220). But even for such a trivial problem, no connectionist network has passed the Wug-test (Prasada & Pinker 1993, Pinker 1999), and, as we shall see in Chapter, much of the complexity in past tense acquisition is not covered by these works.

As suggested in section 1.2.2, there is reason to believe that these challenges are formidable for generalized learning models such as an artificial neural network. Given the power of computational tools available today, it would not be remarkable to construct a (GSL) system that learns something. What would be remarkable is to discover whether the constructed system learns in much the same way that human children learn. (10) shows that child language and adult language display significant disparities in statistical distributions; what the GSL approach has to do, then, is to find an empiricist (learning-theoretic) alternative to the learning biases introduced by innate UG. This seems difficult, given the simultaneous constraints—from both child language acquisition and comparative studies of the world's languages—that such an alternative must satisfy. That is, an empiricist must account for, say, systematic utterances like me riding horse (meaning 'I am riding a horse') in child language and island constraints in adult language, at the same time. But again, nothing can be said unless the GSL approach faces the challenges from the quantitative and crosslinguistic study of child language; as pointed out by Lightfoot (1998), Fodor & Crowther (in press), and others, there is nothing on offer.

We thus focus our attention on the other leading approach to language acquisition, which is most closely associated with generative linguistics. We will not review the argument for innate linguistic knowledge; see section 1.1 for a simple yet convincing example. The restrictiveness in the child language learner's hypothesis space, coupled with the similarities revealed in comparative studies of the world's languages, have led linguists to conclude that human languages are delimited in a finite space of possibilities, the Universal Grammar. The Principles and Parameters (P&P) approach (Chomsky 1981) is an influential instantiation of this idea by attempting to constrain the space of linguistic variation to a set of parametric choices.

In generative linguistics, the dominant model of language acquisition (e.g. Chomsky 1965, Wexler & Culicover 1980, Berwick 1985, Hyams 1986, Dresher & Kaye 1990, Gibson & Wexler 1994) can be called the transformational learning (TL) approach. It assumes that the state of the learner undergoes direct changes, as the old hypothesis is replaced by a new hypothesis. In the Aspectsstyle framework (Chomsky 1965), it is assumed (Wexler & Culicover 1980, Berwick 1985) that when presented with a sentence that the learner is unable to analyze with the present set of rules, an appropriate rule is added to the current hypothesis. Hence, a new hypothesis is formed to replace the old. With the advent of the P&P framework, acquiring a language has been viewed as setting the appropriate parameters. An influential way to implement parameter setting is the triggering model (Chomsky 1981, Gibson & Wexler 1994). In a typical triggering algorithm, the learner changes the value of a parameter in the present grammar if the present grammar cannot analyze an incoming sentence and the grammar with the changed parameter value can. Again, a new hypothesis replaces the old hypothesis. Note that in all TL models, the learner changes hypotheses in an all-or-nothing manner; specifically for the triggering model, the UG-defined parameters are literally 'triggered' (switched on and off) by the relevant evidence. For the rest of our discussion, we will focus on the triggering model (Gibson & Wexler 1994), representative of the TL models in the UG-based approach to language acquisition.

Formal Insufficiency of the Triggering Model

It is by now well known that Gibson & Wexler's triggering model has a number of formal problems (see Berwick & Niyogi 1996, Frank & Kapur 1996, Dresher 1999). The first problem concerns the existence of local maxima in the learning space. Local maxima are non-target grammars from which the learner can never reach the target grammar. By analyzing the triggering model as a Markovian process in a finite space of grammars, Berwick & Niyogi (1996) have demonstrated the pervasiveness of local maxima in Gibson and Wexler's (very small) three-parameter space. Gibson & Wexler (1994) suggest that the local maxima problem might be circumvented if the learner starts from a default parameter setting, a 'safe' state, such that no local maximum can ever be encountered. However, Kohl (1999), using an exhaustive search in a computer implementation of the triggering model, shows that in a linguistically realistic twelve-parameter space, 2,336 of the 4,096 grammars are still not learnable even with the best default starting state. With the worst starting state, 3,882 grammars are unlearnable. Overall, there are on average 3,348 unlearnable grammars for the triggering model. A second and related problem has to do with the ambiguity of input evidence. In a broad sense, ambiguous evidence refers to sentences that are compatible with more than one grammar. For example, a sentence with an overt thematic subject is ambiguous between an English-type grammar, which obligatorily uses subjects, and a Chinese-type grammar, which optionally uses subjects. When ambiguous evidence is presented, it may select any of the grammars compatible with the evidence and may subsequently be led to local maxima and unlearnability. To resolve the ambiguity problem, Fodor's (1998) Structural Trigger Learner (STL) model assumes that the learner can determine whether an input sentence is unambiguous by attempting to analyze it with multiple grammars. Only evidence that unambiguously determines the target grammar triggers the learner to change parameter values. Although Fodor shows that there is unambiguous evidence for each of the eight grammars in Gibson & Wexler's three-parameter space, such optimistic expectations may not hold for a large parametric space in general (Clark 1992, Clark & Roberts 1993; we return to this with a concrete example in section 2.3.3). Without unambiguous evidence, Fodor's revised triggering model will not work. Lastly, the robustness of the triggering model has been called into question. As pointed out by Osherson et al. (1984), Randall (1990), and Valian (1990), even a small amount of noise can lead the triggering-like transformational models to converge on a wrong grammar. In a most extreme form, if the last sentence the learner hears just before language acquisition stops happens to be noise, the learning experience during the entire period of language acquisition is wasted. This scenario is by no means an exaggeration when a realistic learning environment is taken into account. Actual linguistic environments are hardly uniform with respect to a single idealized grammar. For example, Weinreich et al. (1968: 101) observe that it is unrealistic to study language as a 'homogeneous object', and that the 'nativelike command of heterogeneous structures is not a matter of multidialectalism or "mere" performance, but is part of unilingual linguistic competence'. To take a concrete example, consider again the acquisition of subject use. English speakers, who in general use overt subjects, do occasionally omit them in informal speech, e.g. Seems good to me. This pattern, of course, is compatible with an optional subject grammar. Now recall that a triggering learner can alter its hypothesis on the basic of a single sentence. Consequently, variability in linguistic evidence, however sparse, may still lead a triggering learner to swing back and forth between grammars like a pendulum.

Developmental Incompatibility of the Triggering Model

While it might be possible to salvage the triggering model to meet the formal sufficiency condition (e.g. via a random-walk algorithm of Niyogi & Berwick 1996; but cf. Sakas & Fodor 2001), the difficulty posed by the developmental compatibility condition is far more serious. In the triggering model, and in fact in all TL models, the learner at any one time is identified with a single grammar. If such models are at all relevant to the explanation of child language, the following predictions are inevitable:

memory lapses (Pinker 1999) fails to explain much of the developmental data reported in Marcus et al. (1992). Phonological rules and structures in irregular verbs must be taken into account to obtain a fuller explanation. And in Chapter , we will see additional developmental data from several studies of children's syntax, including the subject drop phenomenon, to show the empirical problems with the performance-based approach. If we tentatively reject (11a) as, at least, a less favorable research strategy, we must rely on (11b) to explain child language. But exactly how is child competence different from adult competence? Here again are two possibilities:

(12) a. Child competence and adult competence are qualitatively different.
b. Child competence and adult competence are quantitatively different.

(12a) says that child language is subject to different rules and constraints from adult language. For example, it could be that some linguistic principle operates differently in children from adults, or a piece of grammatical knowledge is absent in younger children but becomes available as a matter of biological maturation (Gleitman 1981, Felix 1987, Borer & Wexler 1987). It is important to realize that there is nothing unprincipled in postulating a discontinuous competence system to explain child language. If children systematically produce linguistic expressions that defy UG (as understood via adult competence analysis), we can only conclude that their language is governed by different laws. However, in the absence of a concrete theory of how linguistic competence matures (12a) runs the risk of 'anything goes'. It must therefore remain a last resort only when (12a)—the approach that relies on adult competence, for which we do have concrete theories—is shown to be false. More specifically, we must not confuse the difference between child language and adult language with the difference between child language and Universal Grammar. That is, while (part of) child language may not fall under the grammatical system the child eventually attains, it is possible that it falls under some other, equally principled grammatical system allowed by UG. (Indeed, this is the approach taken in the present study.) This leaves us with (12b), which, in combination with (11b), gives the strongest realization of the Continuity Hypothesis: that child language is subject to the same principles and constraints in adult language, and that every utterance in child language is potentially an utterance in adult language. The difference between child and adult languages is due to differences in the organization of a continuous grammatical system. This position further splits into two directions:

(13) a. Child language reflects a *unique* potential adult language.
b. Child grammar consists of a *collection* of potential adult languages.

(13a), the dominant view ('triggering') in theoretical language acquisition will be rejected in Chapter. Our proposal takes the position of (13b): child language in development reflects a statistical combination of possible grammars allowed by UG, only some of which are eventually retained when language acquisition ends. This perspective will be elaborated in the rest of this book, where we examine how it measures up against the criteria of formal sufficiency, developmental compatibility, and explanatory continuity

A Road Map

This book is organized as follows. Chapter first gives a short but critical review of previous approaches to language acquisition. After an encounter with the populational and variational thinking in biological evolution that inspired this work, we propose to model language acquisition as a population of competing grammars, whose distribution changes in response to the linguistic evidence presented to the learner. We will give a precise formulation of this idea, and study its formal/computational properties with respect to the condition of formal sufficiency. Chapter applies the model to one of the biggest developmental problems in language, the learning of English past tense. It will be shown that irregular verbs are organized into classes, each of which is defined by special phonological rules, and that learning an irregular verb involves the competition between the designated special rule and the default -ed rule. Again, quantitative predictions are made and checked against children's performance on irregular verbs. Along the way we will develop a critique of Pinker and his colleagues' Words and Rules model (Pinker 1999), which holds that irregular verbs are individually and directly memorized as associated pairs of root and past tense forms. Chapter continues to subject the model to the developmental compatibility test by looking at the acquisition of syntax. First, crosslinguistic evidence will be presented to highlight the model's ability to make quantitative predictions based on adult-to-child corpus statistics. In addition, a number of major empirical cases in child language will be examined, including the acquisition of word order in a number of languages, the subject drop phenomenon, and Verb Second. Chapter extends the acquisition model to the study of language change. The quantitativeness of the acquisition model allows one to view language change as the change in the distribution of grammars in successive generations of learners. This can again incorporate the statistical properties of historical texts in an evolving, dynamic system. We apply the model of language change to explain the loss of Verb Second in Old French and Old English. Chapter concludes with a discussion on the implications of the acquisition model in a broad context of linguistic and cognitive science research.

A Variational Model of Language Acquisition

It is a simple observation that young children's language is different from that of adults. However, this simple observation raises profound questions: What results in the differences between child language and adult language, and how does the child eventually resolve such differences through exposure to linguistic evidence? These questions are fundamental to language acquisition research. (6) in Chapter, repeated below as (14), provides a useful framework within to characterize approaches to language acquisition:

(14) $\mathcal{L}: (S_0, E) \rightarrow S_T$

Language acquisition can be viewed as a function or algorithm, L, which maps the initial and hence putatively innate state (S_0) of the learner to the terminal state (S_T), the adult-form language, on the basis of experience, E, in the environment. Two leading approaches to L can be distinguished in this formulation according to the degree of focus on S_0 and L. An empiricist approach minimizes the role of S_0, the learner's initial (innate) and domain-specific knowledge of natural language. Rather, emphasis is given to L, which is claimed to be a generalized learning mechanism cross-cutting cognitive domains. Models in this approach can broadly be labeled generalized statistical learning (GSL): learning is the approximation of the terminal state (S_T)

based on the statistical distribution of the input data. In contrast, a rationalist approach, often rooted in the tradition of generative grammar, attributes the success of language acquisition to a richly endowed S_0, while relegating L to a background role. Specifically, S_0 is assumed to be a delimited space, a Universal Grammar (UG), which consists of a finite number of hypotheses that a child can in principle entertain. Almost all theories of acquisition in the UG-based approach can called transformational learning models, borrowing a term from evolutionary biology (Lewontin 1983): the learner's linguistic hypothesis undergoes direct transformations (changes), by moving from one hypothesis to another, driven by linguistic evidence. This study introduces a new approach to language acquisition in which both S_0 and L are given prominent roles in explaining child language. We will show that once the domain-specific and innate knowledge of language (S_0) is assumed, the mechanism language acquisition (L) can be related harmoniously to the learning theories from traditional psychology, and possibly, the development of neural systems.

Against Transformational Learning

Recall from Chapter the three conditions on an adequate acquisition model:

(15) a. formal sufficiency
b. developmental compatibility
c. explanatory continuity

If one accepts these as guidelines for acquisition research, we can put the empiricist GSL models and the UG-based transformational learning models to the test. In recent years, the GSL approach to language acquisition has (re) gained popularity in cognitive sciences and computational linguistics (see e.g. Bates & Elman 1996, Seidenberg 1997). The GSL approach claims to assume little about the learner's initial knowledge of language. The child learner is viewed as a generalized data processor, such as an artificial neural network, which approximates the adult language based on the statistical distribution of the input data. The GSL approach claims support (Bates & Elman 1996) from experiments showing that infants are capable of extracting statistical regularities in (quasi)linguistic information (e.g. Saffran et al. 1996).

Despite this renewed enthusiasm, it is regrettable that the GSL approach has not tackled the problem of language acquisition in a broad empirical context. For example, a main line of work (e.g. Elman 1990, 1991) is dedicated to showing that certain neural network models are able to capture some limited aspects of syntactic structures—a most rudimentary form of the formal sufficiency condition—although there is still debate on whether this project has been successful (e.g. Marcus 1998). Much more effort has gone into the learning of irregular verbs, starting with Rumelhart & McClelland (1986) and followed by numerous others, which prompted a review of the connectionist manifesto, Rethinking Innateness (Elman et al. 1996), to remark that connectionist modeling makes one feel as if developmental psycholinguistics is only about 'development of the lexicon and past tense verb morphology'(Rispoli 1999: 220). But even for such a trivial problem, no connectionist network has passed the Wug-test (Prasada & Pinker 1993, Pinker 1999), and, as we shall see in Chapter, much of the complexity in past tense acquisition is not covered by these works.

As suggested in section 1.2.2, there is reason to believe that these challenges are formidable for generalized learning models such as an artificial neural network. Given the power of computational tools available today, it would not be remarkable to construct a (GSL) system that learns something. What would be remarkable is to discover whether the constructed system learns in much the same way that human children learn. (10) shows that child language and adult language display significant disparities in statistical distributions; what the GSL approach has to do, then, is to find an empiricist (learning-theoretic) alternative to the learning biases introduced by innate UG. This seems difficult, given the simultaneous constraints—from both child language acquisition and comparative studies of the world's languages—that such an alternative must satisfy. That is, an empiricist must account for, say, systematic utterances like me riding horse (meaning 'I am riding a horse') in child language and island constraints in adult language, at the same time. But again, nothing can be said unless the GSL approach faces the challenges from the quantitative and crosslinguistic study of child language; as pointed out by Lightfoot (1998), Fodor & Crowther (in press), and others, there is nothing on offer.

We thus focus our attention on the other leading approach to language acquisition, which is most closely associated with generative linguistics. We will not review the argument for innate linguistic knowledge; see section 1.1 for a simple yet convincing example. The restrictiveness in the child language learner's hypothesis space, coupled with the similarities revealed in comparative studies of the world's languages, have led linguists to conclude that human languages are delimited in a finite space of possibilities, the Universal Grammar. The Principles and Parameters (P&P) approach (Chomsky 1981) is an influential instantiation of this idea by attempting to constrain the space of linguistic variation to a set of parametric choices.

In generative linguistics, the dominant model of language acquisition (e.g. Chomsky 1965, Wexler & Culicover 1980, Berwick 1985, Hyams 1986, Dresher & Kaye 1990, Gibson & Wexler 1994) can be called the transformational learning (TL) approach. It assumes that the state of the learner undergoes direct changes, as the old hypothesis is replaced by a new hypothesis. In the Aspectsstyle framework (Chomsky 1965), it is assumed (Wexler & Culicover 1980, Berwick 1985) that when presented with a sentence that the learner is unable to analyze with the present set of rules, an appropriate rule is added to the current hypothesis. Hence, a new hypothesis is formed to replace the old. With the advent of the P&P framework, acquiring a language has been viewed as setting the appropriate parameters. An influential way to implement parameter setting is the triggering model (Chomsky 1981, Gibson & Wexler 1994). In a typical triggering algorithm, the learner changes the value of a parameter in the present grammar if the present grammar cannot analyze an incoming sentence and the grammar with the changed parameter value can. Again, a new hypothesis replaces the old hypothesis. Note that in all TL models, the learner changes hypotheses in an all-or-nothing manner; specifically for the triggering model, the UG-defined parameters are literally 'triggered' (switched on and off) by the relevant evidence. For the rest of our discussion, we will focus on the triggering model (Gibson & Wexler 1994), representative of the TL models in the UG-based approach to language acquisition.

Formal Insufficiency of the Triggering Model

It is by now well known that Gibson & Wexler's triggering model has a number of formal problems (see Berwick & Niyogi 1996, Frank & Kapur 1996, Dresher 1999). The first problem concerns the existence of local maxima in the learning space. Local maxima are non-target grammars from which the learner can never reach the target grammar. By analyzing the triggering model as a Markovian process in a finite space of grammars, Berwick & Niyogi (1996) have demonstrated the pervasiveness of local maxima in Gibson and Wexler's (very small) three-parameter space. Gibson & Wexler (1994) suggest that the local maxima problem might be circumvented if the learner starts from a default parameter setting, a 'safe' state, such that no local maximum can ever be encountered. However, Kohl (1999), using an exhaustive search in a computer implementation of the triggering model, shows that in a linguistically realistic twelve-parameter space, 2,336 of the 4,096 grammars are still not learnable even with the best default starting state. With the worst starting state, 3,892 grammars are unlearnable. Overall, there are on average 3,348 unlearnable grammars for the triggering model. A second and related problem has to do with the ambiguity of input evidence. In a broad sense, ambiguous evidence refers to sentences that are compatible with more than one grammar. For example, a sentence with an overt thematic subject is ambiguous between an English-type grammar, which obligatorily uses subjects, and a Chinese-type grammar, which optionally uses subjects. When ambiguous evidence is presented, it may select any of the grammars compatible with the evidence and may subsequently be led to local maxima and unlearnability. To resolve the ambiguity problem, Fodor's (1998) Structural Trigger Learner (STL) model assumes that the learner can determine whether an input sentence is unambiguous by attempting to analyze it with multiple grammars. Only evidence that unambiguously determines the target grammar triggers the learner to change parameter values. Although Fodor shows that there is unambiguous evidence for each of the eight grammars in Gibson & Wexler's three-parameter space, such optimistic expectations may not hold for a large parametric space in general (Clark 1992, Clark & Roberts 1993; we return to this with a concrete example in section 2.3.3). Without unambiguous evidence, Fodor's revised triggering model will not work. Lastly, the robustness of the triggering model has been called into question. As pointed out by Osherson et al. (1984), Randall (1990), and Valian (1990), even a small amount of noise can lead the triggering-like transformational models to converge on a wrong grammar. In a most extreme form, if the last sentence the learner hears just before language acquisition stops happens to be noise, the learning experience during the entire period of language acquisition is wasted. This scenario is by no means an exaggeration when a realistic learning environment is taken into account. Actual linguistic environments are hardly uniform with respect to a single idealized grammar. For example, Weinreich et al. (1968: 101) observe that it is unrealistic to study language as a 'homogeneous object', and that the 'nativelike command of heterogeneous structures is not a matter of multidialectalism or "mere" performance, but is part of unilingual linguistic competence'. To take a concrete example, consider again the acquisition of subject use. English speakers, who in general use overt subjects, do occasionally omit them in informal speech, e.g. Seems good to me. This pattern, of course, is compatible with an optional subject grammar. Now recall that a triggering learner can alter its hypothesis on the basic of a single sentence. Consequently, variability in linguistic evidence, however sparse, may still lead a triggering learner to swing back and forth between grammars like a pendulum.

Developmental Incompatibility of the Triggering Model

While it might be possible to salvage the triggering model to meet the formal sufficiency condition (e.g. via a random-walk algorithm of Niyogi & Berwick 1996; but cf. Sakas & Fodor 2001), the difficulty posed by the developmental compatibility condition is far more serious. In the triggering model, and in fact in all TL models, the learner at any one time is identified with a single grammar. If such models are at all relevant to the explanation of child language, the following predictions are inevitable: To the best of my knowledge, there is in general no developmental evidence in support of either (16a) or (16b). A good test case is again children's null subjects (NS), where we have a large body of quantitative and crosslinguistic data. First, consider the prediction in (16a), the consistency of child language with respect to a single grammar defined in the UG space. Working in the P&P framework, Hyams (1986), in her groundbreaking work, suggests that English child NS results from missetting their language to an optional-subject grammar such as Italian, in which subject drop is grammatical. However, Valian (1991) shows that while Italian children drop subjects in 70% of all sentences, the NS ratio is only 31% for American children in the same age group. This statistical difference renders it unlikely that English children initially use an Italian-type grammar. Alternatively, Hyams (1991) suggests that during the NS stage, English children use a discourse-based, optional-subject grammar like Chinese. However, Wang et al. (1992) show that while subject drop rate is only 26% for American children during the NS stage (2;0–3;0),4 Chinese children in the same age group drop subjects in 55% of all sentences. Furthermore, if English children did indeed use a Chinese-type grammar, one predicts that object drop, grammatical in Chinese, should also be robustly attested (see section 4.3.2 for additional discussion). This is again incorrect: Wang et al. (1992) find that for 2-year-olds, Chinese children drop objects in 20% of sentences containing objects and American children only 8%. These comparative studies conclusively demonstrate that subject drop in child English cannot be identified with any single adult grammar.

Turning now to the triggering models' second prediction for language development (16b), we expect to observe abrupt changes in child language as the learner switches from one grammar to another. However, Bloom (1993) found no sharp changes in the frequency of subject use throughout the NS stage of Adam and Eve, two American children studied by Brown (1973). Behrens (1993) reports similar findings in a large longitudinal study of German children's NS stage. Hence, there is no evidence for a radical reorganization—parameter resetting (Hyams & Wexler 1993)—of the learner's grammar. In section 4.1 we will show that for Dutch acquisition, the percentage of V2 use in matrix sentences also rises gradually, from about 50% at 2;4 to 85% at 3;0. Again, there is no indication of a radical change in the child's grammar, contrary to what the triggering model entails. Overall, the gradualness of language development is unexpected in the view of all-or-none parameter setting, and has been a major argument against the parameter-setting model of language acquisition (Valian 1990, 1991, Bloom 1990, 1993), forcing many researchers to the conclusion that child and adult language differ not in competence but in performance.

Imperfection in Child Language?

So the challenge remains: what explains the differences between child and adult languages? As summarized in Chapter and repeated below, two approaches have been advanced to account for the differences between child and adult languages:

(17) a. Children and adults differ in linguistic performance.
b. Children and adults differ in grammatical competence.

The performance deficit approach (17a) is often stated under the Continuity Hypothesis (Macnamara 1982, Pinker 1984). It assumes an identity relation between child and adult competence, while attributing differences between child and adult linguistic forms to performance factors inherent in production, and (nonlinguistic) perceptual and cognitive capacities that are still underdeveloped at a young age (e.g. Pinker 1984, Bloom 1990, 1993, Gerken 1991, Valian 1991).

The competence deficit approach (17b) is more often found in works in the parameter-setting framework. In recent years it has been claimed (Hyams 1996, Wexler 1998), in contrast to earlier ideas of parameter mis-setting, that the parameter values are set correctly by children very early on. The differences between child language and adult language have been attributed to other deficits in children's grammatical competence. For example, one influential approach to the OI phenomenon reviewed in section 1.2.2 assumes a deficit in the Tense/Agreement node in children's syntactic representation (Wexler 1994): the Tense/Agreement features are missing in young children during the ROI stage. Another influential proposal in Rizzi's (1994) Truncation Hypothesis holds that certain projections in the syntactic representation, specifically CP, are missing in young children's knowledge of language. The reader is referred to Phillips (1995) for a review and critique of some recent proposals along these lines.

Despite the differences between the two approaches, a common theme can be identified: child language is assumed to be an imperfect form of adult language, perturbed by either competence or performance factors. In section 1.2.3, we have already noted some methodological pitfalls associated with such explanatorily discontinuous accounts. More empirically, as we shall see in Chapters and, the imperfection perspective on child language leaves many developmental patterns unexplained. To give a quick preview, we will see that children's overregularization errors (hold-holded) reveal important clues on how phonology is structured and learned, and should not be regarded as simple memory retrieval failures as in Pinker (1999). We will see that when English children drop subjects in Wh questions, they do so almost always in adjunct (where, how) questions, but almost never in argument (who, what) questions: a categorical asymmetry not predicted by any imperfection explanation proposed so far. We will document the robust use (approximately 50%) of V2 patterns in children acquiring V2: hence, 50% of 'imperfection' to be explained away. This concludes our very brief review of the leading approaches to language acquisition. While there is no doubt that innate UG knowledge must play a crucial role in constraining the child's hypothesis space and the learning process, there is one component in the GSL approach that is too sensible to dismiss. That is, statistical learning seems most naturally suited to modeling the gradualness of language development. In the rest of this chapter we propose a new approach that incorporates this useful aspect of the GSL model into a generative framework: an innate UG provides the hypothesis space and statistical learning provides the mechanism. To do this, we draw inspiration from Darwinian evolutionary biology.

The Variational Approach to Language Acquisition

The Dynamics of Darwinian Evolution

We started the discussion of child language by noting the variation between child and adult languages. It is a fundamental question how such variation is interpreted in a theory of language acquisition. Here, the conceptual foundation of Darwinian evolutionary thinking provides an informative lesson. Variation, as an intrinsic fact of life, can be observed at many levels of biological organizations, often manifested in physiological, developmental, and ecological characteristics. However, variation among individuals in a population was not fully recognized until Darwin's day. As pointed out by Ernst Mayr on many occasions (in particular, 1963, 1982, 1993), it was Darwin who first realized that the variations among individuals are 'real': individuals in a population are inherently different, and are not mere 'imperfect' deviations from some idealized archetype. Once the reality of variation and the uniqueness of individuals were recognized, the correct conception of evolution became possible: variations at the individual level result in fitness variations at the population level, thus allowing evolutionary forces such as natural selection to operate. As R. C. Lewontin remarks, evolutionary changes are hence changes in the distribution of different individuals in the population:

> Before Darwin, theories of historical change were all transformational. That is, systems were seen as undergoing change in time because each element in the system underwent an individual transformation during its history. Lamarck's theory of evolution was transformational in regarding species as changing because each individual organism within the species underwent the same change. Through inner will and striving, an organism would change

its nature, and that change in nature would be transmitted to its offspring. In contrast, Darwin proposed a variational principle, that individual members of the ensemble differ from each other in some properties and that the system evolves by changes in the proportions of the different types. There is a sorting-out process in which some variant types persist while others disappear, so the nature of the ensemble as a whole changes without any successive changes in the individual members. (Lewontin 1983: 65–6; italics original.)

For scientific observations, the message embedded in Darwinian variational thinking is profound. Non-uniformity in a sample of data often should, as in evolution, be interpreted as a collection of distinct individuals: variations are therefore real and expected, and should not be viewed as 'imperfect' forms of a single archetype. In the case of language acquisition, the differences between child and adult languages may not be the child's imperfect grasp of adult language; rather, they may actually reflect a principled grammatical system in development and transition, before the terminal state is established. Similarly, the distinction between transformational and variational thinking in evolutionary biology is also instructive for constructing a formal model of language acquisition. Transformational learning models identify the learner with a single hypothesis, which directly changes as input is processed. In contrast, we may consider a variational theory in which language acquisition is the change in the distribution of I-language grammars, the principled variations in human language.

In what follows, we present a learning model that instantiates the variational approach to language acquisition. The computational properties of the model will then be discussed in the context of the formal sufficiency condition on acquisition theories.

Language Acquisition as Grammar Competition

To explain the non-uniformity and the gradualness in child language, we explicitly introduce statistical notions into our learning model. We adopt the P&P framework, i.e. assuming that there is only a finite number of possible human grammars, varying along some parametric dimensions. We also adopt the strongest version of continuity hypothesis, which says, without evidence to the contrary, that UG-defined grammars are accessible to the learner from the start.

Each grammar G_i is paired with a weight p_i, which can be viewed as the measure of prominence of G_i in the learner's language faculty. In a linguistic environment E, the weight p_i (E, t) is determined by the learning function L, the linguistic evidence in E, and the time variable t, the time since the outset of language acquisition. Learning stops when the weights of all grammars are stabilized and do not change any further, possibly corresponding to some kind of critical period of development. In particular, in an idealized environment where all linguistic expressions are generated by a 'target' grammar T—again, keeping to the traditional terminology—we say that learning converges to target if $p_T = 1$ when learning stops. That is, the target grammar has eliminated all other grammars in the population as a result of learning.

The learning model is schematically shown below:

(18) Upon the presentation of an input datum *s*, the child
   a. selects a grammar G_i with the probability p_i
   b. analyzes *s* with G_i
   c. • if successful, reward G_i by increasing p_i
      • otherwise, punish G_i by decreasing p_i

Metaphorically speaking, the learning hypotheses—the grammars defined by UG—compete: grammars that succeed in analyzing a sentence are rewarded and those that fail are punished. As learning proceeds, grammars that have overall more success with the data will be more prominently represented in the learner's hypothesis space. An example illustrates how the model works. Imagine the learner has two grammars, G_1, the target grammar used in the environment, and G_2, the competitor, with associated weights of p_1 and p_2 respectively. Initially, the two grammars are undifferentiated, i.e. with comparable weights. The learner will then have comparable probabilities of selecting the grammars for both input analysis and sentence production, following the null hypothesis that there is a single grammatical system responsible for both comprehension/learning and production. At this time, sentence sequences produced by the learner will look like this:

(19) Early in acquisition:
   $S_{G1}, S_{G1}, S_{G2}, S_{G1}, S_{G2}, S_{G2}, \ldots$

where S_G indicates a sentence produced by the grammar G. [7] As learning proceeds, G_2, which by assumption is incompatible with at least some input data, will be punished and its weight will gradually decrease. At this stage of acquisition, sequences produced by the learner will look like this:

(20) Intermediate in acquisition:
   $S_{G1}, S_{G1}, S_{G2}, S_{G1}, S_{G1}, S_{G1} \ldots$

where G_1 will be more and more dominantly represented. When learning stops, G_2 will have been eliminated ($p_2 \approx 0$) and G_1 is the only grammar the learner has access to:

(21) Completion of acquisition:
$S_{G1}, S_{G1}, S_{G1}, S_{G1}, S_{G1}, S_{G1}, \ldots$

Of course, grammars do not actually compete with each other: the competition metaphor only serves to illustrate (a) the grammars' coexistence and (b) their differential representation in the learner's language faculty. Neither does the learner play God by supervising the competition of the grammars and selecting the winners.We will also stress the passiveness of the learner in the learning process, conforming to the research strategy of a 'dumb' learner in language acquisition. That is, one does not want to endow the learner with too much computational power or too much of an active role in learning. The justification for this minimum assumption is twofold. On the one hand, successful language acquisition is possible, barring pathological cases, irrespective of 'general intelligence'; on the other, we simply don't have a theory of children's cognitive/computational capacities to put into a rigorous model of acquisition—an argument from ignorance. Hence, we assume that the learner does not contemplate which grammar to use when an input datum is presented. He uses whichever happens to be selected with its associated weight/probability. He does not make active changes to the selected grammar (as in the triggering model), or reorganize his grammar space, but simply updates the weight of the grammar selected and moves on.

Some notations. Write $s \in E$ if a sentence s is an utterance in the linguistic environment E. We assume that during the time frame of language acquisition, E is a fixed environment, from which s is drawn independently. Write $G \rightarrow s$ if a grammar G can analyze s, which, as a special case, can be interpreted as parsability (Wexler & Culicover 1980, Berwick 1985), in the sense of strong generative capacity. Clearly, the weak generative notion of string-grammar acceptance does not affect formal properties of the model. However, as we shall see in Chapter, children use their morphological knowledge and domain-specific knowledge of UG—strong generative notions—to disambiguate grammars. It is worth noting that the formal properties of the model are independent of the definition of analyzability: any well-defined and empirically justified notion will suffice. Our choice of string-grammar compatibility obviously eases the evaluation of grammars using linguistic corpora. Suppose that there are altogether N grammars in the population. For simplicity, write pi for $p_i(E, t)$ at time t, and p_i' for $p_i(E, t + 1)$ at time t + 1. Each time instance denotes the presentation of an input sentence. In the present model, learning is the adaptive change in the weights of grammars in response to the sentences successively presented to the learner. There are many possible instantiations of competition-based learning.Consider the one in (22):

(22) Given an input sentence s, the learner selects a grammar G_i with probability p_i :

a. if $G_i \rightarrow s$ then $\begin{cases} p'_i = p_i + \gamma(1 - p_i) \\ p'_j = (1 - \gamma)p_j \quad \text{if } j \neq i \end{cases}$

b. if $G_i \not\rightarrow s$ then $\begin{cases} p'_i = (1 - \gamma)p_i \\ p'_j = \dfrac{\gamma}{N-1} + (1 - \gamma)p_j \quad \text{if } j \neq i \end{cases}$

(22) is the Linear reward-penalty (L_{R-P}) scheme (Bush & Mosteller 19951, 1958), one of the earliest, simplest, and most extensively studied learning models in mathematical psychology. Many similar competition-based models have been formally and experimentally studied, and receive considerable support from human and and animal learning and decision-making; see Atkinson et al. (1965) for a review.

Does the employment of a general-purpose learning model from the behaviorist tradition, the L_{R-P}, signal a return to the Dark Ages? Absolutely not. In competition learning models, what is crucial is the constitution of the hypothesis space. In the original L_{R-P} scheme, the hypothesis space consists of simple responses conditioned on external stimulus; in the grammar competition model, the hypothesis space consists of Universal Grammar, a highly constrained and finite range of possibilities. In addition, as discussed in Chapter , it seems unlikely that language acquisition can be equated to data-driven learning without prior knowledge. And, as will be discussed in later chapters in addition to numerous other studies in language acquisition, in order adequately to account for child language development, one needs to make reference to specific characterization of UG supplied by linguistic theories. There is yet another reason for having an explicit account of the learning process: because language is acquired, and thus the composition, distribution, and other properties of the input evidence, in principle, matter. The landmark study of Newport et al. (1977) is best remembered for debunking the necessity of the so-called 'Motherese' for language acquisition, but it also shows that the development of some aspects of language does correlate with the abundance of linguistic data. Specifically, children who are exposed to more yes/no questions tend to use auxiliary verbs faster and better. An explicit model of learning that incorporates the role of input evidence may tell us why such correlations exist in some cases, but not others (e.g. the null subject phenomenon). The reason, as we shall see, lies in the Universal Grammar. Hence, our emphasis on L is simply a plea to pay attention to the actual mechanism of language development, and a concrete proposal of what it might be.

The Dynamics of Variational Learning

We now turn to the computational properties of the variational model in (22).

Asymptotic Behaviors

In any competition process, some measure of fitness is required. Adapting the formulation of Bush & Mosteller (1958), we may offer the following definition:

(23) The penalty probability of grammar G_i in a linguistic environment E is

$$c_i = \Pr(G_i \nrightarrow s \mid s \in E)$$

The penalty probability c_i represents the probability that a grammar G_i fails to analyze an incoming sentence and gets punished as a result. In other words, c_i is the percentage of sentences in the environment with which the grammar G_i is incompatible. Notice that penalty probability is a fixed property of a grammar relative to a fixed linguistic environment E, from which input sentences are drawn.

For example, consider a Germanic V2 environment, where the main verb is situated in the second constituent position. A V2 grammar, of course, has the penalty probability of 0. [10] An English-type SVO grammar, although not compatible with all V2 sentences, is nevertheless compatible with a certain proportion of them. According to a corpus analysis cited in Lightfoot (1997), about 70% of matrix sentences in modern V2 languages have the surface order of SVO: an SVO grammar therefore has a penalty probability of 30% in a V2 environment. Since the grammars in the delimited UG space are fixed—it is only their weights that change during learning—their fitness values defined as penalty probabilities are also fixed if the linguistic environment is, by assumption, fixed.

It is crucial to realize that penalty probability is an extensionally defined property of grammars. It is a notion used, by the linguist, in the formal analysis of the learning model. It is not a component of the learning process. For example, the learner needs not and does not keep track of frequency information about sentence patterns, and does not explicitly compute the penalty probabilities of the competing grammars. Nor is penalty probability represented or accessed in during learning, as the model in (22) makes clear.

The asymptotic properties of the L_{R-P} model have been extensively studied in both mathematical psychology (Norman 1972) and machine learning (Narendra & Thathachar 1989, Barto & Sutton 1998). For simplicity but without loss of generality, suppose that there are two grammars in the population, G_1 and G_2 , and that they are associated with penalty probabilities of c_1 and c_2

respectively. If the learning rate g is sufficiently small, i.e. the learner does not alter his 'confidence' in grammars too radically, one can show (see Narendra and Thathachar 1989: 162–5) that the asymptotic distributions of p_1 (t) and p_2 (t) will be essentially normal and can be approximated as follows:

(24) Theorem:

$$\lim_{t \to \infty} p_1(t) = \frac{c_2}{c_1 + c_2}$$

$$\lim_{t \to \infty} p_2(t) = \frac{c_1}{c_1 + c_2}$$

(24) shows that in the general case, grammars more compatible with the input data are better represented in the population than those less compatible with the input data as the result of learning.

Stable Multiple Grammars

Recall from section 2.1.1 that realistic linguistic environments are usually heterogeneous, and the actual linguistic data cannot be attributed to a single idealized 'grammar'. This inherent variability poses a significant challenge for the robustness of the triggering model. How does the variational model fare in realistic environments that are inherently variable? Observe that non-homogeneous linguistic expressions can be viewed as a probabilistic combination of expressions generated by multiple grammars. From a learning perspective, a non-homogeneous environment induces a population of grammars none of which is 100% compatible with the input data. The theorem in (24) shows that the weights of two (or more, in the general case) grammars reach a stable equilibrium when learning stops. Therefore, the variability of a speaker's linguistic competence can be viewed as a probabilistic combination of multiple grammars. We note in passing that this interpretation is similar to the concept of 'variable rules' (Labov 1969, Sankoff 1978), and may offer a way to integrate generative linguists' idealized grammars with the study of language variation and use in linguistic performance. In Chapter, we extend the acquisition model to language change. We show that a combination of grammars as the result of acquisition, while stable in a single (synchronic) generation of learners, may not be diachronically stable. We will derive certain conditions under which one grammar will inevitably replace another in a number of generations, much like the process of natural selection. This formalizes historical linguists' intuition of grammar competition as a mechanism for language change.

Consider the special case of an idealized environment in which all linguistic expressions are generated by an input grammar G_1 . By definition, G_2 has a penalty probability of 0, while all other grammars in the population have positive penalty probabilities. It is easy to see from (24) that the p_1 converges to 1, with the competing grammars eliminated. Thus, the variational model meets the traditional learnability condition.

Empirically, one of the most important features of the variational model is its ability to make quantitative predictions about language development via the calculation of the expected change in the weights of the competing grammars. Again, consider two grammars, target G_1 and the competitor G_2, with $c_1 = 0$ and $c_2 > 0$ At any time $p_1 + p_2 = 1$. With the presentation of each input sentence, the expected increase of p_1, $E[\Delta p_1]$ can be computed as follows:

(25)
$$\begin{aligned} E[\Delta p_1] &= p_1\gamma(1-p_1) + && \text{with Pr. } p_1,\ G_1 \text{ is chosen and } G_1 \rightarrow s \\ &\quad p_2(1-c_2)(-\gamma)p_1 + && \text{with Pr. } p_2(1-c_2),\ G_2 \text{ is chosen and } G_2 \rightarrow s \\ &\quad p_2c_2\gamma(1-p_1) && \text{with Pr. } p_2c_2,\ G_2 \text{ is chosen and } G_2 \not\rightarrow s \\ &= c_2\gamma(1-p_1) \end{aligned}$$

Although the actual rate of language development is hard to predict—it would rely on an accurate estimate of the learning parameter and the precise manner in which the learner updates grammar weights—the model does make comparative predictions on language development. That is, ceteris paribus, the rate at which a grammar is learned is determined by the penalty probability (c_2) of its competitor. By estimating penalty probabilities of grammars from CHILDES (25) allows us to make longitudinal predictions about language development that can be verified against actual findings. In Chapter, we do just that.

Before we go on, a disclaimer, or rather, a confession, is in order. We in fact are not committed to the L_{R-P} model per se: exactly how children change grammar weights in response to their success or failure, as said earlier, is almost completely unknown. What we are committed to is the mode of learning: coexisting hypotheses in competition and gradual selection, as schematically illustrated in (18), and elaborated throughout this book with case studies in child language. The choice of the L_{R-P} model is justified mainly because it allows the learner to converge to a stable equilibrium of grammar weights when the linguistic evidence is not homogeneous (24). This is needed to accommodate the fact of linguistic variation in adult speakers that is particularly clear in language change, as we shall see in Chapter . There are doubtlessly many other models with similar properties.

Unambiguous Evidence

The theorem in (24) states that in the variational model, convergence to the target grammar is guaranteed if all competitor grammars have positive penalty probabilities. One way to ensure this is to assume the existence of unambiguous evidence (Fodor 1998): sentences that are compatible only with the target grammar, and not with any other grammar. While the general existence of unambiguous evidence has been questioned (Clark 1992, Clark & Roberts 1993), the present model does not require unambiguous evidence to converge in any case. To illustrate this, consider the following example. The target of learning is a Dutch V2 grammar, which competes in a population of (prototype) grammars, where X denotes an adverb, a prepositional phrase, and other adjuncts that can freely appear at the initial position of a sentence:

(26) a. Dutch: SVO, XVSO, OVS
b. Hebrew: SVO, XVSO
c. English: SVO, XSVO
d. Irish: VSO, XVSO
e. Hixkaryana: OVS, XOVS

The grammars in (26) are followed by some of the matrix sentences word orders they can generate/analyze. Observe that none of the patterns in (26a) alone could distinguish Dutch from the other four human grammars, as each of them is compatible with certain V2 sentences. Specifically, based on the input evidence received by a Dutch child (Hein), we found that in declarative sentences, for which the V2 constraint is relevant, 64.7% are SVO patterns, followed by XVSO patterns at 34% and only 1.3% OVS patterns. Most notably, Hebrew, and Semitic in general, grammar, which allows VSO and SVO alternations (Universal 6: Greenberg 1963; see also Fassi-Fehri 1993, Shlonsky 1997), is compatible with 98.7% of V2 sentences.

Despite the lack of unambiguous evidence for the V2 grammar, as long as SVO, OVS, and XVSO patterns appear at positive frequencies, all the competing grammars in (26) will be punished. The V2 grammar, however, is never punished. The theorem in (24) thus ensures the learner's convergence to the target V2 grammar. The competition of grammars is illustrated in Fig. 2.1, based on a computer simulation.

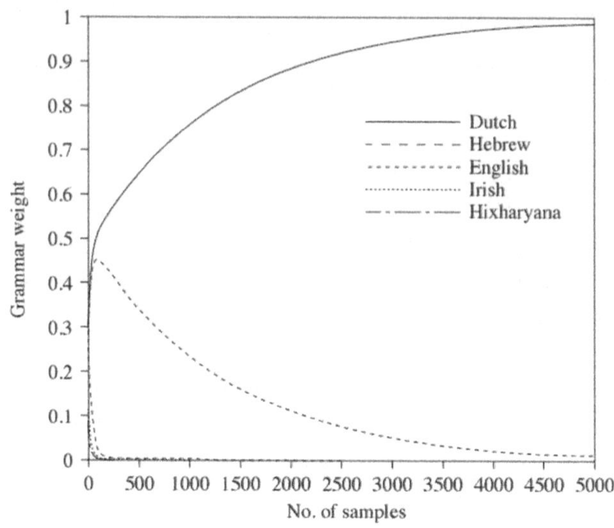

Figure .1: The convergence to the V grammar in the absence of unambiguous evidence

Learning Grammars in a Parametric Space

The variational model developed in the preceding sections is entirely theory-neutral. It only requires a finite and non-arbitrary space of possible grammars, a conclusion accepted by many of today's linguists. Some interesting questions arise when we situate the learning model in a realistic theory of grammar space, the P&P model.

Parameter Interference

So far we have been treating competing grammars as individual entities; we have not taken into account the structure of the grammar space. Although the convergence result in (24) for two grammars generalizes to any number of grammars, it is clear that when the number of grammars increases, the number of grammar weights that have to be stored also increases. According to some estimates (Clark 1992; cf. Kayne 2000, Baker 2001), 30–40 binary parameters are required to give a reasonable coverage of the UG space. And, if the grammars are stored as individual wholes, the learner would have to manipulate 2^{30}–2^{40} grammar weights: now that seems implausible

It turns out that a parametric view of grammar variation, independently motivated by comparative theoretical linguistics, dramatically reduces the computational load of learning. Suppose that there are n binary parameters, $\alpha_1, \alpha_2, \ldots, \alpha_n$, which can specify 2^n grammars. Each parameter α_1 is associated with a weight p_i , the probability of the parameter α_i being 1. The weights constitute an n-dimensional vector of real numbers between [0, 1]: $P = (p_1, p_2, \ldots, p_n)$.

Now the problem of selecting a grammar becomes the problem of selecting a vector of n 0s and 0s, which can be done independently according to the parameter weights. For example, if the current value of pi is 0.7, then the learner has a 70% chance of selecting 1 and a 30% chance of selecting 0. As the value of pi changes, so will the probability of selecting 0 or 1. Now, given a current parameter weight vector $P = (p_1, p_2, \ldots, p_n)$, the learner can non-deterministically generate a string of 0s and 0s, which is a grammar, *G*. Write this as $P \Rightarrow G$, and the probability of $P \Rightarrow G$ is the product of the parameter weights with respect to G's parameter values. P gives rise to all 2^n grammars; as P changes, the probability of $P \Rightarrow G$ also changes. When P reaches the target vector, then the probability of generating non-target grammars will be infinitely small.

(27) describes how P generates a grammar to analyze an incoming sentence:

(27) For each incoming sentence *s*
  a. For parameter i, $i = 1, 2, \ldots, n$
    - with probability p_i, choose the value of α_i to be 1;
    - with probability $1 - p_i$, choose the value of α_i to be 0.
  b. Let *G* be the grammar with the parameter values chosen in (27a).
  c. Analyze *s* with *G*.
  d. Update the parameter values to $\mathbf{P}' = (p_1', p_2', \ldots, p_n')$ accordingly.

Now a problem of parameter interference immediately arises. Under the parametric representation of grammars, grammar selection is based on independent parameters. By contrast, fitness measure and thus the outcome of learning—reward or punishment—is defined on whole grammars. How does the learner infer, backwards, what to do with individual parameter weights, from their collective fitness as a composite grammar? In other words, what is the proper interpretation of accordingly in the parameter learning model (27)?

To be concrete, suppose we have two independent parameters: one determines whether the language has overt Wh movement (as in English but not Chinese), and the other determines whether the language has verb second (V2), generally taken to be the movement of inflected verbs to matrix Complementizer position, as in many Germanic languages. Suppose that the language to be acquired is German, which has [+Wh] and [+V2]. When the parameter combination [+Wh, –V2] is chosen, the learner is presented with a declarative sentence. Now although [+Wh] is the target value for the Wh parameter, the whole grammar [+Wh, –V2] is nevertheless incompatible with a V2 declarative sentence and will fail. But should the learner prevent the correct parameter value [+Wh] from being punished? If so, how? Similarly, the grammar [–Wh, +V2] will succeed at any declarative German sentence, and the wrong parameter value [–Wh], irrelevant to the input, may hitch a ride and get rewarded.

So the problem is this. The requirement of psychological plausibility forces us to cast grammar probability competition in terms of parameter probability competition. This in turns introduces the problem of parameter interference: updating independent parameter probability is made complicated by the success/failure of the composite grammar. In what follows, we will address this problem from several angles that, in combination, may yield a decent solution.

Independent Parameters and Signatures

To be sure, not all parameters are subject to the interference problem. Some parameters are independent of other parameters, and can be learned independently from a class of input examples that we will call signatures. Specifically, with respect to a parameter a, its signature refers to s_a, a class of sentences that are analyzable only if a is set to the target value. Furthermore, if the input sentence does not belong to s_a, the value of a is not material to the analyzability of that sentence.

In the variational model, unlike the cue-based learning model to be reviewed a little later, the signature–parameter association need not be specified a priori, and neither does the learner actively search for signature in the input. Rather, signatures are interpreted as input whose cumulative effect leads to correct setting of parameters. Specifically, both values of a parameter are available to the child at the outset. The non-target value, however, is penalized upon the presentation of 'signatures', which, by definition, are only compatible with the target value. Hence, the nontarget value has a positive penalty probability, and will be eliminated after a sufficient number of signatures have been encountered. The existence of signatures for independent parameters is useful in two important ways. On the one hand, it radically reduces the problem of parameter interferences. For every parameter that is independent, the learning space is in effect cut by half; we will clarify this claim shortly, in section 2.4.4.[14] On the other hand, parameters with signatures lead to longitudinal predictions that can be directly related to corpus statistics. For two such parameters, we can estimate the frequencies of their respective signature, and predict, on the basis of (24), that the parameter with more abundant signatures be learned sooner than the other. In Chapter , we will see the acquisition of several independent parameters that can be developmentally tracked this way. So what are these independent parameters? Of the betterestablished parameters, a few are obviously independent. The Wh movement parameter is a straightforward example. Wh words move in English questions, but not in Chinese questions, and Wh questions will serve to unambiguously determine the target values of this parameter, regardless of the values of other parameters. For non-Wh sentences, the Wh parameter obviously has no effect.

Another independent parameter is the verb raising parameter that determines whether a finite verb raises to Tense: French sets this parameter to 1, and English, 0 (Emonds 1978, Pollock 1989). The 1 value for this parameter is associated with signature such as (28), where finite verbs precede negation/adverb:

(28) a. Jean ne mange pas de fromage.
Jean *ne* eats no of cheese.
'John does not eat cheese.'
b. Jean mange souvent du fromage.
Jean eats often of cheese.
'John often eats cheese.'

Yet another independent parameter is the obligatory subject parameter, for which the positive value (e.g. English) is associated with the use of pure expletives such as there in sentences like There is a train in the house.

What about the parameters are not independent, whose values can not be directly determined by any particular type of input data? In section 2.4.3 we review two models that untangle parameter interference by endowing the learner with additional resources. We then propose, in section 2.4.4, a far simpler model and study its formal sufficiency. Our discussion is somewhat technical; the disinterested reader can go straight to section 2.5. A fuller treatment of the mathematical and computational issues can be found in Yang (in press).

Interference Avoidance Models

One approach is to give the learner the ability to tease out the relevance of parameters with respect of an input sentence. Fodor's (1998) Structural Trigger Learner (STL) takes this approach. The STL has access to a special parser that can detect whether an input sentence is parametrically ambiguous. If so, the present parameter values are left unchanged; parameters are set only when the input is completely unambiguous. The STL thus aims to avoid the local maxima problem, caused by parametric inference, in Gibson & Wexler's triggering model.

The other approach was proposed by Dresher & Kaye (1990) and Dresher (1999); see Lightfoot (1999) for an extension to the acquisition of syntax. They note that the parameters in metrical stress can be associated with a corresponding set of cues, input data that can unambiguously determine the values of the parameters in a language. Dresher & Kaye (1990) propose that for each parameter, the learner is innately endowed with the knowledge of the cue associated with that parameter. In addition, each parameter has a default value, which is innately specified as well. Upon the presentation of a cue, the learner sets the value for the corresponding parameter. Crucially, cues are ordered. That is, the cue for a parameter may not be usable if another parameter has not been set. This leads to a particular sequence of parameter setting, which must be innately specified. Suppose the parameter sequence is $\alpha_1, \alpha_2, \ldots \alpha_n$, associated with cues $s_1, s_2, \ldots, s_n$, respectively. (29) schematically shows the mechanisms of the cue-based learner:

(29) a. Initialize $\alpha_1, \alpha_2, \ldots, \alpha_n$ with their respective default values.
b. For $i = 1, 2, \ldots, n$
- Set α_i upon seeing s_i.
- Leave the set parameters $\alpha_1, \ldots, \alpha_i$ alone.
- Reset $\alpha_{i+1}, \ldots, \alpha_n$ to respective default values.

In the present context, we do not discuss the formal sufficiency of the STL and the cue-based models. The STL model seems to introduce computational cost that is too high to be realistic: the learner faces a very large degree of structural ambiguity that must be disentangled (Sakas & Fodor 2001). The cue-based model would only work if all parameters are associated with cues and default values, and the order in which parameters are set must be identified as well. While this has been deductively worked out for about a dozen parameters in metrical stress (Dresher 1999), whether the same is true for a non-trivial space of syntactic parameters remains to be seen.

Both models run into problems with the developmental compatibility condition, detrimental to all transformational learning models: they cannot capture the variation in and the gradualness of language development. The STL model may maintain that before a parameter is conclusively set, both parameter values are available, to which variation in child language are be attributed. However, when a parameter is set, it is set in an all-ornone fashion, which then incorrectly predicts abrupt changes in child language. The cue-based model is completely deterministic. At any time, a parameter is associated with a unique parameter value—correct or incorrect, but not both—and hence no variation in child language can be accounted for. In addition, the unset parameters are reset to default values every time a parameter is set. This predicts radical and abrupt reorganization of child language: incorrectly, as reviewed earlier. Finally, the cue-based model entails that learners of all languages will follow an identical learning path, the order in which parameters are set: we have not been able to evaluate this claim.

Naive Parameter Learning

In what follows, we will pursue an approach that sticks to the strategy of assuming a 'dumb' learner. Consider the algorithm in (30), a Naive Parameter Learner (NPL):

(30) Naive Parameter Learning (NPL)
  a. Reward *all* the parameter values if the composite grammar succeeds.
  b. Punish *all* the parameter values if the composite grammar fails.

The NPL model may reward wrong parameter values as hitchhikers, and punish correct parameter values as accomplices. The hope is that, in the long run, the correct parameter values will prevail. To see how (30) works, consider again the learning of the two parameters [Wh] and [V2] in a German environment. The combinations of the two parameters give four grammars, of which we can explicitly measure the fitness values (penalty probabilities). Based on the CHILDES corpus, we estimate that about 30% of all sentences children hear are Wh questions, which are only compatible with the [+Wh] value. Of the remaining declarative sentences, about 49% are SVO sentences that are consistent with the [–V2] value. The other 21% are VS sentences with a topic

in [Spec,CP], which are only compatible with the [+V2] value. We then have the penalty probabilities shown in Table 1.

Fig. 2 shows the changes of the two parameter values over time. We see that the two parameters, which fluctuated in earlier stages of learning—the target values were punished and the nontarget values were rewarded—converged correctly to [1, 1] in the end. It is not difficult to prove that for parameters with signatures, the NPL will converge on the target value, using the Martingale methods in Yang & Gutmann (1999); see Yang (in press) for

Table 1: The penalty probabilities of four grammars composed of two parameters

	[+Wh]	[–Wh]
[+V2]	0	0.3
[–V2]	0.21	0.51

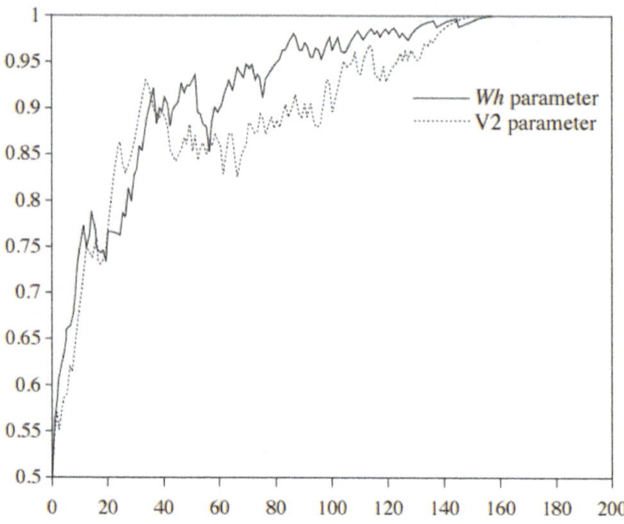

Figure 2: The independent learning of two parameters, Wh and V2

details. We now turn to the more difficult issue of learning parameters that are subject to the interference problem. Fitness distribution In what follows, we will suggest that (some variant) of the NPL may be a plausible model of learning that distangles the interference effects from parameter interaction. First, our conclusion is based on results from computer simulation. This is not the preferred move, for the obvious reason that one cannot simulate all possibilities that may arise in parameter learning. Analytical results—proofs—are much better, but so far they have been elusive. Second, as far as feasible, we will study the behavior of the model in an actual learning environment. As the example of the Wh and V2 learning (Fig. 2) shows, the relative fitness values of the four composite grammars will determine the outcome of parameter learning. In that example, if the three competitors have high penalty probabilities, intuition tells us that the two parameters rise to target values quickly. So the actual behavior of the model can be understood only if we have a good handle on the fitness distribution of actual grammars. This is a departure from the traditional linguistic learnability study, and we believe it is a necessary one. Learnability models, in general, do not consider convergence in relation to the actual (statistical) distribution of the learning data. Rather, learning is studied 'in the limit' (Gold 1967), with the assumption that learning can take an arbitrary amount of data as long as it converges on the correct grammar in the end: hence, no sample complexity considerations. However, it is clear that learning data is not infinite. In Chapter we show that it is possible to establish bounds on the amount of linguistic data needed for actual acquisition:

if the learning data required by a model greatly exceed such bounds, then such a model will fail the formal sufficiency condition. Sample complexity, even if it is formally studied, means very little unless placed in an actual context. For example, suppose one has found models that require exactly n or n^2 specific kinds of input sentences to set n parameters. The sample complexity of this model is very small: a (low) polynomial function of the problem size. But to claim this is an efficient model, one must show that these n^2 sentences are in fact attested with robust frequencies in the actual input: a model whose theoretical convergence relies on twenty levels of embedded clauses with parasitic gaps is hopeless in reality. In a similar vein, a model that fails under some hypothetical conditions may not be doomed either: it is possible that such cases never arise in actual learning environments. For example, computer simulation shows that the NPL model does not converge onto the target parameter values in a reasonable amount of time if all of the $2^n - 1$ composite grammars have the penalty probability of 0.1: that is, all non-target grammars are equally good, compatible with 90% of input data. But this curious (and disastrous) scenario does not occur in reality.

It is very difficult to know what actual penalty probability distributions are like. To do so, one would have to consider all, at least a large portion, of the 2^n grammars. For each grammar, which is a parameter value vector, one needs to find a corresponding existing language, take a large sample of sentences from it, and then analyze the sample with all the other $2^n - 1$ competitors. It is obvious that each of these steps poses enormous practical problems for large numbers of n. Our experience working with corpora (suggests that there are relatively few competing grammars with low penalty probabilities, i.e. very close to the target grammar, whereas the vast majority of them are bad. The example in (26), the V2 grammar in competition with four other grammars, is a case in point. This assumption seems compatible with the fact that most (but not all) parameters are acquired fairly early, which would not be possible if the relative compatibilities among grammars were very high.

Furthermore, we believe that it is reasonable to assume that the badness of a grammar is in general correlated with how 'far away' it is from the target grammar, where distance can be measured by how many parameter values they differ: the Hamming distance. In particular, we assume that as grammars get further and further away, their fitness values deteriorate rapidly. It is true that the change of some parameter may induce radical changes on the overall grammar obtained, e.g. [±Wh], scrambling (though some of these parameters may be independent, and thus free of parameter interference). Hence, what we assume is only a statistical tendency: it is possible that a grammar closer to the target (in terms of the Hamming distance) is worse than one that is further away, but it is unlikely. Specifically, we assume that the penalty probabilities of the competing grammars follow a standard Gaussian distribution:

(31) $c(x) = 1 - e - \frac{x^2}{2\sigma^2}$, where $\sigma = 1/3$

To choose penalty probabilities, we first divide the interval (0, 1) into n equal segments, where n is the number of parameters. A grammar G_h with Hamming distance h is expected to fall in the hth interval. However, to simulate the effect that grammars further from the target are generally (but not always) worse than the closer ones, we assume that G_h falls in the hth region with probability s, in the h ± 1st regions with probability s^2, in the h ± 2nd regions with probability s^3, etc. This is our assumption of exponential decay of grammar fitness with respect to its Hamming distance. Thus, a grammar farther away can be still be compatible with many sentences from the target grammar, but the likelihood of it being so vanishes very quickly. Similarly, a grammar that differs from the target by few paprameters can also be fairly bad. But overall, further away grammars are on average worse than those that are closer to the target. To verify our assumptions of penalty probability distributions, we consider a very small case, for n = 3 with three parameters, in Gibson & Wexler (1994): Spec-Head, Comp-Head, and V4. And even here we will make simplified assumptions; see Appendix A for details. First, we only consider the matrix clauses, as in Gibson & Wexler (1994). Second, some essential distributional statistics are based on English and Germanic languages, and then extrapolated (not unreasonably, we believe) to other grammars. Averaging over the pairwise penalty probabilities of eight grammars, we have:

(32) a. The average penalty probability for grammars one parameter away is 0.571312.
b. The average penalty probability for grammars two parameters away is 0.687908.
c. The average penalty probability for grammars three parameters away is 0.727075.

This is clearly consistent with our assumption about fitness distribution. Penalty probability in general correlates with the Hamming distance from the target. The pairwise penalty probabilities (Table 3 in Appendix A) are also consistent with our assumption of distance-related exponential decay.

Learning Rates and Random Walks

If one runs the NPL on the distribution of penalty probabilities as in (31), a number of problems arise, all having to do with the choice of the learning parameter, g, which controls the rapidity with which the learner adjusts the parameters. First, if g is too small—the learner modifies parameter weights very slightly upon success/failure—the learner takes an incredibly long time to converge. And second, if g is too big, the learner will modify the parameter weights very abruptly, resulting in a 'jumpy' learning curve, not so unlike the original triggering model rejected on the ground of developmental incompatibility (section 2.1.2).

It is not hard to understand why this may be the case. Consider the current parameter weight vector $P = (p_1, p_2, \ldots, p_n)$, and the target values are T, which is an n-ary vector of s and . When P is far from T, e.g. $P = (0.5, 0.5, \ldots, 0.5)$, the learner has no idea what T may be. As P gets closer to T, the learner will be able to analyze incoming sentences more often. Thus, the learner may have increasingly higher confidence in P, which now works better and better. It then seems reasonable to assume that the learner ought to be more conservative when P is far from the target, but more assured when P gets close. There are a number of ways of implementing this intuition. One may assume that the gradual increase in g is a matter of biological maturation. There are also many algorithms in computer science and machine learning that formally—and computationally expensively—modify the learning rate with respect to the confidence interval. But these approaches will alter the mathematical properties of the L_{R-P} model (22), which requires a fixed learning rate. Furthermore, they deviate from the guidelines of psychological plausibility and explanatory continuity that acquisition models are advised to follow An alternative is suggested by Morgan Sonderegger (personal communication). It is based on two observations. First, note that having a high g is equivalent to having a fixed g and using it often. Second, the overall goodness of P can be related to how often P successfully analyzes incoming sentences. This leads to a very simple measure of how close P is to the target, by introducing a small batch counter b, which is initialized to , and a batch bound B, a small positive integer (usually between 2 and 5, in practice). Formally,.

(33) The Naive Parameter Learner with Batch (NPL+B)

a. For an input sentence *s*, select a grammar *G* based on P following the procedure in (27)

b. • If $G \rightarrow s$, then $b = b + 1$.
   • If $G \not\rightarrow s$, then $b = b - 1$.

c. • If $b = B$, reward *G* and reset $b = 0$.
   • If $b = -B$, punish *G* and reset $b = 0$.

d. Go to (33a).

Note that the use of 'batch' in NPL+B (33) is very different from the standard one. Usually, 'batch' refers to a memory that stores a number of data points before processing them. In NPL+B, b is simply a counter that tracks the success or failure of sentence analysis, without recording what sentences have been presented or what grammars selected. The cost of additional memory load is trivial. Yet the effect of this batch is precisely what we wanted: it slows down the learning rate when P is bad, and speeds it up when P gets better. To see this, consider that P is very close to T. Now almost every sentence is compatible with the grammars given by P, because most of the non-target grammars now have a very low probability of being selected. Then, almost every B sentences will push the batch counter b to its bound (B). Weights will be updated very frequently, driving P to T ever more rapidly. By contrast, if P is quite far from T, then it generally takes a longer time for b to reach its bound—reward and punishment are then less frequent, and thus slow down learning. This batch process can be understood precisely by considering the problem of the Gambler's Ruin. A gambler has n dollars to start the game. Every gamble he makes, there is a probability p of making a dollar, and a probability q = 1 – p of losing a dollar. The gambler wins if he ends up with 2n dollars, and is ruined if he is down to 0. Since every gamble is independent of all others, the gambler's fortune takes a random walk. It is not difficult to show—the interested reader may consult any textbook on stochastic processes—that the probability of the gambler winning (i.e. getting 2n dollars), w, is:

(34) $$w = \frac{(q/p)^n - 1}{(q/p)^{2n} - 1}$$

Our batch counter b does exactly the same thing. It gains 1 when P yields a succesful grammar, and loses 1 when P yields a failing grammar. b wins if it reaches B, and loses if it reaches –B.

Let p be the probability of P yielding a successful grammar. Then w_B, the probability of b reaching the batch bound B is

(35) $$w(B, p) = \frac{(q/p)^B - 1}{(q/p)^{2B} - 1}$$

Clearly, as p gets bigger, w_B gets larger, and as B increases, w_B gets larger still. Fig. 3 shows w(B, p) as a function of B and p. B = 1 means that there is no batch: the learning parameter would be uniform throughout learning.

The assumptions of the normal distribution of grammar fitness, the exponential decay of fitness with respect to the Hamming distance, and the use of a small batch counter together give rise to a satisfactory learner, the NPL+B model. A typical result from a simulation of learning a ten-parameter grammar is given in Fig. 2.4. The learning curve is generally smooth, with no abrupt changes. And the learner converges in a reasonable amount of time. About 600,000 sentences were needed for converging on ten interacting parameters.

It must be conceded that the formal sufficiency condition of the NPL model is only tentatively established. Future research lies in two directions. First, and obviously, much more work is needed to establish whether the assumptions of Gaussian distribution and exponential decay are accurate. Second, one may (manually) determine how many parameters are in fact independent, and thus do not lead to parameter interference.

The most important consequence of the NLP model, if vindicated, lies in the dramatic reduction of computational cost: the memory load reduced from storing 2^n grammar weights to n parameter weights. This makes the variational model psychologically plausible, and in turn gives a computational argument for the conception of UG as a parametric space.

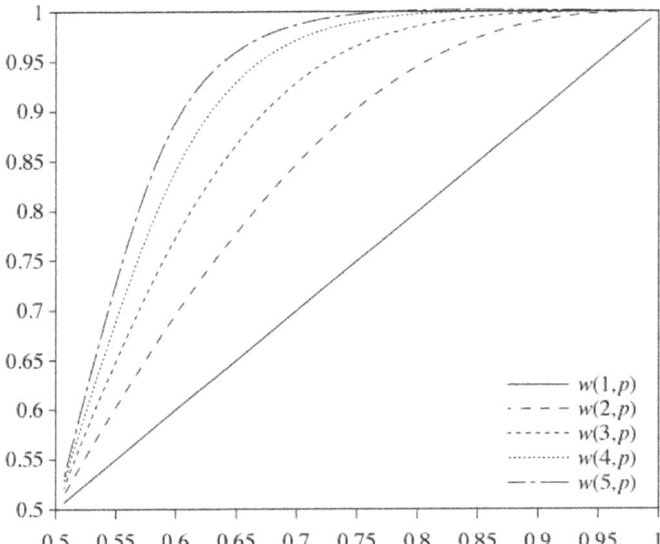

Figure 3: The probability function $w(B, p) = \frac{(q/p)^B - 1}{(q/p)^{2B} - 1}$

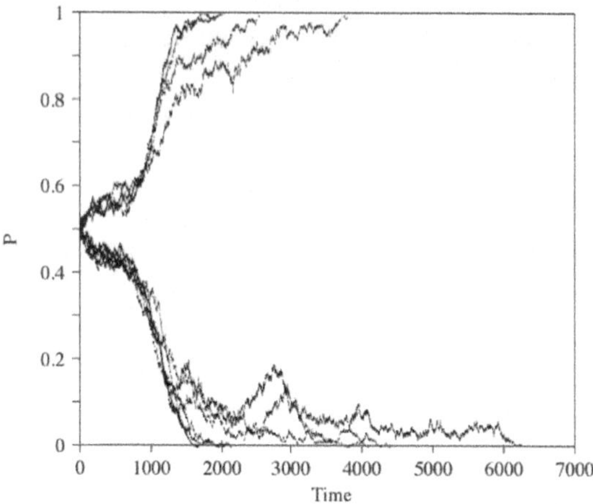

Figure4: NPL+B learning of the grammar (1 0 0 0 0 1 0 1 1 0). B = 5, γ = 0.002, s = 5/6

Learning in a parametric space gives rise to 'hybrid' grammars. Since the successful acquisition of a grammar is accomplished only when all parameters are set correctly, children may go through an extended period of time in which some parameters are already in place while others are still fluctuating. For example, an English child may have learned that his language moves Wh words overtly, but has not conclusively learned that it also obligatorily uses overt subjects. Now what the child possesses are partial fragments of grammars that may not correspond to any attested adult language—something that is, say, English-like in one respect but Chinese-like in another. And it is precisely these hybrid languages that confirms the reality of grammar coexistence and competition. A number of such cases in child languages will be documented in Chapter.

Related Approaches

The idea of language acquisition as grammar competition has occasionally surfaced in the literature, although it has never been pursued systematically or directly related to quantitative data in language development.

To the best of our knowledge, Jakobson (1941) was the first to interpret 'errors' in child phonology as possible phonological forms in non-target adult languages. This position was echoed in Stampe (1979), and seems to be accepted by at least some researchers in phonological acquisition (Macken 1995). Recent studies on infants' gradual loss of universal ability for phonetic discrimination (Kuhl et al. 1992; cf. de Boysson-Bardies 1999) seem to suggest that the variational model, in which the hypothesis space goes from 'more' to 'less' through competition, may hint at a general process that also governs the development of phonetic perception. Since the advent of the P&P framework, some linguists have claimed that syntactic acquisition selects a grammar out of all possible human grammars (Piattelli-Palmarini 1989, Lightfoot 1991), but nothing has been formalized. That children may have simultaneous access to multiple hypotheses has been suggested by Berwick & Weinberg (1984) and Pinker (1984), among others. The possibility of associating grammars with weights has been raised by Valian (1990), Weinberg (1990), and Bloom (1993), either for learnability considerations or to explain the gradual developmental patterns in child language. These authors, however, opted for different solutions to the problems under study.

Here we will put forward an alternative approach, the Rules and Competition (RC) model. The RC model treats both irregular and regular verbs within a single component of the cognitive system: generative phonology. Like the WR model, we assume the presence of a default rule, which attaches the -d suffix to the stem and in principle applies to all verbs. In contrast to the WR model, we claim that irregular past tense is also formed by phonological rules. That is, errors such as overregularization are not memory lapses, but result from failures to apply appropriate irregular phonological rules over the default rule. The RC model derives from the variational approach to language acquisition, which holds that systematic errors in child language are reflections of coexisting hypotheses in competition. These hypotheses are associated with weights, and it is the weights, or the distribution of the grammars, that change during learning from data. For the problem of past tense, the hypothesis space for each irregular verb x includes an irregular rule R, defined over a verb class S of verbs of which x is a member. For example, the rule [-t suffixation & Vowel Shortening] applies to irregular verbs such as lose, deal, and dream. The acquisition of x involves a process of competition between R and the default -d rule, the latter of which in principle could apply to all verbs, regular and irregular. The child learns from experience that for irregular verbs, irregular rules must apply, and thus the default -d rule must not. Before learning is complete, the default rule will be probabilistically accessed, leading to overregularization errors. presents the RC model in detail, including a description of the past tense formation rules in the computational system and a learning algorithm that specifies how rules compete. We will also give a learning-theoretic interpretation and revision of the Blocking Principle that underlies the WR model as well as much of generative phonology. compares the WR and RC models, based on the child acquisition data reported in Marcus et al. (1992). Specifically, we show that children's performance on an irregular verb strongly correlates with the weight of its corresponding phonological rule, which explains a number of class-based patterns in the acquisition of irregular verbs. These patterns receive no explanation under the WR model, to the extent that the WR model is explicitly formulated. Section examines, and rejects, the proposal of pairing stem and past tense with analogy or phonological similarity in the WR model, which one might consider a partial remedy for the problems revealed in section gives a critical review of ten arguments in support of the WR model (Pinker 1995). We show that each of them is either empirically flawed or can be accommodated equally well in the RC model.

REFERENCES

1. Ainsworth, Janet. "In a Different Register: The Pragmatics of Powerlessness in Police Interrogation." 103 Yale L.J. 259 (1993).
2. Ainsworth, Janet. Linguistics as a Knowledge Domain in the Law, 54 Drake L. Rev. 651 (2006).
3. Asprey, Michèle M. Plain Language for Lawyers. 2d ed. Leichhardt, N.S.W.: The Federation Press, 1996.
4. Atkinson, J. Maxwell, and Paul Drew. Order in the Court: The Organization of Verbal Behavior in Judicial Settings. Atlantic Highlands, N.J.: Humanities Press, 1979.
5. J. Baldwin & P. French. Forensic Phonetics. (London: Pinter, 1990).
6. Bennett, W.L. & M.S. Feldman, Reconstructing Reality in the Courtroom. London: Tavistock Publications (1981).
7. Benson, Robert W. "The End of Legalese: The Game Is Over." 13 N.Y.U. Rev. L. & Soc. Change 519 (1985).
8. BerkSeligson, Susan. The Bilingual Courtroom Court Interpreters in the Judicial Process (1990).
9. Bhatia, Vijay. "Cognitive Structuring in Legislative Provisions." In Language and the Law, edited by John Gibbons, 136. London and New York: Longman, 1994.
10. Bosmajian, Haig. Metaphor and Reason in Judicial Opinions. Carbondale: Southern Illinois University Press, 1992.
11. Bowers, Frederick. Linguistic Aspects of Legislative Expression. Vancouver: University of British Columbia Press, 1989.
12. Charrow, Robert P., and Veda R. Charrow. "Making Legal Language Understandable: A Psycholinguistic Study of Jury Instructions." 79 Colum. L. Rev. 1306 (1979).
13. Chaski, Carole E. Empirical evaluations of language-based author identification techniques. 8 Forensic Linguistics 1 (2001).

14. Conley, John M., et al. «The Power of Language: Presentational Style in the Courtroom.» 78 Duke L.J. 1375 (1978).
15. Conley, John M., and William M. O›Barr. Just Words: Law, Language, and Power. Chicago: University of Chicago Press, 1998.
16. Conley, John M., and William M. O›Barr. Rules versus Relationships: The Ethnography of Legal Discourse. Chicago: University of Chicago Press, 1990.
17. Cotterill, Janet. Language in the legal process. Hampshire, U.K.: Palgrave, 2002.
18. Janet Cotterill. Language and Power in Court : A Linguistic Analysis of the O.J. Simpson Trial. Plagrave.
19. Coulthard, Malcolm. On the use of corpora in the analysis of forensic texts. 1 Forensic Linguistics 27 (1994).
20. Coulthard, Malcolm. Powerful evidence for the defence: an exercise in forensic discourse analysis. In J. Gibbons (Ed.), Language and the Law, 414 (1994).
21. Crystal, David, and Derek Davy. Investigating English Style. Bloomington: Indiana University Press, 1969.
22. Cunningham, Clark D., et al. «Plain Meaning and Hard Cases.» 103 Yale L.J. 1561 (1994).
23. Danet, Brenda. «›Baby› or ‹Fetus›? Language and the Construction of Reality in a Manslaughter Trial.» 32 Semiotica 187 (1980).
24. Danet, Brenda. «Language in the Legal Process.» 14 Law & Society Rev. 445 (1980).
25. Danet, Brenda, et al. «An Ethnography of Questioning in the Courtroom.» In Language Use and Uses of Language, edited by Roger W. Shuy and Anna Shnukal, 225. Washington, D.C.: University of Georgetown Press, 1980.
26. Danet, Brenda, and Bryna Bogoch. «Orality, Literacy and Performativity in Anglo-Saxon Wills.» In Language and the Law, edited by John Gibbons, 100. London and New York: Longman, 1994.
27. Dickerson, Reed. The Interpretation and Application of Statutes. Boston: Little, Brown and Co., 1975.
28. Duarte i Montserrat, C., & A. Martinez. El Lenguaje Juridico. (Buenos Aires: AZ editora, 1995).
29. Dumas, Bethany K. «Adequacy of Cigarette Package Warnings: An Analysis of the Adequacy of Federally Mandated Cigarette Package Warnings.» 59 Tenn. L. Rev. 261 (1992).

30. Eades, Diana. «A Case of Communicative Clash: Aboriginal English and the Legal System.» In Language and the Law, edited by John Gibbons, 234. London and New York: Longman, 1994.

31. Eades, Diana. Aboriginal English and the Law: Communication with Aboriginal English speaking clients: A handbook for legal practitioners. (Brisbane, Queensland Law society, 1992).

32. Eades, Diana (ed.). Language in Evidence: Linguistic and Legal Perspectives in Multicultural Australia. (Sydney: University of New South Wales Press, 1995).

33. Eagleson, Robert D. Forensic analysis of personal written texts: A case study, in Language and the Law (J. Gibbons ed.) 363 (Harlow: Longman, 1994).

34. Eagleson, Robert D. «The Plain English Movement in Australia and the United Kingdom.» In Plain English: Principles and Practice, edited by Erwin R. Steinberg, 30. Detroit: Wayne State University Press, 1991.

35. Ehrlich, Susan. Representing Rape: Language and Sexual Consent. London: Routledge, 2001.

36. Elwork, Amiram, Bruce D. Sales, and James J. Alfini. Making Jury Instructions Understandable. Charlottesville, Va.: The Michie Co., 1982.

37. Eskridge, William N. «The New Textualism.» 37 UCLA L. Rev. 621 (1990).

38. Finegan, Edward. «Form and Function in Testament Language.» In Linguistics and the Professions, edited by Robert J. Di Pietro, 113. Norwood, N.J.: Ablex Publishing Co., 1982.

39. Flesch, Rudolf. How to Write Plain English: A Book for Lawyers and Consumers. New York: Harper and Row, 1979.

40. Foster, Don. Author unknown: on the trail of Anonymous. New York: Henry Holt, 2000.

41. Friedman, Lawrence M. «Law and Its Language.» 33 Geo. Wash. L. Rev. 563 (1964).

42. Garner, Bryan A. A Dictionary of Modern Legal Usage. 2d ed. Oxford: Oxford University Press, 1995.

43. Gibbons, John. Forensic Linguistics: An Introduction to Language in the Justice System. Oxford: Blackwell Publishing.

44. Gibbons, John. Language and the Law. London and New York: Longman, 1994.

45. Goodrich, Peter. Languages of Law: From Logics of Memory to Nomadic Masks. London: Weidenfeld, 1990.

46. Goodrich, Peter. Legal Discourse. London: Macmillan, 1987.
47. Green, Georgia M. Linguistic analysis of conversation as evidence regarding the interpretation of speech events, in J. N. Levi & A. G. Walker (eds.), Language in the judicial Process 247. New York, NY: Plenum Press, 1990.
48. Gumperz, John. Fact and inference in courtroom testimony, in John Gumperz (ed.), Language and Social Identity 163. Cambridge: Cambridge University Press, 1982.
49. Gustafsson, Marita. Some Syntactic Properties of English Law Language. University of Turku, Publications of the Department of English, 1975.
50. Hiltunen, Risto. Chapters on Legal English: Aspects Past and Present of the Language of the Law. Helsinki: Suomalainen Tiedeakatemia, 1990.
51. Hollien, Harry. The Acoustics of Crime: The New Science of Forensic Phonetics. New York, NY: Plenum, 1990.
52. Jackson, Bernard S. Making Sense in Law: Linguistic, Psychological and Semiotic Perspectives. Liverpool: Deborah Charles Publications, 1995.
53. Jacquemet, M. Credibility in Court: Communicative practices in the Camorra trials. Cambridge: Cambridge University Press, 1966.
54. Kaplan, Jeffrey P. «Syntax in the Interpretation of Legal Language: The Vested versus Contingent Distinction in Property Law.» 68 Am. Speech 58 (1993).
55. Kettridge, Richard, and John Lehrberger. Sublanguage: Studies of Language in Restricted Semantic Domains. Berlin: W. de Gruyter, 1982.
56. Klinck, Dennis R. The Word of the Law: Approaches to Legal Discourse. Ottawa: Carlton University Press, 1992.
57. Kniffka, Hannes (ed.), Recent Developments in Forensic Linguistics (Frankfurt am Main: Peter Lang, 1996).
58. Kniffka, Hannes. Der Linguist als Gutachter bei Gericht, in G. Peuser and S. Winter (eds.), Angewandte Sprachwissenschaft (Bonn: Bouvier Verlag, 1981).
59. Komter, Martha L. Dilemmas in the Courtroom: A Study of Trials of Violent Crime in the Netherlands. Mahwah, N.J.: Lawrence Erlbaum, 1998.
60. Kurzon, Dennis. «Clarity and Word Order in Legislation.» 5 Oxford J. Legal Stud. 269 (1985).
61. Kurzon, Dennis. It Is Hereby Performed: Explorations in Legal Speech Acts. Amsterdam: John Benjamins Publishing Co., 1986.

62. Labov, William, and Wendell A. Harris. Addressing social issues through linguistic evidence, in Language and the law (John Gibbons ed.) 265 (London: Longman, 1994).
63. Robin Tolmach Lakoff, Talking Power: The Politics of Language. Basic Books, 1990.
64. Levi, Judith N. Language as evidence: the linguist as expert witness in North American courts. 1 Forensic Linguistics 26 (1994).
65. Levi, Judith N., and Anne Graffam Walker. Language in the Judicial Process. New York and London: Plenum Press, 1990.
66. Loftus, Elizabeth F., and John C. Palmer. «Reconstruction of Automobile Destruction: An Example of the Interaction between Language and Memory.» 13 J. Verbal Learning & Verbal Behavior 585 (1974).
67. Maley, Yon. «The Language of the Law.» In Language and the Law, edited by John Gibbons, 11. London and New York: Longman, 1994.
68. Martineau, Robert J. Drafting Legislation and Rules in Plain English. St. Paul, Minn.: West Publishing Co., 1991.
69. Matoesian, Gregory M. Law and the Language of Identity: Discourse in the William Kennedy Smith Rape Trial. Oxford, University Press, 2001.
70. Matoesian, Gregory. Reproducing Rape: Domination through Talk in the Courtroom. Chicago: Chicago University Press, 1993.
71. Maynard, Douglas W. Inside Plea Bargaining: The Language of Negotiation. New York: Plenum Press, 1984.
72. McMenamin, Gerald. R. Forensic Stylistics. Amsterdam: Elsevier, 1993.
73. Mellinkoff, David. Language of the Law. Boston: Little, Brown and Company, 1963.
74. Mellinkoff, David. «The Language of the Uniform Commercial Code.» 77 Yale L.J. 185 (1967).
75. Mertz, Elizabeth. The Language of Law School: Learning to «Think Like a Lawyer» (Oxford: University Press, 2007).
76. Miller, Geoffrey. «Pragmatics and the Maxims of Interpretation.» 5 Wis. L. Rev. 1179 (1990).
77. Morrison, Mary Jane. «Excursions into the Nature of Legal Language.» 37 Clev. St. L. Rev. 271 (1989).
78. Nolan, Frances. The Phonetic Bases of Speaker Recognition. Cambridge: Cambridge University Press, 1983.
79. O›Barr, William M. Linguistic Evidence: Language, Power, and Strategy in the Courtroom. San Diego: Academic Press, 1982.

80. Philbrick, Frederick A. Language and the Law: The Semantics of Forensic English. New York: Macmillan, 1949.

81. Philips, Susan U. Ideology in the Language of Judges. Oxford, University Press, 1998.

82. Rieber, Robert and William Stewart (eds.). The language scientist as expert in the legal setting. New York: Annals of the New York Academy of Science, 1990.

83. Robinson, Marlyn (ed.). Language and the Law: Proceedings of a Conference. William S. Hein & Co. 2003.

84. Schane, Sanford. «The Corporation Is a Person: The Language of a Legal Fiction.» 61 Tulane L. Rev. 563 (1987).

85. Schauer, Frederick (ed). Law and Language. New York University Press, 1993.

86. Schwarzer, William W. «Communicating with Juries: Problems and Remedies.» 69 Cal. L. Rev. 731 (1981).

87. Shuy, Roger W. The language of confession, interrogation and deception. Thousand Oaks, CA: Sage, 1998.

88. Shuy, Roger W. Language Crimes: The Use and Abuse of Language Evidence in the Courtroom. Cambridge, Mass.: Blackwell Publishers, 1993.

89. Shuy, Roger W. «Warning Labels: Language, Law, and Comprehensibility.» 65 American Speech 291 (1990).

90. Singer, Norman J. Sutherland Statutory Construction. 5th ed. Deerfield, Ill.: Clark Boardman Callaghan, 1992.

91. Smith, Vicky L. When prior knowledge and law collide: Helping jurors use the law. 17 Law and Human Behavior 507(1993).

92. Solan, Lawrence M. Can the legal system use experts in meaning? 66 Tennessee Law Review 1167 (1999).

93. Solan, Lawrence M. The Language of Judges. Chicago: University of Chicago Press, 1993.

94. Lawrence M. Solan, Law, Language, and Lenity, 40 Wm. & Mary L. Rev. 57 (1998).

95. Lawrence N. Solan. Learning Our Limits: The Decline of Textualism in Statutory Cases, 1997 Wis. L. Rev. 235.

96. Solan, Lawrence M. Refocusing the Burden of Proof In Criminal Cases: Some Doubt about Reasonable Doubt, 78 Texas L. Rev. 105 (1999).

97. Solan, Lawrence. «When Judges Use the Dictionary.» 68 American

Speech 50 (1993).

98. Solan, Lawrence M, and Peter M. Tiersma. Hearing Voices: Speaker Identification in American Courts, 54 Hastings Law Journal 373 (2003)

99. Solan, Lawrence M, and Peter M. Tiersma. Speaking of Crime: The Language of Criminal Justice. Chicago: University of Chicago Press. To appear, 2005.

100. Sontag, Lorelei. Deciding Death: A Legal and Empirical Analysis of Penalty Phase Jury Instructions and Capital Decision-making. Ann Arbor: University Microfilms International, 1990.

101. Steinberg, Edwin R. Plain English: Principles and Practice. Detroit: Wayne State University Press, 1991.

102. Stygall, Gail. Trial Language: Differential Discourse Processing and Discursive Formation. Amsterdam: John Benjamins Publishing Co., 1994.

103. Tiersma, Peter M. «Dictionaries and Death: Do Capital Jurors Understand Mitigation?» 1995 Utah L. Rev. 1 (1995).

104. Tiersma, Peter M. «The Language of Perjury: ‹Literal Truth,› Ambiguity, and the False Statement Requirement.» 63 S. Cal. L. Rev. 373 (1990).

105. Tiersma, Peter M. The Language of Silence, 48 Rutgers Law Review 1 (1995).

106. Tiersma, Peter M. Legal Language. Chicago: University of Chicago Press, 1999.

107. Tiersma, Peter M. Linguistic issues in the law. 69 Language 113 (1993)

108. Tiersma, Peter M. A Message in a Bottle: Text, Autonomy, and Statutory Interpretation, 76 Tulane Law Review 431 (2001).

109. Tiersma, Peter M. Nonverbal Communication and the Freedom of «Speech». 1993 Wisconsin Law Review 1525.

110. Tiersma, Peter M. «Reforming the Language of Jury Instructions.» 22 Hofstra L. Rev. 37 (1993).

111. Tiersma, Peter M. and Lawrence M. Solan. The Linguist on the Witness Stand: Forensic Linguistics in American Courts, 78 Language 221 (2002).

112. Tiersma, Peter M. and Lawrence M. Solan. Cops and Robbers: Selective Literalism in American Criminal Law, 38 Law and Society Review 229 (2004).

113. Walker, Anne Graffam. «Language at Work in the Law: The Customs, Conventions, and Appellate Consequences of Court Reporting.» In

Language in the Judicial Process, edited by Judith N. Levi and Anne Graffam Walker, 203. New York and London: Plenum Press, 1990.

114. Wallace, William D. The admissibility of expert testimony on the discourse analysis of recorded conversations. 38 University of Florida Law Review 69 (1986).
115. Walsh, Michael. Interactional styles in the courtroom. In J. Gibbons (ed.), Language and the Law 217 (Harlow: Longman, 1994).
116. Walter, Bettyruth. The Jury Summation as Speech Genre: An Ethnographic Study of What It Means to Those Who Use It. Amsterdam: John Benjamins Publishing Co., 1988.
117. Winter, Stephen L. «Transcendental Nonsense, Metaphoric Reasoning, and the Cognitive Stakes for Law.» 137 U. Pa. L. Rev. 1105 (1989).
118. Woodbine, George E. «The Language of English Law.» 18 Speculum 395 (1943).
119. Woodbury, Hanni. «The Strategic Use of Questions in Court.» 48 Semiotica 197 (1984).
120. Wydick, Richard C. Plain English for Lawyers. 3d ed. Durham, N.C.: Carolina Academic Press, 1994.

Chapter 8

COMMUNICATION STRATEGY USE BY HEALTHCARE TRAINEES IN MONOLOGUES AND DIALOGUES DURING STRATEGY TRAINING

Megawati Soekarno, Su-Hie Ting

Universiti Malaysia Sarawak

ABSTRACT

The study examined the use of communication strategies in monologues and dialogues by Malaysian healthcare trainees with limited English proficiency during communication strategy training. The training focused on the use of circumlocution in individual presentation, appeal for assistance in role-play, offering assistance and lexical repetition in group discussion, stress (tonicity) in responding to questions after a presentation, and filled pauses in interviews. The speech of eight participants in the five speaking tasks were recorded and transcribed. The analysis of the 6,137-word transcript showed that monologues called into use more communication strategies than dialogues which are jointly negotiated. The participants used pauses and lexical repetition as communication strategies most often, which, in fact, is predictable considering their language proficiency. Most of the pauses were pauses filled with sounds like umm and uhh rather than fillers taught during the strategy training. The analysis revealed that the participants could use lexical repetition to appeal for assistance, request clarification and confirm comprehension but the frequencies for these strategies were low compared to discourse maintenance and topic salience marking. The strategy training helped the participants to use the strategy that was taught immediately after the training but automatisation in strategy use had not taken place.

INTRODUCTION

The study aims to examine the use of communication strategies in monologues and dialogues by healthcare trainees during English communication strategy training in Malaysia. The specific objectives of the study were to: (1) compare the frequency in which different communication strategies are used in monologues and dialogues; and (2) determine the impact of communication strategy training on the use of the strategies. The paper begins by presenting the related literature that leads to the focus of this study, followed by the method of the study. Finally, the results are discussed with reference to findings of previous studies.

The use of communication strategies is a manifestation of strategic competence, which is the ability to use verbal and nonverbal communication strategies "to compensate for breakdowns in communication due to limiting conditions in actual communication or to insufficient competence in one or more areas of communicative competence" (Canale, 1983, p.12).

In research on the use of communication strategies, the attention has been on the problem solving role. Faerch and Kasper (1983a, p. 36) viewed communication strategies as "potentially conscious plans for solving what to an individual presents itself as a problem in reaching a particular communicative goal". Examples of linguistic strategies are code-switching, foreignising, literal translation, word coinage, substitution, description, exemplification, and restructuring. Other researchers who share Faerch and Kasper's (1980) psycholinguistic problem-solving perspective of communication strategies are Bialystok and Frohlich (1980), Haastrup and Phillipson (1983), Paribakht (1985), Poulisse, Bongaerts, and Kellerman (1987), Poulisse and Schils (1989), Kellerman, Ammerlaan, Bongaerts, and Poulisse (1990), and Lafford (2004).

Another view of communication strategies is Tarone's (1981, p.292) social interactional view which is premised on the need to "bridge the gap between the linguistic knowledge of the second-language learner and the linguistic knowledge of the target language interlocutor in real communication situations." The main difference between her typology and Faerch and Kasper's (1980, 1984) typology is the addition of appeal for assistance which highlights the joint effort to reach shared meaning (see also Yule & Tarone, 1991). Tarone's (1980, 1981) work has been cited in the language learning literature but her framework has not been employed as the theoretical underpinning of communication strategy research.

To our knowledge, the only framework that is strongly anchored to the message enhancing role of communication strategies is that of Clennell (1995). Clennell (1995, p.6) described strategies in previous frameworks

(Faerch & Kasper, 1980, 1984; Tarone, 1980, 1981) as "local lexically based strategies" which are used to "overcome specific obstacles in the process of communication". According to Clennell (1994a, 1994b), the more useful strategies for negotiating meaning are global discourse strategies, namely, lexical repetition, tonicity and topic fronting. The discourse-based strategies can perform short-term functions like appealing for assistance as well as discourse functions such as topic salience marker and conversational maintenance. Since proficient speakers are better at using discourse strategies for meaning enhancement (Ting & Phan, 2008), it is beneficial to train less proficient speakers to develop "collaborative discourse skills" (Clennell, 1995, p.16).

Thus far, Dörnyei (1995) and co-researchers have demonstrated the benefits of communication strategy training. Dörnyei's (1995) pioneering study on 109 Hungarian learners of English showed that they improved in the quality and quantity of circumlocution and fillers after the 6-week training. Dörnyei (1995) was instrumental in getting stalling strategies (i.e., pause-fillers and hesitation gambits) to be accepted as a communication strategy because prior to this, Tarone (1980) had considered filler as a speech production strategy and Faerch and Kasper (1983b) had considered filler as a temporal variable (Dörnyei & Scott, 1997). The six principles of communication strategy training used by Dörnyei and Thurrell (1991) were raising awareness, instilling risk taking, modelling use of communication strategies, highlighting cross-cultural differences, directly teaching communication strategies, and giving opportunities for practice. Using these principles, Lam and Wong (2000) conducted strategy training on Hong Kong sixth formers and found that they demonstrated better use of meaning negotiation strategies (seeking clarification, clarifying themselves) after the training but their limited linguistic resources prevented them from using them effectively. The strategy training carried out by Naughton (2006) also helped the Spanish EFL learners to use more interaction strategies in discussions, namely, asking follow-up questions, requesting and giving clarification, and requesting and giving help. After Nakatani's (2010) 12-week communication strategy training, the Japanese EFL learners with greater communicative ability in English used more achievement communication strategies (active response, shadowing, confirmation check, comprehension check, clarification request) and became more fluent.

Findings from communication strategy training concur on the teachability of meaning negotiation strategies (Lam & Wong, 2000; Nakatani, 2010; Naughton, 2006). Since these jointly directed strategies help speakers to navigate potential communication breakdowns (Clennell, 1995), it is useful to focus on these during communication strategy training. It may not be worthwhile to teach lexically based strategies (e.g., paraphrase, restructuring, approximation) because speakers with limited English proficiency in Nakatani's (2010) study were unable to learn to use them due to lack of lexical resources. Naughton's (2006) strategy training also did not bring about much increase in the use of repair strategies. Naughton (2006) explains the results in terms of the considerable cognitive load required to use repair strategies and the Spanish EFL learners' reluctance to use strategies which hinder fluency and conversational flow.

Task type may affect strategy use. For example, Rossiter (2003) found that object description tasks brought out more paraphrase strategies than narrative tasks. However, some previous studies have used one task type such as group discussion (Lam & Wong, 2000; Naughton, 2006) and picture or object description (Rossiter, 2003). There were other researchers used several task types, namely, cartoon description, topic description, definition formulation (Dörnyei, 1995), role play (Dörnyei & Scott, 1997) or interview (Kongsom, 2009). However, these researchers reported the results for the strategy use as a whole rather than segregated by task. In this paper, we show that segregating the results by task type provides a better understanding of task demands on strategy use and can lead to a better matching of strategy with task type for communication strategy training.

METHODOLOGY

A case study was conducted to understand how communication strategies are used differently in monologues and dialogues, and why certain strategies are more useful to less proficient English speakers. In addition to the "how" and "why" questions which need to be answered, this research requires an extensive and in-depth description of strategy use, thereby making case study a suitable research design (Yin, 2014). The in-depth description of strategy use in the present study is made possible because of the data triangulation.

Participants

The eight participants in this study were healthcare trainees in a private university in Sabah, Malaysia (referred to as Participants 1 to 8 in this paper). They were undergoing vocational studies and training that prepared them for employment as pharmacy assistants, laboratory technicians, physiotherapists and assistant health officers. Most of them were in their twenties and from various language backgrounds. Their proficiency in English is considered average to weak based on their English grades in the Sijil Pelajaran Malaysia (SPM, translated as Malaysian Certification of Education) examination, a public examination at the end of the five years of secondary education in the Malaysian education system. To these participants, English is a foreign language because it does not have much recognised function in their daily lives although they have learnt it as a subject in school (Richards, Platt, & Weber, 1985). They do not hold English to be part of their linguistic and cultural identity (Nayar, 1997). This is because most of their daily interactions take place in Malay (the national language and its dialects) or their respective ethnic languages. If they work in government departments like hospitals, they would be using mostly Malay but if they work in the private sector, they may use English for official communication and rely on Malay for informal communication even in the workplace (Ting, 2002, 2012).

Communication Strategy Training and Data Collection

In this case study, eight healthcare trainee with weak to fairly low knowledge of English were recorded during communication strategy training when delivering monologue and dialogue sequences in English. The monologues consisted of a short presentation and a response to a question posed after the presentation. The dialogue comprised of a role play on medical issues, an interview and a group discussion.

This study used speech data from five different types of speaking tasks (Table 1). No co-triangulation with other forms of data was carried out because the different types of speech data allow the patterns of communication strategy use to be discerned based on the task type.

The communication strategy training, conducted by the first researcher, consisted of six sessions spread over six weeks as shown in Table 1. The second column shows the six communication strategies taught in the present study. Two of the strategies are among the three strategies considered crucial by Dörnyei and Thurrell (1991), that is, circumlocution and appealing for help. Dörnyei and Thurrell (1991) also considered going off the point smoothly and evading answers as crucial in real communication situations but we decided not to include this because such evasive responses would cause the participants to lose marks if they were assessed in language classroom contexts. Instead, fillers were included based on Dörnyei (1995), and lexical repetition and stress were adapted from Clennell (1995) because of their potential to facilitate information transfer.

TABLE 1: Communication strategies taught in six weekly sessions in communication strategy training

Week/ Session	Communication strategy taught	Speaking task for data collection
1	Circumlocution for conversational repair	Individual presentation
2	Appeal for assistance for joint negotiation of meaning	Role play
3	Offer help for joint negotiation of meaning	Group discussion
4	Lexical repetition for facilitating information transfer	
5	Stress for conversational maintenance	Question and answer
6	Fillers for time gaining	Interview

The communication strategies were chosen to fit the topics of the English course they were enrolled in (English for Occupational Purposes) and the skills they were expected to demonstrate (e.g., giving directions). For each weekly session, the teaching procedures followed Nakatani's (2006) five-step sequence: review of previous performance; presentation of new task and strategy; rehearsal of roles; performance; and evaluation of strategy use. The last column in Table 1 shows the five sets of data collected (two monologues and three dialogues).

The first session was on the use of the circumlocution strategy where the participants were taught to describe characteristics or elements of the object or action when they could not retrieve the appropriate target language structure to use. This session involved descriptions of an accident and the participants were taught phrases such as it is a kind of and for example to initiate the description. They were given a visual stimulus of the accident and asked to discuss possible terms to use with a partner before making an individual report of the accident. Although the participants had some time to prepare for their individual presentations, compensation strategies are relevant because they did not read out a script and they made impromptu changes.

The second session was a dyadic presentation session where participants were trained to utilise help seeking statements in a role play on giving directions in the hospital. For instance, I don't understand or I don't follow you or what does ... mean? Other than these expressions, participants were not given other target vocabulary items for their role play. The participants were told to complete the task within two minutes as giving directions is not supposed to be a lengthy activity.

The third and fourth sessions focused on negotiation of meaning in the context of group discussions on possible issues related to Corporate Social Response (CSR) activities and internship training. The communication strategies taught were offering help for joint negotiation of meaning and lexical repetition for facilitating information transfer respectively. Lexical repetitions are techniques where speakers repeat words or phrases with a system of tones (e.g., rise, fall, rise–fall) for discourse and topic maintenance, topic salience marker, appeal for assistance, request for clarification and to indicate comprehension (Clennell, 1995). In pairs, the participants discussed topics such as prevention of epidemic and hospital malpractice.

In the fifth session, participants were taught how to use stress and pitch to mark key information or to differentiate given from new information when they respond to questions after a presentation. Abstract topics such as Pharmacovigilance and the Importance of Risk Management made it necessary for the participants to use strategies to facilitate information transfer.

In the final session, the participants were taught how to use fillers during pauses in the context of interviews. Interjections for conversational maintenance include well, let me see. However, they were told to avoid the excessive use of unfilled pauses in interviews as these indicate lack of fluency.

Data Analysis Procedures

The audio-recordings of the five speaking tasks were transcribed. Unfinished utterances were marked with ellipsis (...). Pauses were indicated on the transcripts; an example of a filled pause is Well, I guess and [umm]. Unfilled pauses are indicated by {pauses} on the transcript. Stress is shown by the use of capital letters and rising or falling intonation with a / and \ respectively.

The 6,137 word-transcript was analysed using a framework of analysis as shown in Appendix 1. The frameworks from which the communication strategies were taken (Clennell, 1995; Faerch & Kasper, 1980; Nakatani, 2006; Tarone, 1981) are indicated in superscripts in the first column.

The two researchers analysed the transcript to ensure consistency in the identification of communication strategies. Initially, it was difficult to differentiate between message abandonment and pauses. With rereading of the transcript, it became clear that if the participant continues with the message after a break in vocalisation, the break is a pause but if the participant leaves the message as incomplete, then it is message abandonment.

The number of communication strategies used was counted (raw frequencies). As the five sets of data were of variable word lengths, it is necessary to give equal weight to each set of frequencies. For a meaningful comparison, the raw frequencies need to be converted to a form of standard score, and that is frequencies per thousand words (ptw) which is calculated as follows:

$$\frac{\text{Raw frequency}}{\text{Number of words in transcript}} \times 1000 = \text{Frequency per thousand words}$$

For the analysis of the functions of lexical repetition, the parts of the transcript coded for lexical repetition were read many times to determine the purpose of the repetition from the context. Clennell's (1995) descriptions of possible functions of lexical repetition was used as a guide but we were open to other functions that might emerge. Shadowing to acknowledge points made by the interlocutor was the only function of lexical repetition that was not described by Clennell (1995). In the process of identifying the functions of lexical repetition, descriptors of the functions were formulated and refined until the typology is clear, as shown in Table 3. Using this typology, the transcripts were analysed to find out the participants' purposes in using lexical repetition and the results are shown in Table 4.

RESULTS AND DISCUSSION

3.1 Comparison of frequency of communication strategies used in monologues and dialogues

The participants used 845 communication strategies in five speaking tasks comprising two monologues and three dialogues (transcript word-length: 6,137). More strategies were used in monologues (160.1 ptw) than in dialogues (124.6 ptw). The most frequently used communication strategy in both monologues and dialogues was pausing followed by lexical repetition.

Table 2: Frequency per thousand words for use of communication strategies in monologues and dialogues

Communication strategies		Monologue		Dialogue			Total
		Individual report	Response to question	Role play	Interview	Group discussion	
Pauses		73.6	74.3	37.8	49.6	54.5	58.5
Lexical repetition		17.3	36.2	35.1	36.6	54.5	38.8
Stress		1.4	40.0	0	0	0.6	10.6
Paraphrase		31.7	5.1	0	5.2	4.4	7.3
Examples		1.4	7.0	0	7.2	1.9	4.2
Appeal for assistance		1.4	0.6	32.4	0	1.3	7.6
Restructuring		1.4	4.4	2.7	1.3	5.6	6.9
Abandonment of message		5.8	1.3	6.8	1.3	0.6	2.3
Reduction of message		0	0.6	0	3.9	2.5	3.0
Confirmation checks		0	0	2.7	0	1.9	0.8
Offer of help		0	0	4.1	0	3.1	1.3
Clarification requests		0	0	0	0	4.4	1.1
Gestures and facial expressions		1.4	0	4.1	0	3.8	1.5
Comprehension checks		0	0	5.4	0	0.6	1.0
Rhythm and intonation		0	0.6	0	0	0	0.2
Make pronunciation clear		3	0	0	0.7	0	0.2
Information for calculation of frequency per thousand words (ptw)	Raw frequency of communication strategies	93	254	94	155	208	804
	Transcript word-length	693	1575	740	1532	1597	6137

Pauses

The results show that pausing is the communication strategy that was used the most frequently by the eight healthcare trainees. The frequency in Table 2 is given for filled and unfilled pauses. As the participants in this study had limited proficiency in English, they paused frequently to think about other options to compensate for missing vocabulary or grammar when talking. Table 2 shows that the participants paused more frequently in monologues (73.6 ptw in individual presentations and 74.3 ptw in their response to their instructor's question) than in dialogues (37.8 ptw in role-play, 49.6 ptw in interview and 54.5 ptw in role-play). The following excerpts and explanation show that the shared responsibility of taking the floor minimises the pressure to speak continuously, reducing the need to pause.

Excerpt 1 Individual Presentation, Participant 1: L1-5 When I see, I see {lexical repetition} the boot of the red car is crushed and [umm] I

think, have many [umm] things in the boot [umm] bags or [umm] everything, things I think {pause} so the cause of the incident of the [high tone] boot is crushed because the red, the black is hit the boot of the red car.

Excerpt 1 shows that Participant 1 paused to grope for words to describe the car crash in the picture (Figure 1), and repeated boot because she did not have the words to describe the situation of a black car crushed underneath the red car. Participant 1's presentation has the appearance of hesitant speech because of the frequent pausing.

Figure 1: Picture description task for individual presentation.

The frequency of pauses is even higher in the same participant's response to a question on pharmacovigilance, the practice of monitoring effects of medical drugs (Excerpt 2).

Excerpt 2 Response to Question, Participant 1: L1-8 What I'm [umm] understand about pharmacovigilance is WHAT the action of the pharmacovigilance in the body and what the, what the, what the certain people, what the certain people CONTROL the drug. So I have THREE people [umm] I have three people {lexical repetition} that control the drug, the drug {lexical repetition} it is the authorizer, regulatory authorizer, pharmaceutical industry and [pause] healthcare profession, professional. [But] they all are most, more KEY player to control the drug {lexical repetition} ehh the medicine. [Ok]. [So] [umm] for example, I can [umm] I know for example {lexical repetition} is [uhh] analgesic [uhh] analgesic {lexical repetition}, antibiotic to, to prevent the growth of the fungal or bacteria and [umm] antiseptic, and another.

When Participant 1 responded to the instructor's question on what pharmacovigilance was, she could define pharmacovigilance without much pausing but when she gave an example of an antiseptic, the frequency of pauses increased. She was probably more familiar with the definition of pharmacovigilance than with the example. Hence, she also repeated words until she came to the appropriate medical term to use (analgesic, antibiotic, antiseptic).

The nature of pausing is different in dialogues. In Excerpt 3 showing a group discussion of hospital malpractice, Participant 4 led the discussion.

Excerpt 3

Group Discussion, Participants 3, 4 and 5: L18-31

Participant 4 First we will, we will discuss about?
Participant 5 How to improve, we reduce the hospital malpractice//
Participant 4 Among our, among our//
Participant 5 Among our government hospital.
Participant 4 Among our organization in this hospital. We need to interview the patients or the victim of this hospital malpractice. Firstly, we should ask them what are we working, what are we going to, what our staff or nurse mis [uhh] misdiagnose or miss [uhh] miss action. [And] then we will covered the and we'll come, we will cover//
Participant 3 Cover, cover what?
Participant 4 Cover [*uhh*] cover the improve the quality so the malpractice doesn't occur//
Participant 3 Occur again.
Participant 4 We will minimize the, the error.

She went on coherently on the need to interview patients or victims of hospital malpractice until she reached the part on the misdiagnosis by the nurse (line 25) and what to cover. That was when she paused. However, the frequency of pauses in group discussion is lower than in monologues because other group members could step in to continue the utterance, like Participant 3 (lines 27 and 30). Participant 3's repetition of the Participant 4's last word also gave the latter time to think and continue speaking. The turn-taking and shared responsibility in speaking brought about less pausing in dialogues (49.4

ptw) than in monologues (74.1 ptw). So far, the description has been on pauses marked by sounds like uhh and umm. Sometimes the participants used fillers when they could not think of what to say. For example, in the group discussion (Session 4), Participant 3 said We also need to take account, I mean, we also need to consider the hospital staff also. After Participant 3 said I mean, she restructured her utterance and decided not to proceed with the use of the verb take account but changed to consider. This was an easier sentence structure to manage and she could continue with her point that the hospital staff could also be the victims of hospital malpractice. In the transcript of the five speaking tasks, the use of fillers such as I mean and I guess are infrequent compared to okay. Excerpt 4 shows how Participant 5 used okay (transcribed as Ok, line 8) when she needed to get her thoughts together on the causes of headache. Participant 5's explanation is marked by many pauses (umm) as she moved from one cause to another.

Excerpt 4 Interview, Participant 5: L5-12

Instructor	Can you please give me an example of a risky situation?
Participant 5	I want to explain about risk of headache.
Instructor	Headache? {correct pronunciation}
Participant 5	Headache. [Ok] [umm] the factor of the what happen that human get headache when they have less of sleep [umm] turn on lamp when they go to sleep and have many thinking at get [umm] at get more thinking about that problem that can makes the, the, the, that can make the human have a headache.

Besides filled pauses comprising either fillers (e.g., okay) or sounds (e.g., umm), the participants sometimes paused by remaining silent (referred to as unfilled pauses). The frequency of unfilled pauses is low. Out of 359 pauses identified in the 6,137-word transcript, 313 (or 87.2%) were filled pauses and 46 (or 12.8%) were unfilled pauses (figures are not in Table 2). In the context of communication, pauses filled with phrases are better because their use gives the impression of continuous speech. Fillers enable learners to gain time to think and to keep the communication channel open (Dörnyei, 1995). Dörnyei and Thurrell (1991, p.19) stated that "the knowledge and confident use of fillers are a crucial part of learners' strategic competence since these invaluable delaying or hesitation devices can be used to carry on the conversation at times of difficulty." However, in the present study, 61.3% of filled pauses consisted of sounds (umm, uhh, ahh) which gives an impression of hesitancy rather than fluency in communication. However, as the results of the communication strategy training show, it is not easy for participants to incorporate the use of lexical fillers (e.g., well, let me think) into their speech.

Lexical Repetition

Lexical repetition was overall the second most frequently used communication strategy. Table 2 shows that the average frequency for the use of lexical repetition is 38.8 ptw; the highest in group discussion (54.5 ptw) and the lowest in individual presentation (17.3 ptw). As the participants had some time to prepare for the individual presentation, they were more certain of what they wanted to say and there was less repetition of lexical items. The frequencies are similar for the other three speaking tasks: response to question (36.2 ptw), role-play (37.8 ptw) and interview (36.6 ptw).

Excerpt 5 Role play, Participants 2 and 6: L1-15

Participant 6	I'm sorry. Can I ask you something? You know the direction to the medical lab?
Participant 2	Oh! Ya, sure I can help you. You go straight and then you will turn left, after that you will see a building Block A and you will found the medical lab.
Participant 6	What? I don't understand. Can you repeat it again?
Participant 2	Never mind. Ok, I can repeat. You go straight, ok? Straight {lexical repetition} and then you, you {lexical repetition} turn left. You know where left? {lexical repetition} You will found the building of Block A and when you found the building A {lexical repetition}, can see the signboard to the medical lab.
Participant 6	Block A, right?
Participant 2	Yes.
Participant 6	Thank you.
Participant 2	No problem.

Excerpt 5 shows the complete role-play on asking for and giving directions. The direction to the medical lab was straightforward but when Participant 6 asked for a repetition, Participant 2 realised that she ought to slow down. Lines 7 to 11 show that Participant 2 repeated key phrases (straight, left, building A). One of the lexical repetitions (you know where left?) functioned as a comprehension check, where Participant 2 directly asked Participant 6 whether she understood what was said. At the end of the direction, Participant 6 repeated Block A, right? to check whether she had understood the directions correctly. This lexical repetition functioned as a confirmation check. In a dialogue, it is also common to repeat words to get back into conversation. Because of the varied functions of lexical repetition, the functions of the 238 lexical repetitions in the transcript were further analysed and the results are shown in Table 3.

Table 3: Framework for functions of lexical repetition

Functions of lexical repetition	Description	Examples from data set
Discourse maintenance	The speaker repeats a phrase before continuing with the message. The repetition is usually consecutive.	Yes, sure. From here you just look there and then you turn left and then you can see the, **you can see the** {discourse maintenance} pharmacy. And then the end of the building you can see the ICU room.
Topic salience marker	The speaker repeats an earlier point to emphasise its importance. The repetitions are interspersed by other utterances and may not be using exactly the same words.	Firstly **we need to double triple check** our every own preparation, especially for us pharmacists, pharmacy assistant. **We need to double check** {topic salience marker} prescription from the doctors and maybe, you know doctor's handwriting can be very hard to read so we need to {pause} call up, call up the doctor to ask for confirmation.
Clarification request	The speaker repeats the interlocutor's utterance to show that he/she does not understand something, usually using a questioning intonation. This is an indirect appeal for assistance.	Speaker 4: Then you explain **surgical risk** to the patient. Speaker 1: **Surgical what?** Speaker 4: **Surgical risk** to the patient. Speaker 1: Oh! Amputating?
Confirm comprehension	The speaker repeats the interlocutor's utterance to show that he/she understands, usually using a falling intonation.	Speaker 2: Wear mask, seek doctor Speaker 3: **Hand wash?** Speaker 2: **Hand wash**, this one *apa tu* [what's that] ahh? Hand washing, yeah, practice hand *apa* [what], hand *apa* [what]? Practice hand hygiene that's what I want to *tau* [know]. Hygienes, practice hand hygienes.
Shadowing	The speaker repeats the last part of what the interlocutor has said to acknowledge the point made. The repetitions may be exact, partial or expanded versions of the interlocutor's utterances. However, it is not shadowing if the speaker repeats his/her own utterances, sometimes across turns intercepted by other speakers.	Speaker 3: **Reduce the activity** outdoor Speaker 1: Yeah, **reduce the activity** {shadowing} for a while Speaker 2: Ok, **reduce activity** {shadowing}. What else?

The framework for the functions of lexical repetition (Table 3) was used to analyse the transcript of the five speaking tasks performed by the eight healthcare trainees. The results in Table 4 show that lexical repetitions are mainly used for discourse maintenance (32.9 ptw) and marking topic salience (27.2 ptw) in both monologues and dialogues. Because of the turn-taking, there is a greater need to use lexical repetition for discourse maintenance in dialogues (21.5 ptw) than in monologues (11.5 ptw). However, the need to capture the audience's attention makes lexical repetition more useful in monologues (19.0 ptw) than in dialogues (8.3 ptw). Discourse maintenance and marking topic salience are the two most important functions of lexical repetition.

Table 4: Frequency per thousand words for functions of lexical repetition in monologues and dialogues

Functions of lexical repetition		Monologues	Dialogues	Total
Discourse maintenance		11.5	21.5	32.9
Topic salience marker		19.0	8.3	27.2
Shadowing		0	11.4	11.4
Clarification request		0.0	1.3	1.3
Confirm comprehension		0.0	0.8	0.8
Appeal for assistance		0.0	0.5	0.5
Information needed for the calculation of frequency per thousand words (ptw)	Raw frequency	69	125	194
	Transcript word-length	2268	3869	6137

* Monologues include the individual presentation and response to question after the presentation whereas dialogues include role play, interview and group discussion.

Shadowing is categorised as lexical repetition because of its form, that is, the speaker repeats words or phrases with a system of tones (Appendix 1). However, in its function, shadowing or back-channelling serves to acknowledge points made by the interlocutor. An example of shadowing can be seen in Table 3 (last row). Shadowing is only relevant in dialogues (11.4 ptw). Shadowing serves the purpose of showing that the speaker is paying attention to the interlocutor, and is not used with the intention of showing either comprehension (which would be a comprehension confirmation) or incomprehension (which would be a clarification request). Lexical repetition used with the purpose of shadowing aids in conversational maintenance. It is a simple strategy for contributing to the conversation if speakers have limited English proficiency and cannot formulate extended utterances to keep the conversation going.

Lexical repetition is a useful communication strategy because its use does not require additional linguistic resources. Although speakers can request clarification (e.g., sorry, I didn't catch you) and confirm comprehension (e.g., I get what you mean) using some stock phrases, this requires ability to incorporate these expressions into their speech. Similarly, lexical repetition takes the place of stock phrases to maintain discourse (e.g., as I was saying) and to highlight salience of topics (e.g., listen to this, this is really important). It is easier for speakers with limited language proficiency to achieve these same functions by repeating words with the appropriate intonation at strategic points of the interaction. On this basis, speakers with low language proficiency can use lexical repetition to facilitate information transfer and prevent communicative gaps from occurring. Because of the characteristic of lexical repetition which does not require additional lexical resources, Clennell (1995) referred to lexical repetition as a discourse-based communication strategy, as opposed to lexically-based strategies like paraphrase and restructuring. The results of the present study showed that the participants with limited English proficiency were capable of using lexical repetition for various functions.

The further analysis that was conducted on the functions of lexical repetition brought to light a methodological issue in research on communication strategies. If the focus of the analysis is strictly on the form of utterances and not on the functions, then the results would be like those presented in Table 2. A review of the main frameworks of communication strategies revealed that the focus has been on form1 (e.g., Clennell, 1995; Dörnyei, 1995; Faerch & Kasper, 1984; Tarone, 1981). The focus on form suffice for the identification of communication strategies in research but it is not sufficient in the context of communication strategy training because learners need to be taught the different forms that can be used to fulfil a particular function, such as asking for clarification which can be achieved through lexical repetition or phrases. If the identification of communication strategies takes note of both form and functions, then there would be ambiguity in whether to classify a repetition of words as lexical repetition (focus on form) or comprehension check (focus on function). The ambiguity surfaces in the identification of negotiation/ interaction strategies (Clennell, 1995) which include clarification request, confirmation check, comprehension check and appeal for assistance. As lexical repetition can perform many of these functions, to resolve this ambiguity in the present study, the first stage of the analysis focused on form (Table 2) and the second stage of the analysis focused on functions (Table 4).

Other Communication Strategies

Table 2 shows that other than pauses and lexical repetition, the other communication strategies are less frequently used. Stress is third highest in frequency (average of 10.6 ptw) and mostly used when participants responded to a question posed after their individual presentation (40.0 ptw). Saying certain words loudly and clearly (for example, there and identify in Excerpt 6) draws the interlocutor's attention to the information that follow the stressed words.

Excerpt 6 Response to Question, Participant 4: L12-15 [umm] THERE are a few step that can be taken while [uhh] to investigate whether the drug is [uhh] comprehensive or effective such as [umm] identify, IDENTIFY what the problem is happen at the market or the public. Participant 4 paused and repeated the word identify while trying to think of how to explain identification of adverse drug reactions among users. When she was ready, she signaled to the interlocutor to pay attention to what she was going to say next by stressing identify. The tendency to stress a repeated word immediately prior to explanation, after some hesitancy, is also found in Ting and Sim's (2013) transcripts of English teacher trainees' interaction in a group discussion. While the manner in which the healthcare trainees use stress may be similar, their frequency of using stress is much lower compared to the English teacher trainees in Ting and Sim's (2013) study who used stress more than any other communication strategy in group discussions, that is, 41.09% of 2,913 communication strategies. Stress is also the most frequently used strategy in oral presentations for this group of English teacher trainees (Ting, Musa, & Sim, 2013), and accounts for 51.52% of 1,935 communication strategies identified. The healthcare trainees in the present study, who had lower English proficiency than the English teacher trainees in Ting and Sim's (2013) study, had not learnt to make the most of stress to convey different kinds of meaning, for example, stress with a falling tone for emphasis and stress with a rising tone for surprise.

As the frequencies of the other communication strategies are below 10 ptw (Table 2), the general patterns will be described. The participants used lexical strategies to some extent to explain when communicative problems were encountered, and these included paraphrase (7.3 ptw), restructuring (6.9 ptw) and giving examples (4.2 ptw). The participants paraphrased their utterances the most in the individual presentation task. This could be because circumlocution, a paraphrasing strategy, was taught during the first session of the communication strategy training and the individual presentation was conducted immediately after that. In contrast, the participants restructured their utterances more frequently in group discussions and in their response to a question posed after their individual presentation. These frequencies are not due to the communication strategy training because restructuring was not taught. Reformulating the syntax of utterances is a natural tendency when speakers cannot express intended meanings, regardless of whether they are proficient or less proficient speakers (Ting & Kho, 2009; Ting et al., 2013; Ting & Phan, 2008). While this may be the case for non-native speakers of English, Tarone and Yule (1989) found that native English speakers do not use much circumlocution and approximation compared to non-native English speakers. These are short-term lexical strategies to overcome specific lexical difficulties when they have occurred but they do not help to prevent communication breakdown before they occur (Clennell, 1995). The strategies that can alleviate communication difficulties are negotiation/interaction strategies which include comprehension checks, clarification requests, confirmation checks, and asking for and giving assistance but these were hardly used by the participants. Taken together, the results show that the healthcare trainees' speech was peppered with pauses and attempts to express intended meanings but they were able to use lexical repetitions to move on with their speech, particularly in dialogic interactions.

An examination of the pattern of communication strategy use for the five speaking tasks revealed that the use of a particular strategy increased right after the training session (Table 2). In the first training session in Week 1, circumlocution was taught and the results showed that the frequency of paraphrase was the highest for individual presentation (31.7 ptw), compared to the other four speaking tasks which had frequencies below 6 ptw.

In the second training session, participants were taught to appeal for assistance when they faced communication difficulties. It turned out that the frequency for appeal for assistance was the highest for role-play (32.4 ptw) conducted in Week 2 of the training. The frequencies for appeal for assistance in the other four speaking tasks were between 0 and 1.

In the third session (Week 3), participants were taught to offer help to their interlocutor if the latter could not continue the message. In the fourth session, lexical repetition was taught. After these two sessions, they participated in a group discussion in Week 4 of the training. The group discussion had the highest frequency for lexical repetition (54.5 ptw) but the frequencies of lexical repetitions in the response to question, role-play and interview (between 35 and 36 ptw) are not far behind. The results suggest that speakers might naturally use lexical repetition, whether or not they were taught to use it because lexical repetition was frequently used by the proficient and less proficient speakers in Ting and Phan's (2008) study although they did not participate in any communication strategy training. The group discussion had the second highest frequency for offering help (3.1 ptw). Incidentally, the participants offered help the most frequently during their role-plays (4.1 ptw) conducted after the second session of training in Week 2 but the frequency is too low for implications to be drawn.

In the fifth session, the participants learnt to use stress to respond to questions after the individual presentation. Indeed the frequency for stress was the highest for this speaking task (40.0 ptw). We do not know how long the effect of the training would last because Ting and Phan (2008) reported that less proficient speakers were less likely to use stress to convey intended meanings compared to proficient speakers in paired interactions. In the sixth and final session, the training focused on using fillers during pauses to gain time during interviews but the frequency of pausing was not particularly high in the group discussion task which was conducted right after the session on fillers. It may not be a matter of whether or not fillers can be learnt from training because participants may feel that they do not want to appear hesitant in their speech, and they may choose to slow down their speech to gain time to think during the speaking tasks.

In short, the results indicate that communication strategy training can increase speakers' use of paraphrase (circumlocution) in individual presentation, appeal for assistance in role-play, offer of assistance in group discussion, and stress in their response to a question but only on a short-term basis. The frequencies of these communication strategies in the subsequent speaking tasks were low, indicating that the participants did not remember to use these strategies in the next session. The present study did not assess their use of communication strategies some time after the training, and therefore cannot offer conclusive evidence on the retention of strategies.

CONCLUSION

The study on the use of communication strategies by healthcare trainees with limited English proficiency yielded three noteworthy findings. First, the two mostly frequently used strategies were pauses and lexical repetition. The participants had to pause frequently to gain time to think because of their inadequate linguistic knowledge. This study revealed that lexical repetition was also used as a stalling device, indicated by the large proportion of their lexical repetitions which were coded as having a discourse maintenance function. In other words, the participants repeated words while thinking of how to express their intended meanings. Lexical repetition is a relatively easy discourse strategy for speakers with limited English proficiency to use because additional lexical resources are not required. It only involves repetition of words with the appropriate tone to convey different kinds of meanings (Clennell, 1995) such as marking topic salience and acknowledging interlocutor's responses. To make the conversational flow better, the participants need to be taught to incorporate fillers into pauses to replace the sounds of hesitation (uhh, umm) which suggest lack of fluency.

Second, communication strategies play a bigger compensatory role in monologues than in dialogues, as indicated by the larger number of strategies used in monologues. The participants frequently paraphrased their utterances during the individual presentation and when answering a question after the presentation. Paraphrasing, which encompasses circumlocution, word coinage and approximation in this study, is a lexical strategy and its use places a high cognitive load on the speakers (Naughton, 2006). In contrast, when participants take turns to speak in dialogues, the collaborative discourse gives them the opportunity to assist one another to reach shared meaning, evident in the high frequency of appeals for assistance in role plays. Since other studies (Lam & Wong, 2000; Nakatani, 2010; Naughton, 2006) have shown that meaning negotiation strategies are more teachable than lexical strategies involving reformulation of the message, it is more worthwhile to focus on meaning negotiation strategies in the context of dialogues. Using interactive task types in communication strategy instruction would provide room for practicing strategy use in collaborative discourse.

Third, the findings indicate that the strategy training helped the participants to use the strategy that was taught immediately after the training. The results showed noticeably higher frequencies for paraphrase (circumlocution) in individual presentations, appeal for assistance in role plays, offering assistance and lexical repetition in group discussion, and stress in responding to questions. The frequencies of these strategies in subsequent speaking tasks were low, indicating that automatisation had not taken place. The present study might have raised awareness on the usefulness of communication strategies but more opportunities for specific focused practice may be needed for automatisation and "the transfer of the new strategies to new tasks" (Dörnyei, 1995, p.65). It is also important in further studies to have a delayed post-test (Rossiter, 2003) to find out the long-term retention of the strategies and to incorporate fluency measures because the ultimate goal of communication strategy training is to enhance the strategic competence of speakers.

ENDNOTE

1 The focus of the main frameworks of communication strategies is form. For example, Tarone (1981, p.286) describes literal translation as "the learner translates word for word from the native language". A similar approach is used by Faerch and Kasper (1984, p.50) to explain the difference between literal translation and foreignising. Faerch and Kasper (1984) state that "If the non-IL [interlanguage] element is adapted to the IL system phonologically and/or morphologically, the strategy is termed foreignizing, whereas the verbatim selection and combination of IL lexical items on the basis of Ll/L3 has been called literal translation." The Nijmegen research group criticised the traditional typologies of communication strategies as being "product-oriented, focussing on surface structures of underlying psycholinguistic processes" (Dörnyei, 1995, p.57). However, the focus of Nijmegen research group's conceptualisation of communication strategies as shown in Dörnyei (1995) is also on form. Although Clennell (1995) emphasised the pragmatic functions of communication strategies in interactive discourse, his classification of discourse-based strategies is also based on form. For instance, in describing

the topic + comment syntactic structuring, Clennell (1995) explains that the topic is stated first and it is usually the subject (e.g., my picture) and then a comment is added after a pause (e.g., no pencil).

Appendix 1: Framework of analysis for communication strategies

Strategy	Description	Examples from data set
Abandon message[N]	The speaker begins to talk about a concept but is unable to continue due to lack of linguistic resources, stops in mid-utterance, and moves on to another idea.	[umm] There are many other term that can be used such as antibiotic, anti ana.. anal.. {abandon} antiseptic such as DETTOL or cream *lah*.
Reduce message[N]	The speaker replaces the original message with another message which is less than what is intended.	S3: Cover [uhh] cover the improve the quality so the malpractice doesn't occur// S1: Occur again. S3: ***We will minimize the, the error.***
Appeal for assistance[T]	The speaker asks for the correct item or structure.	I'm sorry. ***Can I ask you something? You know the direction to the medical lab?***
Offer help[T]	The speaker offers the target item to the interlocutor.	S2: We do the [umm] check from village to village. [umm] what I'm talking// S1:[uhh] [umm] [Aah] *tu*// S2: movement bus S1: ***I know tu, roadshow!***
Pay attention to pronunciation[N]	The speaker pays attention to his/her pronunciation.	A: I want to explain about risk of headache. Q: Headache? {correct pron.} A: ***Headache*** {corrected}
Use stress[N, C]	The speaker tries to speak clearly and loudly to make him/herself heard.	[umm] THERE are a few step that can be taken while [uhh] to investigate whether the drug is [uhh] comprehensive or effective such as [umm] identify, IDENTIFY what the problem is happen at the market or the public.
Use rhythm & intonation[N, C]	The speaker pays attention to his/her rhythm and intonation.	Ok, pharmacovigilance, improving ok [umm] /\ ***pharmacovigilance*** [ahh] my ***grandfather***.
Lexical repetition[N, C]	The speaker repeats words or phrases with a system of tones (e.g. rise, fall, rise-fall) for discourse and topic maintenance, topic salience marker, appeal for assistance, request for clarification, indicate comprehension.	The silver car is the back of the red car where's the red car make cannot control, ***cannot control*** his car or her car and, and bump into, ***bump*** the black car.
Use gestures & facial expressions[N]	The speaker uses non-verbal communication to convey meaning.	

Restructure utterances [FK, N]	The speaker reformulates the syntax of the utterance.	They're ***still talking about improvement***. Yeah, the way, ***the way on improve it***.
Paraphrase [T] **(approximation, coinage, circumlocution)**	The speaker uses other ways of explaining when problems are encountered: Approximation: The speaker uses a single target language vocabulary item which he/she knows is not correct but shares enough semantic features in common with the desired item to satisfy the speaker. Structure is excluded. Word coinage: The speaker makes up a new word in order to communicate a desired concept. Circumlocution: The speaker describes characteristics or elements of the object or action instead of using the appropriate target language structure.	Approximation: So, I think [umm] the another car, another car, not really, not really have a impact more than the red car have a impact... {approximation for the word "damage"} Coinage: ***Ugly frog*** *for toad*, ***Malaysian monkey*** *for Orang Utan* (example is not from this data set as the participants did not use coinage) Circumlocution: This is [uhh] maybe some kind, not some kind [uhh] is a ***situations that can make others people think that there is no one will survive.***
Give examples [N]	The speaker gives examples if the listener doesn't understand what is said. Some examples of phrases are *for example* and *like in the case of*	Commonly there are adverse reaction on the drug whether, such as, we can see on the skin. You can see such as ***the skin burn or others*** [uhh] the example of it.
Comprehension checks [N, T]	The speaker directly asks the listener if he/she understands what is said. Some examples of phrases are *You see what I mean?, Do you understand?, Get what I mean?, Got it?* and *Clear?*	Straight and then you, you turn left. ***You know where left?***
Confirmation checks [N, T]	The speaker rewords what others say to check whether he/she has understood something correctly. Some examples of phrases are *You mean there is no …? and Let me get this right, is it like …?*	S1: You know bribe? Bribe [pause] it's when you give extra money. If we compensate the hospital staff, they will not report the malpractice. S3: ***Compensation is example of "prep-ping"{bribing}?***
Clarification requests [T]	The speaker asks others to explain when he/she does not understand something. Some examples of phrases are *Sorry, I didn't catch you, Can you repeat that? I'm not clear on the meaning.*	S1: Before, before talk, check. S2: ***Check?*** S1: Check. S2: ***Check what?***
Pauses [N]	The speaker pauses and sometimes uses fillers when he/she cannot think of what to say. Some examples of phrases to gain time are *well, let me see, actually, I guess, It's like this and in fact.* Other sounds indicating pauses are *umm, uhh* and *ahh*. Unfilled pauses are marked by silence.	But if the people cannot follow the instruction of the pharmacy [*umm*] we cannot do, we must force the patient and [*umm*] we can, ***actually*** we can do the, the, the checkup every week.

Note: The superscripts in the first column show the frameworks from which these communication strategies were taken from: C for Clennell (1995), FK for Faerch and Kasper (1980), N for Nakatani (2006), and T for Tarone (1981).

REFERENCES

1. Bialystok, E., & Frohlich, M. (1980). Oral communication strategies for lexical difficulties. Interlanguage Studies Bulletin – Utrecht, 5(1), 3-30.
2. Canale, M. (1983). From communicative competence to communicative language pedagogy. In J. Richards & R. Schmidt (Eds.), Language and communication (pp. 2-27). London: Longman.
3. Clennell, C. (1994a). Collaborative discourse strategies or communication strategies? Problems of identifying interlanguage communication strategies in low level learners of English. In J. Burton (Ed.), Perspectives on the Classroom. Research on Language and Learning Series 1. CALUSA: University of South Australia.
4. Clennell, C. (1994b). Investigating the use of communication strategies in adult second language learners: A case for trusting your own judgment in SL classroom research. TESOL Journal, 4(1), 32-35.
5. Clennell, C. (1995). Communication strategies of adult ESL learners: A discourse perspective. Prospect, 10(3), 4-20.
6. Dörnyei, Z. (1995). On the teachability of communication strategies. TESOL Quarterly, 29(1), 55-85.
7. Dörnyei, Z., & Scott, M. L. (1997). Communication strategies in a second language: Definitions and taxonomies. Language Learning, 47(1), 173-210.
8. Dörnyei, Z., & Thurrell, S. (1991). Strategic competence and how to teach it. ELT Journal, 45(1), 16-23.
9. Faerch, C., & Kasper, G. (1980). Processes and strategies in foreign language learning and communication. Interlanguage Studies Bulletin – Utrecht, 5(1), 47-118.
10. Faerch, C., & Kasper, G. (1983a). Plans and strategies in interlanguage communication. In C. Faerch & G. Kasper (Eds.), Strategies in Interlanguage Communication (pp. 20-60). London: Longman.
11. Faerch, C., & Kasper, G. (1983b). On identifying communication strategies in interlanguage production. In C. Faerch & G. Kasper (Eds.), Strategies in interlanguage communication (pp. 210-238). Harlow: Longman.
12. Faerch, C., & Kasper, G. (1984). Two ways of defining communication strategies. Language Learning, 34(1), 45-63.
13. Haastrup, K., & Phillipson, R. (1983). Achievement strategies in learner/native speaker interaction. In C. Faerch & G. Kasper (Eds.), Strategies in interlanguage communication (pp. 140-158). London: Longman.

14. Kellerman, E., Ammerlaan, T., Bongaerts, T., & Poulisse, N. (1990). System and hierarchy in L2 compensatory strategies. Developing communicative competence in a second language, 163-178.
15. Kongsom, T. (2009). The effects of teaching communication strategies to Thai learners of English. Unpublished Ph.D dissertation, University of Southampton.
16. Lafford, B. A. (2004). The effect of the context of learning on the use of communication strategies by learners of Spanish as a second language. Studies in Second Language Acquisition, 26(2), 201.
17. Lam, W., & Wong, J. (2000). The effects of strategy training on developing discussion skills in an ESL classroom. ELT Journal, 54(3), 245-255.
18. Nakatani, Y. (2006). The effects of awareness-raising training on oral communication strategy use. The Modern Language Journal, 89(1), 76-91.
19. Nakatani, Y. (2010). Identifying strategies that facilitate EFL learners' oral communication: a classroom studying using multiple data collection procedures. The Modern Language Journal, 94(1), 116-136.
20. Naughton, D. (2006). Cooperative strategy training and oral interaction: Enhancing small group communication in the language classroom. The Modern Language Journal, 90(2), 169-184.
21. Nayar, P. B. (1997). ESL/EFL dichotomy today: Language politics or pragmatics? TESOL Quarterly, 31(1), 9-37. DOI: 10.2307/3587973
22. Paribakht, T. (1985). Strategic competence and language proficiency. Applied Linguistics, 6(2), 132-146.
23. Poulisse, N., Bongaerts, T., & Kellerman, E. (1987). The use of retrospective verbal reports in the analysis of compensatory strategies. In C. Faerch & G. Kasper (Eds.), Introspection in Second Language Research (pp. 100-112). Clevedon, UK: Multilingual Matters.
24. Poulisse, N., & Schils, E. (1989). The influence of task and proficiency-related factors on the use of compensatory strategies: A quantitative analysis. Language Learning, 39(1), 15-48.
25. Richards, J., Platt, J. J., & Weber, H. (1985). The Longman dictionary of applied linguistics. London: Longman.
26. Rossiter, M. J. (2003). "It's like chicken but bigger": Effects of communication strategy in the ESL classroom. Canadian Modern Language Review, 60(2), 105-121.
27. Tarone, E. (1980). Communication strategies, foreigner talk and repair in interlanguage. Language Learning, 30(2), 417-431.

28. Tarone, E. (1981). Some thoughts on the notion of communication strategy. TESOL Quarterly, 15(3), 285-295.
29. Tarone, E., Yule, G., & Yule, G. (1989). Focus on the language learner: Approaches to identifying and meeting the needs of second language learners (pp. 34-39). Oxford: Oxford University Press.
30. Ting, S. H. (2002). Is English needed in a Malay workplace? RELC Journal, 33(1), 137-153.
31. Ting, S. H. (2012). Variable impact of Malaysia's national language planning on non-Malay speakers in Sarawak. Revista Brasileira de Linguistica Aplicada, 12(2), 381-403.
32. Ting, S. H., & Kho, T. P. (2009). Gender and communication strategy use in learning English as a second language. International Journal of Applied Linguistics, 157(1), 93-108.
33. Ting, S. H., Musa, M. K., & Sim, J. S. E. (2013). Advanced ESL learners' use of communication strategies during oral presentations. In S. Ibrahim, N. A. Adzmi, & M. W. Omar (Eds.), TESSHI 2012 chapters on Humanities and Social Sciences (pp. 117-135). Kedah, Malaysia: UiTM Kedah Press.
34. Ting, S. H., & Phan, G. Y. L. (2008). Adjustment in communication strategy use to interlocutor's language proficiency. Prospect (Australian TESOL Journal), 23(1), 28-36.
35. Ting, S. H., & Sim, S. E. (2013). Communication strategy use in oral academic discussions. Paper presented at SOLLs.INTEC 2013, Cyberjaya, Malaysia.
36. Yin, R. K. (2014). Case study research: Design and methods (5th ed.). Thousand Oaks, California: SAGE.
37. Yule, G., & Tarone, E. (1991). The other side of the page: Integrating the study of communication strategies and negotiated input in SLA. In R. Phillipson, E. Kellerman, L. Selinker, M. Sharwood Smith, & M. Swain (Eds.), Foreign/Second Language Pedagogy Research (pp. 161-171). Clevedon: Multilingual Matters.

Chapter 9

THE EFFECT OF LISTENING TO COMIC STRIP STORIES ON INCIDENTAL VOCABULARY LEARNING AMONG IRANIAN EFL LEARNERS

Omid Arast[1], Bahman Gorjian[2]

[1]Department of English, Ahvaz Branch, Islamic Azad University, Ahvaz, Iran

[2]Department of English, Abadan Branch, Islamic Azad University, Abadan, Iran

ABSTRACT

The effect of listening to comic strip stories on incidental vocabulary learning is the aim of this study. To this end, two groups including twenty pre-intermediate students as an experimental group and twenty students as a control group were participated. A vocabulary knowledge scale (VKS) was given to all participants as a pre-test and post-test to measure learners' knowledge rest on 18 unknown target vocabularies. An experimental group listened to comic strip stories with watching photos of stories, whereas the control group just listened to comic strip stories without watching any photos of stories. The results showed that both groups had a significant improvement after treatment, and listening to stories had an effect on vocabulary learning. In addition, to compare both groups' performance on post-test, an independent t-test was administered which indicated that there was a significant difference between experimental group and control group whilst, experimental group learners almost performed better than control group learners which conveys watching stories' comic photos can affect on incidental vocabulary learning remarkably.

INTRODUCTION

Vocabulary learning is an essential part of language learning (Yoshii, 2002). There are many definitions of vocabulary learning importance in other researches, and the vocabulary learning enthusiasts revealed the vocabulary significance in their researches. As Shoebottom (2014) ascertains the more words you know, the more you will be able to understand what you hear and read, and the better you will be able to say what you want to when speaking or writing. Words are the currency of communication; speakers will not be able to communicate with each other without words (Alexander, 2014). Ahmad (2011) in his study quotes that vocabulary learning is an indispensable process for *ESL* learners to acquire proficiency and competence in target language.

Having studied vocabulary learning instructions, many techniques are revealed. Finocchiaro and Bonomo (1973) conveyed many techniques for teaching vocabulary; they talked about that we give our students an understanding of the meaning in many ways: we dramatize; we illustrate using ourselves and our students; we show pictures or objects; we paraphrase; we give the equivalent if necessary; we use any appropriate techniques. In the other hand, Claudia Pesce (2012) in her article describes five best ways to instruct new words to learners: show students illustrations, flashcards, posters, synonyms and antonyms, setting a scene or situation and the substitute it with a new word or phrase, miming and total physical response (*TPR*) which many teachers believe learners who learn best by moving their bodies, actions and imperative mood and the last one is the realia (real-life objects in the *ESL* classroom) which can help to present new words.

Many scholars in their studies divide the vocabulary learning into two instructional techniques: incidental learning and intentional learning. Many definitions about these techniques are given by many scholars although Yali (2010) points out the incidental learning is defined as the type of learning that is a by-product of doing or learning something else; whereas, intentional learning is defined as being designed, planned for, or intended by teacher or students. He describes that incidental learning defines the approach of learning vocabulary through texts, working on tasks or doing other activities that are not directly related to vocabulary, whereas the intentional learning always focuses on vocabulary itself, and combines with all kinds of conscious vocabulary learning strategies and means of memorizing words. As stated in Krashen (2013), a large portion of second language (L2) vocabulary knowledge is acquired incidentally in the sense that words are acquired as a natural by-product of children/learners performing everyday linguistics activities and tasks. Incidental learning is the process of learning something without the intention of doing so; It is also learning one thing while intending to learn another (van Zeeland, 2013; Ahmad, 2011).

To acquire vocabulary in incidental mood, many kinds of methods are introduced. Listening, as another way of incidental vocabulary acquisition is the process of receiving, constructing meaning from, and responding to spoken and/or nonverbal messages" (Brownell, 2002). Listening is important for effective communication because 50 percent or more of the time we spend communicating is spent listening. The optimal goal of L2 listening development is to allow for the L2 to be acquired through listening. Vocabulary is precisely one of the language components that can be acquired through training in listening skills (Montero Perez & Desmet, 2012).

Nowadays, there is a tendency toward using media to aid and supplement educational objectives. At real life English, it is believed that language learning should be fun so the better way to enjoy learning the English language through comic strips. The most frequently mentioned asset of comics as an educational tool is its ability to motivate students. A comic strip is defined as a sequence of drawings arranged in interrelated panels to display brief humor or form a narrative, often serialized, and usually arranged horizontally, with text in balloons and captions (Liu, 2004; Haines, 2012; Merc, 2013). Based on Liu (2004), a comic strip is described as a series of pictures inside boxes that tell a story. Among visual genres, comic strips catch many researchers' attention because they are communicative, popular, accessible, and readable; Comic strips communicate using two major media—words and images—a somewhat arbitrary separation because comic strips' expressive potential lies in skillfully employing words and images together.

Comics can teach children to infer meaning from the visual first. Comics must include pictures; you can even tell a story without words. The benefits of using comics in the classroom in agreement with Hanies (2012) are certainly great, both in increasing literacy and in addressing the educational needs of differentiated learners, so the teacher chooses and uses world with particular care to keep the students and the other space for growth in vocabulary and language development.

LITERATURE REVIEW

Using Comic Strip Books to Teach English Vocabulary

The use of graphic novels in language classrooms has a short history; therefore its literature is rather limited. Although there are not many comprehensive studies assessing their impact as teaching tools, the feedback from educators and scholars as to the use of graphic novels in language classrooms is a clear indication of their worth as a pedagogical tool (Yildirim, 2013). Comic Book Classroom was founded in Denver, Colorado in 2010. Comic Book Classroom is a standard-based curriculum that examines and explores age-appropriate comic literature with the intent of furthering literacy and introducing students to book culture in the larger scope. As Baker (2011) defines graphic novels are a subset of the comic genre. Both terms will be used in this research. Comics and graphic novels both use graphics and text to tell a story. In addition, the goal is to teach students not just reading and art skills, but engage them in discussions about the texts that may help them tackle problems in their own lives and communities. The use of comics in education is based on the concept of creating engagement and motivation for students.

Wright (2001) claims the effectiveness of comics as medium for effective learning and development has been the subject of debate since the origin modern comic book in the 1930s.The use of comics in education would later attract the attention of Fredric Wertham who noted that the use of comics in education represented "an all-time low in American science. The use of cartoons in your teaching has several advantages: they give life to classrooms, they promote students engagement, they improve students' learning, they prolong student's attention span, and they also enhance student's communicative and linguistic competences.

Liu (2004) in his article talked about the role of comic strips on ESL learners' reading comprehension .He has two different students' levels of proficiency (low & high) with and without a comic strip. This study suggests that the reading comprehension of the low-level students was greatly facilitated when the comic strip repeated the information presented in the text. He noted that the effect of comic strips on reading comprehension largely depends on the quality of the repetition effect. The study's results also imply that the advantage of providing comic strips with reading text diminishes when the student has difficulty comprehending the text. After analyzing the results, it was said that low-level students receiving the high-level text with the comic strip scored significantly higher than their counterparts receiving the high-level text only.

Lang (2009) evaluates comic strip has very consequential role in the English classroom, he defines comics are the most widely read media throughout the world – especially in Japan. As he describes problem of language teachers: constantly searching for new innovative and motivating authentic material to enhance learning in the formal classroom. A textbook is made of material that has been altered and simplified for the learner. He notes some characteristics that make comics thus attractive as an educational tool: a built-in desire to learn through comics, easy accessibility in daily newspapers, ingenious way in which this authentic medium depicts real-life language, people and society and eventually variety of visual and linguistic elements and codes that appeal to students with different learning styles. Furthermore, he suggests comics can be used: a) to practice describing characters using adjectives (e.g., Garfield is a very troublesome cat), b) to learn synonyms and antonyms to expand vocabulary, c) to practice writing direct speech (e.g., 'Hey, move your car!') and reported speech (The man told him to move his car.), d) to practice formation of different verb tenses(i.e., changing the present tense of the action in the strip to the past tense), e) to practice telling the story of a sequentially ordered comic strip that has been scrambled up and finally, f) to reinforce the use of time-sequence transition words to maintain the unity of a paragraph or story (e.g., First, the boy left for school. Next, he . . .).

Based on Bowkett's (2011) book, he uses children's interest in pictures, comics and graphic novels as a way of developing their creative writing abilities, reading skills. The book's strategy is the use of comic art images as a visual analogue to help children generate, organize and refine their ideas when writing and talking about text. In reading comic books children are engaging with highly complex and structured narrative forms. Whether they realize it or not, their emergent visual literacy promotes thinking skills and develops wider Meta-cognitive abilities. Baker (2011) tried to examine the benefits of using comics with English language learners (ELLs). With their bright colors and familiar characters, comics are more appealing than traditional text. The comic represents something different and exciting without sacrificing plot, vocabulary, and other important components of reading comprehension. For these reason and many more, comics might also play an important role in ELL acquisition of literacy. She expresses many graphic novels are high interest with low reading levels, cover diverse genes such as biographies, and cover current events and social issues. Baker (2011) concurs with comics can be used to teach parts of speech, social situations, historical events, and more. She admits that incorporating text and visuals causes readers to examine the relationship between the two and encourages deep thinking and critical thinking.

According to Bowen (2011), comic strips can be very motivating for learners as the story-line is reinforced by the visual element, which can make them easier to understand. He designed many activities for teaching vocabularies through using comic strips in class: for example he used the comic strip stories in one activity that is cutting up the strip into individual boxes and getting the students to rearrange them into an appropriate order. Another activity is to blank out alternate boxes, so

Khoiriyah (2011) in his thesis used comic stories to improve the students' level of vocabulary. He believes the students identify and study words from the context on the comic reading. Story from comic offers a whole imaginary world, created by language which students can learn and enjoy; this story is designed to entertain. Khoiriyah (2011) endeavors to find out whether there is a significant difference in vocabulary score of student taught using comic stories and those taught using non-comic stories or not. The instrument to collect the data were; observation and test. Observation was only used to support the data about students' imagination on reflected on their engagement in learning processes. The researcher gave two times teaching to both classes, after the treatment the researcher analyzed the obtained data and concluded that the performance of experimental group that used the comic stories for learning vocabulary is better than the control group.

Karakas and Sariçoban (2012) in their study, considered the impact of subtitled animated cartoons on incidental vocabulary learning, and found out that the target words were contextualized and it became easy for participants to elicit the meanings of the words. For the aim of this study the researchers selected 42 first grade teaching students in Turkey. To collect data from the subjects, a 5-point vocabulary knowledge scale was used and 18 target words were integrated into the scale. After subjects had been randomly assigned into two groups (one subtitle group and the other no-subtitle group), they were given the same pre- and post-tests. The general findings of this study supported the common assumption that subtitles and captions are powerful instructional tools in learning vocabulary and improving reading and listening comprehension skills of language learners.

Merc (2013) considered the effects of comic strips on reading comprehension of Turkish *EFL* learners. In his study, students read the texts given and wrote what they remembered about the text on a separate answer sheet. The results of the quantitative analyses show that all students with a comic strip effect, regardless of proficiency and text level, performed better than the ones without the comic strips. Yildirim (2013) in his research applies graphic novels in classroom as a teaching tool and provides the necessary background information, the historical evolution of graphic novels. He confesses that in language classrooms graphic novels can be used to boost many different skills. The researcher talks about the historical overview of using the graphic novels in different cultures and compares its use in various literatures around the world.

Cimermanova (2014) believes the role of graphic novels in foreign language teaching, too. Using pictures, storytelling, and creative writing are the activities used more or less regularly in foreign language teaching. She admits that in language teaching picture books present an authentic material. Her article discussed the possibilities of using picture books in language teaching and presents the qualitative case study results focused on effectiveness of using wordless picture books. Cimermanova (2014) conveys reading graphic novels brings authentic material to the EFL class and encourages students' critical thinking. She agrees that the use of picture books contributed to a recognition that it is important to "read" the illustrations that may influence our perception, that details are important for understanding the complexity of the whole.

Statement of the Problem

To learn vocabulary incidentally, the learners may encounter many obstacles and restriction or problems, all researchers that studied these issues proposed to work out these problems. They used many techniques to learn vocabulary through four skills, this study tries to focus the listening techniques for learning vocabulary (the receptive learning) and as you read many articles, there are many ways for learning incidental vocabulary. As Mousavi and Gholami (2014) state new methods of English language teaching should use new materials to draw learners' attention for acquisition of English language. To put it another way, nowadays there is a tendency toward using media to aid and supplement educational objectives. This study used the listening to comic strip books and their funny pictures and checked the role of listening skill on incidental vocabulary acquisition.

After studying the many researches, we understood that many researchers studied large issues about incidental vocabulary learning through many ways, the present study attempts to examine the effect of incidental vocabulary learning on listening through comic strip stories which it is an attractive technique to learn vocabulary. To investigate the role of listening to comic strip books on incidental vocabulary learning, the research question aimed to discover whether listening to the comic strip books affect the incidental vocabulary learning.

METHOD

Participants

The participants of this study were 40 pre-intermediate level EFL learners from Rahyan-Danesh Institute of Ahvaz. All of them are female and the range of their age was between 10 to 16 years old. They were selected based on non-random judgment sampling from 86 students at private language institute through their performance on proficiency test designed based on *Interchange Placement Test* (Lesly, Hansen & Zukowski, 2005). For running this study the participants were randomly pigeonholed into two groups, 20 students as experimental group (Group A), and 20 students as control group (Group B). The participants shared the same linguistic and background knowledge and they were unaware of the purpose of study as vocabulary acquisition.

Materials

Comic Strip Book

The researcher for teaching the incidental vocabulary through listening have selected the seven comic strip stories from *The Brain comic strip series books* (Bang , 1957),which retrieved from the website named www. comicbookplus.com . This comic story book has big hero whose nickname is Brain with several interesting adventures. The words which used in this series books are so simple which are adequate to pre-intermediate readers absolutely.

Research Tests

The *Interchange Placement Test* (Lesly, Hansen & Zukowski, 2005), which includes 70 items (20 listening items, 20 reading items and 30 language use items) was used to determine participants' proficiency level. According to Kuder-Richardson (KR-21) formula, the reliability of the proficiency test was estimated to be (r=.905). In order to choose target words, fifty words from the comic strip stories were selected and placed in vocabulary knowledge scale (VKS) (Wesche & Paribakht, 1996). This test was piloted with 10 learners at pre-intermediate level and those words which learners know their meaning was deleted because the aim of this study is to show that learners incidentally acquired the words which they have not already known them. Finally, the eighteen unknown target words were chosen for the current study based on the results of pilot group.

The researcher has applied the same pre-test and post-test for both experimental and control groups, based on the unknown selected words. This test is five-point self-reported scale of vocabulary knowledge scale (VKS) (Wesche & Paribakht, 1996) was adopted to measure the vocabulary development of the learners before the treatment and after the fulfillment of treatment. This scale which was applied by some scholars (e.g., Rieder, 2003; Mahdavy, 2011; Karakas & Sariçoban, 2012; Mousavi & Gholami, 2014) in previous studies should focus on evaluating the taught target vocabularies or idioms during the treatment. It composed of 5 levels as follows and this scale is scored according the following table (scores apply to each individual target words):

1: I don't remember having seen this word before. (0 point)

2: I have seen this word before but I don't know what it means. (1 point)

3: I have seen this word before and I think it means ________ (synonym or translation). (2 points)

4: I know this word. It means __________ (synonym or translation). (3 points)

5: I can use this word in a sentence. e.g.: __________________ (if you do this section, please

Also do section 4). (4 points)

The reliability coefficient of the pretest and post-test were (r=.976 & r=.947) respectively, which estimated by using Kuder-Richardson (KR-21) formula.

Procedure

The study has lasted for 21 days, 3 sessions a week during the period of one semester (3 weeks, 9 sessions). The teacher chose seven simple stories from *The Brain series books*. He selected just last 30 minutes of each session. The researcher gave proficiency test to all participants for determining their levels in first session .In second session the participants were taken the pre-test VKS and their data were calculated .This treatment has begun from third session to eighth session in third week. In the treatment sessions, the teacher has provided slides for each short story before each session.

Both groups listened to the same stories which were included same vocabularies but in different mediums. For experimental group, researcher provided the power point slides for each story to teach it audio-visually. He has explained the stories by providing them with some more expressions or comic pictures in order to draw their attention to the target vocabularies. This group listened to the teacher who told the story by help of showing the pictures of comic stories on the scope of video projector in front of the classroom. Afterwards, for control group, he utilized his voice which recorded in experimental group sessions formerly. He explained all of the stories in this group without showing any slides to them. The control group has just listened to the recorded voice of teacher who retelling the story, without observing the slides of pictures of comic strip books on video projector. They had to visualize the story in their mind and just listened to the voice of the teacher. The post-test was administered in ninth session in third week of semester after passing the 6 sessions of treatment. The questions of post-test were similar to pre-test (VKS). The post-test was given to both groups on similar condition and time for answering them.

RESULTS

The statistical calculations and results of the study obtained from analyzing the learners' performance on*Interchange Placement Test* as homogeneity test and also vocabulary knowledge scale (VKS) as pre-test and post-test are presented. Next, the analysis went further to find out if there is any difference between both groups (groups A & B) on pre-test and post-test. The analysis on the pre-test was conducted to find any significant differences between two groups' performance on the pre-test through the Independent Samples *t-test* in Table 1.

Table 1: Descriptive Statistics (Pre-test)

Groups	Mean	N	Std. Deviation	Std. Error Mean
Pre-test (Experimental Group)	12.0500	20	3.66312	.81910
Pre-test(Control Group	11.9500	20	3.87264	.86595

Table 4.2 presents both groups' descriptive statistics on pre-test, the means of two groups. The means of both groups are close; however, the Independent Samples t-test may show any significant difference between the groups in Table 2.

Table 2 shows the difference between the mean scores of both groups is not significant since the observed t (.525) is less than the critical t (2.090) with df=19. Thus the two groups' performance in the pre-test is showed no significant difference. The result of the post-test is presented in Table 3.

Table 2: Independent Samples t- Test on the Pre-test of the Groups' Pre-test

	Paired Differences							
Experimental vs. Control Groups	Mean	Std. Deviation	Std. Error Mean	95% Confidence Interval of the Difference		t	df	Sig. (2-tailed)
				Lower	Upper			
	.10000	.85224	.19057	-.29886	.49886	.525	19	.606

Table 3 indicates the descriptive statistics of both groups on the post-test. The means with standard deviations of the two groups reveals that the difference between the post-test means. Thus the significance difference can be got in the Table 4.

Table 3: Descriptive Statistics (Post-test)

Groups	N	Mean	Std. Deviation	Std. Error Mean
Pre-test (Experimental Group)	20	34.3500	12.85250	2.87391
Pre-test (Control Group	20	27.4000	5.49066	1.22775

Table 4 shows the difference between the mean scores of both groups' post-test is significant since the observed t (2.224) is greater than the critical t (2.090) with df=19. Thus the two groups' performance in the post-test is showed a significant difference.

Table 4: Independent Samples t- Test on the Pre-test of the Groups' (Post-test)

	Levene's Test for Equality of Variances		t-test for Equality of Means						
Experimental vs. Control Groups	F	Sig.	t	df	Sig. (2-tailed)	Mean Difference	Std. Error Difference	95% Confidence Interval of the Difference	
								Lower	Upper
Equal variances assumed	14.374	.001	2.224	38	.032	6.950	3.125	.623	13.276
Equal variances not assumed			2.224	25.7	.035	6.950	3.125	.522	13.377

DISCUSSION AND CONCLUSIONS

Discussion

Findings of the study suggest that the mean scores of pre-test of both groups were very close to each other. It is assumed from this finding that both groups had similar knowledge about the target words before they were exposed to the treatment. The development in each group was measured through *t*-test which demonstrated that there was an improvement in each group and also the scores of all participants in two groups on post-test had been progressed. It is clear that high differences in mean score of each group show that both groups after passing the treatment accompanied by using listening to comic strip stories have promoted on post-test scores. Results indicated the differences in mean scores in both groups were significant, ($p < 0.05$). Regarding the comparison of mean differences in groups A and B, it might be concluded that there were significant differences between two groups while progress in group A is slightly more than group B. Thus, it might be concluded that what facilitated the improvement in vocabulary knowledge was listening to comic strip stories while using comic pictures can have more impact on acquiring incidental vocabulary in relation to only listening to these stories. It is concluded that listening to comic strip stories can affect on incidental vocabulary learning. However, by comparing the results of two groups by using independent *t-test*, the difference between two groups was significant, so the experimental group which used watching pictures of the stories could perform better than other group.

The present study confirms the findings of Lang's (2009) study, who evaluates comic strip has very consequential role in the English classroom, he defines comics are the most widely read media throughout the world. Lang (2009) describes problem of language teachers: constantly searching for new innovative and motivating authentic material to enhance learning in the formal classroom. A textbook is made of material that has been altered and simplified for the learner. He agreed by using comic books, the learners can learn different kinds of topics in classroom. Like this current study, Liu (2004) in his article talked about the role of comic strips on ESL learners' reading comprehension .He has two different students' levels of proficiency (low & high) with and without a comic strip. The outcome of the present study is compatible with Bowkett's (2011) book, which in his book the author uses children's interest in pictures, comics and graphic novels as a way of developing their creative writing abilities, reading skills. The book's strategy is the use of comic art images as a visual analogue to help children generate, organize and refine their ideas when writing and talking about text. He agrees in reading comic books children are engaging with highly complex and structured narrative forms.

Bowen (2011) describes that comic strips can be very motivating for learners as the story-line is reinforced by the visual element, which can make them easier to understand. There are a number of different ways to use comic strips. He designed many activities for teaching vocabularies through using comic strips in class: for example he used the comic strip stories in one activity that is cutting up the strip into individual boxes and getting the students to rearrange them into an appropriate order. In another study, Khoiriyah (2011) uses comic stories to improve the students' level of vocabulary. He suggests the students identify and study words from the context on the comic reading. His findings infer that the performance of experimental group that used the comic stories for learning vocabulary is better than the control group.

Karakas and Sariçoban (2012) in their study, considered the impact of subtitled animated cartoons on incidental vocabulary learning, and found out that the target words were contextualized and it became easy for participants to elicit the meanings of the words. Their results were in related to the current study which the general findings of this study supported the common assumption that subtitles and captions are powerful instructional tools in learning vocabulary and improving reading and listening comprehension skills of language learners. Moreover, Merc (2013) considered the effects of comic strips on reading comprehension of Turkish EFL learners. In his study students read the texts given and wrote what they remembered about the text on a separate answer sheet. The results of the quantitative analyses show that all students with a comic strip effect, regardless of proficiency and text level, performed better than the ones without the comic strips.

Conclusions

The present study aimed at investigating the effect of listening to comic strip stories on incidental vocabulary learning of a pre-intermediate Iranian EFL learners group. This study showed Iranian EFL learners picking up the meaning of unfamiliar words encountered incidentally in task materials as they listened to comic strip books. The results of the study showed that listening to comic strip stories had statistically meaningful effect on the performance of language learners on acquiring incidental vocabulary. Findings from the study show that after treatment both experimental group and control group have improved in their results on post-test. In addition, independent sample *t-test* between two groups indicates that the results of experimental group in comparison of the results of control group were better and their performance was more excellent too. As a whole, it seems that listening instruction affected the L2 learners' performance on the incidental vocabulary learning. It can be concluded from the findings of the current study that comic pictures of such strip books can influence on better vocabulary acquisition. Furthermore, the low acquisition rate of word meaning found here, as well as in other incidental learning studies, emphasizes once more the importance of combining incidental learning with some sort of explicit focus. Subsequently, the findings of this study reveal that incidental vocabulary acquisition in listening modes by using various methods can indeed occur and that comic strip story might be an effective tool to support vocabulary learning. The findings of this study also present that vocabulary development is a long lasting process that needs to be supported by contextual clues.

Finally, as the research interest of this study, comic strip use had a significant effect on students' recall of both pre-intermediate EFL learner groups who used the listening method to acquire the new words. This study found that comic strip use noticeably facilitated the listening comprehension of students at pre-intermediate level. Once again, it was proved that students be provided texts with a visual material, the comic strips in particular, in their reading comprehension and listening classrooms.

REFERENCES

1. Ahmad, J. (2011). Intentional vs. Incidental vocabulary learning. Interdisciplinary Journal of Contemporary Research in Business, 3(5), 67-75.
2. Alexander, F. (2014). Understanding vocabulary. Retrieved October 8t h 2014 from www.scholastic.com/teachers/ar ticle.
3. Baker, A. (2011). Using comics to improve literacy in English language learners. Retrieved April 16th 2015 from https://centralspace.ucmo.edu:8443/.../ABaker_LibraryScien ce.pdf.
4. Bang, B. (1957). The Brain comic strip series books. Magazine Enterprises. Retrieved October 14th 2014 from www.comicbookplus.com.
5. Bowen, T. (2011). Methodology: Using comic strips in class. Retrieved July 13th 2014 from http://www.onestopenglish.com.
6. Bowkett, S. (2011). Using comic art to improve speaking, reading and

writing. Florence, KY: Routledge, Taylor & Francis.

7. Brownell, J. (2002). Listening: attitudes, principles and skills. Boston, MA: Allyn and Bacon.
8. Cimermanova, I. (2014). Graphic novels in foreign language teaching. Journal of Language and Cultural Education, 2 (2), 85- 94.
9. Finocchiaro, M. and Bonomo, M. (1973). The foreign language learner: A guide for teachers. New York: Regents Publishing Company, Inc.
10. Haines, J. (2012). Why Teach With Comics? Retrieved July 10th 2014 fromhttp://www.diamondbookshelf.com/Home/1/1/20/182?articleID=109588.
11. Karakas, A., and Sariçoban, A. (2012). The impact of watching subtitled animated cartoons on incidental vocabulary learning of ELT students. Teaching English with Technology, 12(4), 3-15.
12. Khoiriyah, N. (2011). The use of comic stories to improve students' vocabulary. Unpublished Ph.D thesis. Walisongo state institute for Islamic studies faculty.
13. Krashen, S.D. (2013). Second language acquisition: Theory, Applications, and Some Conjectures. Cambridge: Cambridge University Press.
14. Lang, A. (2009). Comic strips in the English classroom. Retrieved April 20th 2015 fromhttp://www.uni-saarland.de/f ak4/teachersday/archive/2009/pdf//Workshop.
15. Lesley, T., Hansen, C., and Zukowski, J. (2005). Interchange Passage Placement Testing Program. Cambridge: Cambridge University Press.
16. Liu, J. (2004). Effects of comic strips on L2 learners' reading comprehension. TESOL Quarterly, 38(2), 225-243.
17. Mahdavy, B. (2011). The role of topic familiarity and rhetorical organization of texts in L2 incidental vocabulary acquisition. Procedia - Social and Behavioral Sciences, 29, 208 – 217.
18. Merc, A. (2013). The effect of comic strips on EFL reading comprehension. International Journal New Trends in Education and Their Implications, 4 (1), 1-11.
19. Mousavi, F., and Gholami, J. (2014). Effects of watching flash stories with or without subtitle And reading subtitles on incidental vocabulary acquisition. Procedia - Social and Behavioral Sciences, 98, 1273 – 1281.
20. Montero Perez, M., and Desmet, P. (2012). The effect of input enhancement in L2 listening on incidental vocabulary learning: A review. Procedia - Social and Behavioral Sciences, 34 (2012), 153 – 157.
21. Pesce, C. (2012). 5 best ways to introduce new vocabulary. Retrieved

February 10th 2015 fromhttp://busyteacher.org/41 97- 5-best-ways-to-introduce-new-vocabulary.html.

22. Rieder, A. (2003). Implicit and explicit learning in incidental vocabulary acquisition. views, 12(2), 24-39.
23. Shoebottom, P. (2014). How to learn vocabulary? Retrieved October 10th 2014 fromhttp://esl.fis.edu/learners/advice/voc ab.htm.
24. Van Zeeland, H. V., & Schmitt, N. (2013). Incidental vocabulary acquisition through L2 listening: a dimensions approach system. Elsevier System, 41, 609-624.
25. Wesche, M. and Paribakht, T.S (1996). Enhancing vocabulary acquisition through reading: A hierarchy of text related exercise types. The Canadian Modern Language Review, 52(2), 155-178.
26. Wright, B (2001). Comic book nation: The transformation of Youth Culture in America. Johns Hopkins University Press
27. Yali, G. (2010). L2 vocabulary acquisition through reading—incidental learning and intentional learning. Chinese Journal of Applied Linguistic (Bimonthly), 33(1), 74-93.
28. Yildirim, A.H. (2013). Using graphic novels in the classroom. Journal of Language and Literature Education, 8,118-131.
29. Yoshii, M. and Flaitz, J. (2002). Second language incidental vocabulary retention: The effect of text and picture annotation.

Chapter 10

A CRITICAL REVIEW OF COMMON VOCABULARY LEARNING STRATEGIES IN IRANIAN EFL CLASSROOMS

Laleh Kohandel Jahromi[1], Amin Marzban[2]

[1]M.A. in TEFL, Department of Foreign Languages, Sepidan Branch, Islamic Azad University, Sepidan, Iran

[2]Assistant Professor, Department of Foreign Languages, Sepidan Branch, Islamic Azad University, Sepidan, Iran

ABSTRACT

Presently, one of the basic challenges that EFL / ESL learners encounter while learning English is vocabulary acquisition, this difficulty in acquiring vocabulary is one of the most prominent aspects of second or foreign language learning process as it can be facilitated through pleasure and ease for EFL / ESL learners. To this end, introducing vocabulary learning strategies to EFL / ESL learners through which their vocabulary knowledge may be improved and applied to real contexts more effectively is central to the realm of language teaching. In this critical review, the importance of vocabulary learning and three commonly used approaches implementing EFL / ESL classrooms including Computer – Assisted Vocabulary Acquisition (CAVOCA), vocabulary learning through games and vocabulary learning through story retelling will be discussed and analyzed.

INTRODUCTION

The significant role of vocabulary acquisition in second or foreign language learning process has been recognized by theorist and researchers such as Rivers. Since it may act like an overpass between main language skills, it has been suggested that teaching vocabulary should not only consist of teaching particular words, but also it should intend to equip learners with strategies necessary to expand vocabulary domain, Hulstijn [1]. Besides, Vocabulary learning strategies (Henceforth VLSs) can be considered as a part of general learning strategies in second or foreign language acquisition.

The first development in learning strategies area began in 1970s with research to recognize the characteristics of good language learners, Rubin [2]. Based on this, numerous kinds of approaches, techniques, and exercises have been introduced through teaching of vocabulary, Hatch & Brown [3]. Based on the prominence of vocabulary knowledge to learning a language research into usefulness of different types of vocabulary learning strategies and methods implementing in EFL / ESL classrooms, it is the instructors' responsibility to make EFL learners familiar with various available strategies and approaches and encourage them to choose the one by which they can improve their vocabulary knowledge. The role of main language skills in successful communication in both spoken and written contexts has its own place in the realm of language learning process, but no matter how well EFL / ESL learners acquire grammar and other language skills, without second language vocabulary items to express a wide range of meanings and thoughts, communication in an second language might not happen in any significant way. Laufer [4] believes that instructors should give their students more responsibilities for vocabulary learning.

However, some researchers including Rivers [5] strive that vocabulary is a part of language that cannot be taught. Instructors can present and explain them; in spite of the fact that students ultimately learn vocabulary items on their own. Therefore, the most crucial issue in vocabulary acquisition is finding an appropriate way to learn them. As mentioned earlier, since vocabulary is an essential feature of language learning, for instance listening, speaking, reading, and writing, EFL / ESL learners ought to be aware of helpful methods; techniques and approaches which can help them learn and recall new vocabularies. Due to diverse learners' outlooks and manners, it is not comprehensible which approach is the best one for learning vocabulary. On the other hand, it is possible to realize which one can be the best or worst approach in the realm of language learning. In contrast, why is it vital to choose an appropriate strategy to acquire vocabulary? One reason is that EFL / ESL learners may not be aware of the wide choice of current strategies and approaches. It could be assumed that it is the knowledge shortage of the VLSs and approaches of both instructors and learners that prevents them from employing the strategies more actively and effectively.

RECENT VLS STRATEGIES

The function of traditional vocabulary methods in EFL / ESL classrooms, including copying definitions, drawing pictures, writing example sentences and Rote Learning, known as RL, which is repeating new vocabulary items without thinking of the meaning until remembering them cannot be doubted in language learning trend. Such methods laid further proof on their positive effect on language learning acquisition; nevertheless, in view of the fact that currently the world is getting more technological and electronic in the communication age, it is the exact time to look for innovated and more updated strategies and approaches to enhance EFL / ESL learners' vocabulary knowledge.

Computer – Assisted Vocabulary Learning (CAVOCA)

Technology will become more famous in future in the world of language learning and teaching, Wang [6]. According to Lu [7] current development in information technologies has led to a sharp increase in the application of technology in instructional environment. Technology has attracted the interest and attention of many researchers in introducing new ways of learning words and lexicons in language, Groot [8]. Groot introduces "*Computer Assisted Vocabulary Acquisition*" (CAVOCA) as a computer program to learn vocabulary in a foreign context.

In this program, a given word to be learnt appears on the screen for a second, and then, definitions, meanings and syntactic functions are given and then exercises along with feedback are presented, too. In an investigation study, Kolich [9] found that students learn a greater load of unknown words by using CALL "Computer – assisted language learning" software that provides synonyms and meaning. Groot [8], in his research with relation to the use of multimedia computers in acquiring vocabulary, found that using bilingual inventories of terms proved to be more efficient than using a computer program for learning scholastic vocabulary. The utilizing of technology in instructional atmosphere, as recommended by Wang [6] is a move from behaviorist viewpoint to a constructivist learning process. Multimedia can make a better condition for learning vocabulary.

Prichard [10] concluded that the efficacy of dictionary use may be affected by new technologies such as handheld electronic dictionaries, online dictionaries, and marginal glosses; referring to an unknown word through an electronic link, for example, takes much less time and sidetracks the reader from the text to a lesser degree. Dehghani et al [11] found that homework assignment provides a superior means of learning new vocabulary for beginner language learners. in point of fact, as one of the significant compensations of using computer – assisted vocabulary acquisition (CAVOCA) in EFL classrooms, learners' motivation can be improved as this approach makes the class more pleasure and without any anxiety, so it might make the progress of learning smoother and expedite learning; moreover, through such method, EFL / ESL learners' time can be saved enough to acquire new vocabularies and focus more on the other aspects of language use and communication skills.

In addition, another advantage of this approach is that by integrating language tasks with computer, learners' excitement in the realm of second / foreign language acquisition might be increased and the stress which is always with learners in language use could be lowered. Pitler, Hubbell, Kuhn & Malenoski [12] praise the impact of technology on increasing learners' motivation and achievement. To put it bluntly, the CAVOCA technique endeavors to replicate the way the first language is taught, which is in the course of a step by step procedure that gradually develops with repeated exposure and constant interaction between the various stages, Groot [8]. The program has four divisions, which embrace accumulating the word in memory; using the word in several sentences to learn the spelling and meaning; giving examples for long-term memory; and a self-assessment.

Regardless the advantages of CAVOCA in EFL / ESL classrooms, the most major question which can influence the benefits of this approach, as a drawback must be taken into consideration is that by lack of using technology knowledge, mainly computer in classrooms the teacher from taking its advantages might be impeded and as Zhao and Zciko [13] oppose the most important cause of not using technology in classroom is not being qualified. As the result, traditional methodologies are being remained by instructors.

In order to increase practice, in the language, instructors have to bring a focus on making and planning learning environments technologically, Hartnell [14]. It is believed that computer assists all language learners and instructors to remove the obstacles on the way of language acquisition. Hence, there should be a severe attempt on removing some obstructions which is related to the lack of familiarity of instructors with the appropriate use of technology, computer programs. Sometimes they do not know about computer programs in order to help learners acquire new vocabularies.

Vocabulary Learning through Story retelling Approach

Another VLS which has been claimed to be an effective instructional strategy in English as a foreign language or English as a second language (ESL) classes is story retelling. Story retelling is meant the process by which the EFL / ESL learners repeat the story that has been learnt. Besides, story retelling approach is a post reading or listening process through which learners promote their comprehension of discourse by memorizing and rearranging what they have read or heard, Stoicovy [15]. As Deacon and Murphey [16] recommend in their study, one of the advantages of this approach is promoting EFL / ESL learners' grammatical structures, pronunciation, and glossary knowledge by endowing them with a variety of conversational topics. Similarly, Rachmawaty & Hermagustiana [17] found another benefit, as participants in their study progressed in retelling the story; they successfully used words different from those in the original text that had similar meanings.

Coupled with this, Rachmawaty and Hermagustiana [17] used the retelling technique to find out its effect on the students' speaking fluency and to know the strategies they used while retelling a story, they found that the students' vocabulary improved as well. The findings revealed that not only students are better able to sort out, put together, come to conclusions, and categorize information, but also they can also take a broad view and speak about ideas that do not exist in the story. This suggests strength of EFL learners' story retelling which is useful for the improvement of vocabulary achievement. The findings of this study confirm the effectiveness of this technique and are in line with the previous studies (Rachmawaty & Hermagustiana [17], Brandi-Muller [18], Scheinkman [19], Stoicovy [15], Deacon & Murphey [16], Lipson & Wixson [20], Gambrell, Koskinen, & Kapinas [21].

Weiss & Hamilton [22] also known as "Beauty and the Beast Storytellers," have been teaching children and adults to tell stories for many years. They suggest storytelling as a teaching tool for the following reasons:

1. Storytelling is the oldest form of education.
2. Stories are the way we store information in the brain, and go straight to the heart.
3. Telling and reading are different. Without the book as an obstruction, the teller stares right into the eyes of the audience and gestures, signs, facial expression, and body movements are free to use by the teller.
4. Listening to stories instills the love of language in children and encourages them to read, in the same way storytelling excites the imagination and thoughts. As scientist Albert Einstein alleged "imagination is more important than knowledge."
5. Stories teach lessons, desirable behaviors and strengthening character.
6. Storytelling develops listening skill. Concentration can be developed by storytelling; accordingly, stories act as a humanizing element. They help to work against the increasing emphasis on technology at home and in school.
7. Telling stories from around the world creates awareness and apprecia-

tion of different cultures, storytelling by instructors motivates students to tell stories as well.

In the same manner of other approaches, techniques and methods, story retelling has its own shortcoming which makes instructors to be more careful about implementing it in their classrooms; story retelling is generally deemed to be time-consuming and difficult, for this reason, it has not been commonly practiced in EFL/ESL classes, Palingo [23]. The main problem of using this practical technique is to be the large number of students in each class; therefore, it could be difficult to find time for each learner involving more actively in this method. Nevertheless, it is not impossible to remove this negative part of story retelling technique by reducing the number of the EFL / ESL learners in classrooms.

Vocabulary Learning through Games

Games can be applied in several ways and at different points in a lesson. Consequently, there is diverse game types designed to stimulate and enhance various aspects of language learning. Some authors such as Pham [24] suggest the following classification of games in EFL: 1) Structure games which provide experience of the use of particular patterns of syntax in communication. 2) Vocabulary games in which the learners' attention is focused mainly on words. 3) Spelling games. 4) Pronunciation games. 5) Number games. 6) Listen – and – do games 7) Games and writing 8) Miming and role play 9) Discussion games.

In the first place, as Yip and Kwan [25] exhibited in their study the main pro of this approach is that students preferred learning that is supported by educational games rather than traditional activity by lessons. In line with their research, EFL / ESL learners who were provided with games became more successful in learning new words compared to those who learned the same vocabulary through activity-based lessons. Therefore, instructors that condemn the insufficiency of the current strategies demanded by language teaching programs might be willing to set up or try new techniques where games could play a major role.

As Allen [26] points out, the use of word games to teach vocabulary does not mean or suggest pleasant ways of passing the time of class. An instructor's responsibility is not the entertainment of students, rather instructors are responsible for creating a constructive class environment, which promotes vocabulary items expansion, and a carefully selected game can assist the learners acquire words correctly and feel that certain words are important and necessary because without those vocabulary items, the intention of the game cannot be materialized. In that case, as Schultz& Fisher [27] advocated game playing is a popular way to engage learners in language learning. Prensky [28] designed twelve elements as to why games engage people. To name a few, games motivate players (to achieve goals), gratify the ego (when winning), are funs (through enjoyment and pleasure) and spark the players' creativity (to solve the game).

Surprisingly, the use of interactive games has impacted on the mode of teaching, Foreman, et al. [29]. According to Wood [30], it can be said another advantage of using learning games as a learning tool and it can be concluded that game-like formats could be more effective at capturing learners' attention than traditional media such as textbooks. Many experienced textbook and methodology manuals writers have argued that games are not just time-filling activities but have a great educational value. Purushotma [31] has suggested that games can be so highly motivating that they can even cause addictive manners. These compensations of games can aid educators create an enthusiastic, ready to learn, active and vigorous atmosphere in their classrooms. The main inspirational idea of this work , Bakar, et al [32]; Sahhuseyinoglu [33]; Bayirtepe and Tuzun [34]; Tuzun [35] is the fact that people feel better, get less tired, and are highly motivated when they do things they enjoy, such as playing games.

Another reason why games are often used in language classes is that they lower students' stress in the class. In conventional classes, a lot of stress put on students trying to master the target language can be easily seen. By the same token, Schultz and Fisher [27] said that stress is a major hindrance in language learning process. Learning language in traditional way is by its nature time consuming and stress provoking and raise the stress level to a point at which it interferes with student attention and efficiency and slowly weaken motivation. Relaxing learners by engaging them in stress-reducing task like games could be one method which has been developed to make students forget that they are in class. Since students know that they are playing games and want to communicate efficiently they do not worry about making mistakes and do not try to correct themselves in every single structure. As a result when students are free from concern, tension and pressure, their fluency and natural speaking styles can be flourished. As Schultz & fisher [27] claimed subsequently learners learn without realizing that they are learning.

Huang [36] came to the conclusion that the operation of certain psychological and intellectual factors may be encouraged by "learning through games" consequently, could facilitate communication heightened self-esteem, inspiration and spontaneity, reinforcing learning, improving inflection and building self-assurance. Besides all the advantages this approach has, its weakness can be: 1) discipline issues, learners may get extremely noisy; hence, playing games are joyful and entertaining by nature, it might be tough to put a scaffold based on the educational aim to control the class, novice instructors may have this problem in the early years of teaching. 2) Straying away from the basic purpose of the game - play activity, perhaps, due to inadequate rules instruction, resulting in playing too much and the lack of learning, in the first place, learners should be given this point that games are not just for passing the time pleasurably. Definitely it is a tutorial tool to facilitate language acquisition process. 3) Due to the fact that there are not many available games, and by repeating them all the time, EFL / ESL learners may become familiar with the games or boring, consequently, not get equally involved. 4) Some learners, especially teenagers, because of their attitudes and characteristics, may find games unnecessary and childish.

A Critical Comparison of the Three Methods

In this section, the implementation of story retelling with the CAVOCA and games approaches are compared from different perspectives such as improving speaking skill in EFL, decreasing anxiety and nervous tension in language acquisition process, etc. The emphasis in this comparison is on story retelling because of its magnificent effect on language skills (i.e. speaking, listening, reading and writing) and the ability of taking advantage of such skills. As already stated, words may function like a bridge between main language skills. From this viewpoint, the role of understanding the vocabulary's meaning comes to account. According to Blachowicz, Fisher, & Watts – Taffe [37], three factors cause difficulties in learning meanings of words such as learners' personalities, complexity levels of words, and feature words; on the other hand, the consequence of these vocabulary learning approaches on developing main skills in EFL contexts varies.

Compared with CAVOCA and vocabulary learning through games, according to Gambrell, Koskinen & Kapinus [21], "Retelling" is an effective instruction of strategy for enhancing the comprehension of proficient and less proficient reader because verbal reconstruction of text helps readers to organize and to deploy their processing capacity more successfully. In contrast, EFL / ESL learners should start reading short stories and literature; in order to be able to use story retelling. Here, getting habituated with the target language's culture and mentality is another significant advantage of this method lies. One advantage of reading literature texts based on a research by Pardede [38], is to supply authentic circumstance for processing new language. By the same token, stories include real examples of grammatical structures and lexical items. Reading text and stories (short or long) aid learners to comprehend the cultures, people, thoughts and philosophy of the target language is another important point about reading and understanding passages that gives more credits to "Story retelling" approach comparing with others. Consequently, reading text makes learners enthusiastic enough to retell the stories through learning vocabularies and improving speaking skill, whereas the VOCACA and Games approach methods are relatively poor in delivering these benefits to learners.

Another advantage of story retelling is the direct and instant feedback that it provides. In contrast with CAVOCA and games, Stoicovy [15] points out that based on several studies, retelling has positive influence in language learning as it promotes students' ability in rearranging information from the text that they have read. On the other hand, story retelling may help instructors as a precious assessment tool in evaluating learners' conception listening, speaking skills. As claimed by Slater [39] "retelling is an important skill often overlooked in regular reading instruction. Students' retelling gives instructors insight into their levels of language competence, comprehension, vocabulary items, and backdrop knowledge that they cannot give in the other two methods. As a matter of fact, story retelling ,the process by which a student listens to or reads a story and then summarize, or "retells" the story in his or her own words is a procedure that ties into these learning experiences and is an effective way to improve students' reading comprehension and consequently their speaking. In comparison, the two other methods, CAVOCA and games may not have strong effect on improving speaking skill.

Nevertheless, there are some critiques on this concept, O'Malley and Pierce, [40] argue that EFL / ESL learners must speak according to that story they had read or listened in this type of teaching speaking. Moreover, retelling story may be good for EFL students in their beginnings. So, this category is a closed assignment. Consequently, it might be assumed that retelling can also be used to determine students' understanding of story structure. As opposed to story retelling, games approach gains advantage in terms of proactively engagement in the learning process; Story retelling and CAVOCA by which learners acquire language intentionally, games provide language learning in an incidental manner. As a result, this leads to making learners concentrate more on learning for the reason that they do not feel they are forced to learn. In point of fact, the compensation of games according to Hansen [41], identically, they are highly motivating and amusing, and more opportunity can be given to shy learners to express their outlook and thoughts, so learners are not anxious about making mistakes, get ready to acquire new language psychologically and expressively as well, while we cannot observe this ability in story retelling method.

However, how to apply games in language learning program is a matter which must be taken into consideration. One weakness of this approach is although games are effective in cooperative learning new words; they cannot be successful if the instructor does not explain the tasks and roles of students clearly in playing games. Another critique upon this method is the limitations that are related to members' characters, using games in the classroom sometimes fails owing to the lack of cooperation among members of the class. Games have need of all learners' participation; For that reason, it is very important that learners have a cooperative attitude. It could be said it is the instructor's job to explain the rules clearly and let learners and prospect to learn, apply and to assess the English language in a pleasant atmosphere. In the event that, the goal of language learning is the communicating with people in real settings, CAVOCA and story retelling are somehow underprivileged in getting this vital end as these two methods do not require learners' contribution.

In spite of the above limits, compared with CAVOCA and story retelling, games due to their fun nature may remove psychological barriers which affect language learning process. It is obvious that games lower learners stress over language learning. In particular, language learning takes place in a stress-free environment and vocabulary learning games reduce the children negative stress. According to a study done by Crookal [42], games are advantageous at this point because they lessen apprehension, enhance positive outlook and improve self-assurance because learners are not afraid of punishment or criticism while practicing the target language freely, while CAVOCA and story retelling may not have strong influence in removing stress and concern in learning atmosphere.

CONCLUSIONS

It can be concluded that vocabulary acquisition strategies is one of the most important aspects of teaching language which must be taken into consideration more masterly by instructors in EFL / ESL classrooms. Since learners' English knowledge can be evaluated by finding out how well they use acquired vocabularies in real contexts, introducing and teaching vocabulary learning strategies, known as VLSs and approaches to learners can be considered as significant job for instructors. The author believes that through vocabulary, EFL / ESL learners can integrate listening; speaking, reading and writing skills together, therefore these skills could be improved by integrating relevant tasks in the second or foreign language acquisition process.

The prominent role of using technology in everyone's life is certainly clear while it can facilitate tasks such as language acquisition that considered difficult in the past. One of the innovated and updated techniques which is used in Iran is "Computer – assisted vocabulary learning" (CAVOCA) as it was discussed earlier, this method has this advantage of improving EFL / ESL learners' motivation, achievement and excitement in the realm of second or foreign language acquisition. Thus, the procedure of language learning can be accelerated. conversely, the most prominent issue is that by lack of using technology knowledge, mainly computer in classrooms the instructor from taking its advantages might be obstructed and as Zhao and Zciko, [13] has shown in his paper the primary cause of not being involved in using technology in classroom is not being taught. As the result, traditional tactics are being chosen to remain by instructors.

Therefore, there should be a serious effort on removing some obstructions which is related to the lack of familiarity of instructors with the appropriate use of technology, computer programs. Sometimes they do not know about computer programs in order to help learners acquire new vocabularies. The author believes that this drawback must not be highlighted since by training instructors to get this knowledge could be removed, nevertheless, these days in Iran; most of the instructors were trained how to use technology in their classrooms.

The second approach which was discussed in the critical review and is used as a practical method in most of EFL classrooms in Iran is vocabulary learning through story retelling. Based on Stoicovy [15] story retelling approach is a post reading or listening process through which learners promote their comprehension of discourse by memorizing and rearranging what they have read or heard. As it was mentioned earlier, instructors can promote learners' knowledge of grammatical structures, pronunciation, and vocabulary by providing them with a variety of conversational topics. According to studies which done by Rachmawaty and Hermagustiana [17], It can be closed that retelling technique effect on the students' speaking fluency and to know the strategies they used while retelling a story, they found that the students' vocabulary improved as well. The findings revealed that students are well able to organize, integrate, make inferences, and classify information.

Moreover, they can also generalize and relate ideas that do not exist in the given story. This suggests that EFL / ESL learners' story retelling approach is useful for the improvement of vocabulary achievement. On the other hand, the author took a closer look at the negative parts of this approach; while Palingo has publicized in his article story retelling is generally deemed to be time-consuming and complicated, it has not been extensive in EFL/ESL classrooms. Consequently, it could be non-manageable to find time for each learner involving more actively in this technique. With the aim of removing this problem and processing this approach more effectively, language training centers can reduce the number of the EFL / ESL learners in classrooms. The last technique which was considered in this article is vocabulary learning through games; it is employed for young learners in Iran, though. In view of the fact that language classrooms always are full of stress resulting in not using language skills more successfully, game playing may have a prominent role in reducing learners' stress and making them prepared to acquire language. Based on Wood [] the use of learning games as learning tool and game-like formats could be more effective at capturing learners' attention than traditional media such as textbooks, having well – chosen game regarding the educational purpose and the learners' level, can help instructors create an enthusiastic, ready to learn, active and vigorous atmosphere in their classes. The author believes this approach like any other approaches has its own unconstructive parts. Discipline issues, learners may get extremely vociferous, straying away from the basic purpose of the game - play activity, perhaps, due to inadequate rules instruction, resulting in playing too much and the lack of learning, already familiar or boring games and finding games unnecessary and childish by some learners, in particular adolescents as negative parts must be taken into account. The author comes to judge by having organized scaffold on games which explains how to play, time, make learners enthusiastic to play and control the class during using this method, these weak points might be eliminated.

REFERENCES

1. Hulstijn, J.H., & Laufer, B. (2001). Some empirical evidence for the involvement load hypothesis in vocabulary acquisition. Language Learning, 51, 539-558.
2. Rubin, J. (1975). What the 'good language learner' can teach us. TESOL Quarterly, 9, 41-51.
3. Hatch, E. and Brown, C. (1995). Vocabulary, semantics, and language education. Cambridge: Cambridge UP.
4. Laufer, B. (1990). Why are some words more difficult than others? Some intralexical factors that affect the learning of words. International Review of Applied Linguistics, 28, 293-307.
5. Rivers, W. (1983). Communicating naturally in a second lan guage. Cambridge: Cambridge University Press.
6. Wang, X. C. (2005, December). Digital photo journal project: Case study of technology integration in early childhood education. Invited presentation in the School of Early Childhood Education, East China Normal University, Shanghai, China.
7. Lu, F. L. (2010). English learners' incidental vocabulary acquisition in

the Video-based CALL program. Asian EFL Journal, 12(4).pp. 51-66.

8. Groot, P.J.M. (2000). Computer assisted second language vocabulary acquisition. Language Learning and Technology, 4(1), 60-81.
9. Kolich, E. M. (1991) Effects of computer-assisted vocabulary training on word knowledge. Journal of Educational Research, 84, 177-182.
10. Prichard, C. (2008). Evaluating L2 readers' vocabulary strategies and dictionary use. Reading in a Foreign Language Volume 20, No. 2.pp.216-231
11. Dehghani, A. P., Motamedi, A. & Mahbudi, A. (2011). Homework Assignment after EFL Beginners' Vocabulary Learning. US- China Foreign Language. Vol 9, (5). Pp. 331-338.
12. Pitler, H., Hubbell, E. R., Kuhn, M., & Malenoski, K. (2007). Using technology with classroom instruction that works. Alexandria, VA: Association for Supervision and Curriculum Development.
13. Zhao, Y., & Cziko, GA. (2001). Teacher adoption of technology: A perceptual control theory perspective. Journal of Technology and Teacher Education, 9(1), 5-30.
14. Hartnell-Young, E. (2006). Teachers Roles' and Professional Learning in Communities of Practice Supported by Technology in Schools. Journal of Technology and Teacher Education, 14(3), 461-480.
15. Stoicovy, C.E. (2004). Using retelling to scaffold English language for pacific island students. The Reading Matrix, 4, (1). Retrieved 25 December, 2011 from http://www.readingmatrix.com/articles/Stoicovy.
16. Deacon, B & Murphey, T. 2001. Deep Impact Storytelling. Forum, Vol. 39, No.4. Retrieved 16 April 2008 from http://exchanges.state.gov/forum/vols/vol39/no4/bio.
17. Rachmawaty, N. & Hermagustiana, I. (2010). Does retelling technique improve speaking fluency? TEFLIN Journal, 21(9), 1-8.
18. Brandi-Muller, J. (2005). Retelling stories. Retrieved 4 January, 2012 from http://www.colorincolorado.org/article/1 3282/
19. Scheinkman, N. (2004). Picturing a story. Teaching Pre K-8, 34(6), 58-59.
20. Lipson, M., & Wixson, K. (1997). Assessment and instruction 36 Laleh Kohandel Jahromi et al.: A Critical Review of Common Vocabulary Learning Strategies in Iranian EFL Classrooms of reading and writing disability. An interactive approach. New York: Addison-Wesley.
21. Gambrell, L.B., Koskinen, P.S. & Kapinus, B.A. (1991). Retelling and the reading.

22. Weiss, M. & Hamilton, M. (2011). Children tell stories: Teaching and using storytelling in the classroom. Retrieved 3 January, 2012 from www.beautyandthebeaststorytellers.com
23. Palingo, T (2003). Literature review of kindergarten story retelling. Retrieved from http://www.bridgew.edu/library/ca gs_projects/tpalingo/web%20page/conlitrev.htm
24. Pham, H. H. (2007). Communicative language teaching: Unity within diversity. ELT Journal, 61(3), 193-201.
25. Yip, F.W.M., and Kwan, A.C.M. (2006). Online vocabulary games as a tool for teaching and Burn & G. Schott (Eds.), Computer games: Text, narrative and play (pp. 119–148). Cambridge: Polity Press.
26. Allen, V.F. (1983). Techniques in teaching vocabulary. Oxford: Oxford University Press.
27. Schultz, M. and Fisher. A.. (1988). Interacting in the Language Classroom. Games for All Reasons. Massachusetts: Addison-Wesley Publishing Company.
28. Prensky, M. (2001). Digital game-based learning. New York: McGraw-Hill.
29. Foreman, J., Gee, J. P., Herz, J. C., Hinrichs, R., Prensky, M. & Sawyer, B. (2004). Game based learning: how to delight and instruct in the 21st century, Educause Review, 39(5), 50–66.
30. Wood, J. (2001) Can software support children's vocabulary development? Language Learning & Technology, 5(1), 166–201.
31. Purushotma, R. (2005). Commentary: You're not studying, you're just… Language Learning Technology, 9(1), 80-96.
32. Bakar. A, Tuzun. H, and Cagiltay. K. (2008). Students' opinions of educational computer game utilization: A social studies course case. H.U. Journal of Education, 35, 27- 37.
33. Sahhuseyinoglu, D. (2007). Educational games for developing critical thinking skills: Pre- Service English language teachers' views. Hacettepe University Journal of Education, 32, 266-273.
34. Bayirtepe, E. & Tuzun, H. (2007). The effects of game-based learning environments on students' achievement and self-efficacy in a computer course. H.U. Journal of Education, 33, 41-54.
35. Tuzun, H. (2006). Educational computer games and a case: Quest Atlantis. Hacettepe University Journal of Education, 30, 220-229.
36. Huang, H. Mi. (2000). Instructional technologies facilitating online courses. Educational Technology, 40 (4), 41-46.

37. Blachowicz, C. L. Z., Fisher, P., & Watts-Taffe, S. (2011). Teaching vocabulary: Leading edge research and instruction. In T. Rasinski (Ed.), Rebuilding the Foundation: Effective Reading Instruction for 21st Century Literacy (pp. 203-222). Bloomington IN: Solution Tree Press.
38. Pardede, P. (2011). Teaching short stories to teach language skills. Journal of English teaching. A Tri-Annual publication on the study of English language teaching, 1 (1). February, 2011. Christian University of Indonesia. Jakarta.
39. Slater, J. M. (2004). Retelling: the overlooked skill. Slater software, Inc. 351 Badger lane. Retrieved: March 7, 2013. From: www.suncastletech.com/presentations/RetellingOverlooked.pdf.
40. O'Malley, J. Michael and Lorraine Valdez Pierce. 1996. Authentic Assessment for English Language Learners. USA: Addison-Wesley Publishing Company.
41. Hansen, M.. (1994). The use of games for vocabulary presentation and revision. Vol 36 No 1, January, March 1998. Available at http://www.Esldepot.com/section.php/4/0.
42. D. Crookal (Ed.), Simulation, Gaming and Language Learning, (1990), New York: Newbury House.

Chapter 11

BUILDING BRIDGES. HOW SECONDARY SCHOOL PUPILS BRING THEIR INFORMAL LEARNING EXPERIENCES INTO A CONTENT AND LANGUAGE INTEGRATED (CLIL) CLASSROOM

Teppo Jakonen

University of Jyväskylä

ABSTRACT

This article explores how students' informal language learning experiences with English find their way into the formal context of content-based language teaching (CLIL). The analysis is focused on stretches of classroom talk in which native Finnish-speaking students draw on their expertise of English-language popular culture, and use their knowledge as a semiotic resource for producing various types of actions. Based on the data, it is argued that the organisation of peer group talk in the language classroom provides students with affordances for participation that are characteristically different from whole-class interaction. In this environment, global popular culture and conversational humour intertwine with the official business of learning. Moreover, the findings are used to problematize a monolithic conceptualisation of 'classrooms' as a formal context for language learning within the dichotomy of formal/informal. Instead, it is suggested that many interactional practices in classrooms, such as those described in this article, share similarities with everyday interaction, the pedagogic implications of which are briefly discussed.

INTRODUCTION

Research in the framework of second language acquisition (SLA) tends to make a distinction between naturalistic and instructed environments of language learning. This allows researchers to map specific contexts such as formal language and immersion classrooms, or study abroad stays (e.g. Collentine & Freed 2004) against a dichotomy of naturalistic/instructed to investigate whether participation in these contexts lead to different learning outcomes. Although there have been proposals to broaden the database of language learning contexts to include settings which do not necessarily involve the identities of 'learner' and 'teacher', along with calls for rethinking traditional SLA concepts and methods to better highlight the role of social context for learning (see e.g. Firth & Wagner 1997), the juxtaposition between instructed and natural settings remains an organising principle in the field. Notwithstanding the obvious merits of such a dichotomy, it nevertheless appears to have the effect of pigeon-holing studies under either of the two macro-contexts, which means the relationship between language instruction and its use outside the classroom is 'under-theorized' (Higgins 2009). Thus, the question how learners' participation in both formal and informal settings together contributes to the increase of their interactional repertoires, and more specifically, through what kinds of practices it happens, is currently largely unaddressed.

As English is a global language of popular culture, ample opportunities for learning it exist outside the formal classroom context, and teenagers in particular can sometimes be quite knowledgeable about films, music and computer games. Consider the following excerpt in which the teacher of an English-medium history classroom is instructing a quiz activity called Blockbusters1, which is to be used for revising previous course contents and involves the students answering questions designed by the teacher and gaining hexagon-shaped blocks after every correct answer. At this stage of the instruction-giving sequence, the teacher is explaining the game grid, which two students have just drawn on the blackboard.

Extract 1. Blockbusters

```
01 T       and there is a passage or pass.
02         SHIFTS GAZE TO THE STUDENTS
03         a:nd we're gonna play a game of blockbusters (0.5)
04         so that you answer questions=
05 Sakari  =gho[stbusters    ]
           {TURNS GAZE TO NEXT STUDENT, SMIRKS AFTERWARDS
06 T           [and (.) this] i-
07         >have you ever heard of blockbusters<
08 Sakari  [no]
09 T       [no] uh (.) ↑this is numbe-
10         team number one is on this side here?
```

As the teacher nominates the game to be played and begins to give instructions (lines 3-4), one of the students mentions Ghostbusters, a well-known film from the 1980s, in a turn that appears to be designed as a humorous commentary, or a 'toss-out' (see Aoki et al. 2006; Lehtimaja 2012: 185–190) to a fellow student based on the lexical similarity between the two popular culture items. The teacher, however, cuts off her instruction-giving immediately after the overlap, and instead attends to the student's turn as a possible expression of familiarity with the game by checking whether it is in fact known to the class (lines 6-7). Although the teacher addresses the whole class, Sakari, by virtue of having made the earlier commentary treats himself as the addressee and claims no knowledge of Blockbusters (cf. Sert 2011). What this achieves is that the humour sequence is abandoned and Sakari re-aligns with the teacher's game-instruction agenda, which continues from line 9 onwards.

This is a fairly straightforward example of how students may draw on language or knowledge of popular culture in a manner that is difficult to conceptualise using traditional SLA research terminology on interaction. For example, it does not quite fit the bill for corrective teacher feedback (Lyster & Ranta 1997; Lyster & Saito 2010) after a linguistically erroneous student response, or negotiation for meaning following non-comprehension of linguistic input (Long 1983, 1996; Varonis & Gass 1985; Gass et al. 2005). Rather, it seems that in this stretch of interaction popular culture is being brought into the classroom by both the student, who draws on his knowledge of cinema to entertain the class, and the teacher, who uses a popular game format to revise history with her class. Before the students' turn, Ghostbusters does not feature in this language learning environment, whereas afterwards it may be referred to and used for other social actions (even if it is not in this particular case).

Even if sequences such as extract 1 tend not to be analysed in mainstream SLA research on classroom interaction, it does not mean 'learning' would not be taking place in and through such sequences. The kind of co-ordination of diverse resources, or affordances (van Lier 2000, 2002), upon which the teacher and the student are drawing forms the basis for some accounts of human learning and cognition (e.g. Hutchins 1995: 287–316; Churchill 2007). Moreover, although the mechanisms through which language learning in one context translates into proficiency and knowledge beyond the original domain are considerably less well known and studied in SLA, they do appear under the lens of learning transfer research (cf. Lobato 2006; Marton 2006). Thus, the aim of this paper is to provide an initial exploration of how pupils in classroom use their previous informal learning experiences as a semiotic resource in a formal learning context. In other words, the article probes how 'bridge-building' between everyday life and formal instruction may be achieved in interaction. I use interactional data from the context of Content and Language Integrated (CLIL) teaching in Finland, a society where students have a decent degree of access to English language outside formal education (see Leppänen & Nikula 2007; Leppänen et al., 2011). Drawing on conversation analytic methodology (CA), my focus is on analysing sequences of talk where pupils make clear that they are bringing into classroom interaction either language or content knowledge they have previously acquired outside the classroom. These can be used in my data to conduct a variety of social actions, such as language play, affiliative teasing and accounting for knowing.

Far from offering a definitive list of all language functions and social actions for which the focal practice can be used, it is nevertheless hoped that the approach will further our understanding of the interactional organisation of language classrooms, as well as contribute to research on language learning affordances by problematizing the notion of 'environment', and the dichotomy between instructed and non-instructed contexts.

BACKGROUND

The dichotomous distinction in language learning research between non-instructed and instructed learning environments (Freeman 2007: 896) echoes a more general dichotomy found in education between informal and formal settings (Eurostat 2006), in which different learning activities are seen to be taking place. In SLA, the distinction is essentially based on differing conditions of exposure to the target language between the settings (Howard 2011: 71–72), being related to yet another conceptual distinction between acquiring a language in naturalistic environments and learning it in instructed settings (Krashen 1976). In this framework, foreign language classrooms, or at home (AH) settings (Collentine & Freed 2004), fall under the heading of 'instructed environments', and stay-abroad periods, or growing up in a bilingual family, are seen as naturalistic settings. Accordingly, previous studies in classroom contexts have shed light on how teacher-student exchanges of corrective feedback, such as recasts (Lyster & Ranta 1997; Lyster 2004), negotiation for meaning (Foster 1998), or form-focused episodes in meaning-oriented classrooms (Spada 1997) have consequences for students' subsequent learning of the focal language items, as set by the teachers. Recently, research has begun probing the role of informal contexts in order to investigate what kinds of resources everyday interaction provides for language learning (Kääntä et al. 2013; Lilja 2010; Piirainen–Marsh & Tainio 2009a, 2009b), but any individual studies have a tendency to examine speakers separately in either informal or formal context instead of probing how participation in different types of speech events might work together to produce learning (although see Sahlström 2011; Slotte-Lüttge, Pörn & Sahlström 2012, as examples of studies that follow speakers in a variety of contexts).

At the same time as more research on language learning is being conducted outside classrooms, these informal contexts have also undergone a change, which is especially salient with English in the Finnish society. This change is part of globalisation-related processes, the effects of which for languages are being probed within a new 'sociolinguistics of globalization' (Blommaert 2010), which has described how the English language is involved with translocal and transcultural flows (Pennycook 2006: 5–8), largely mediated by new technology and various media. As a consequence, English has become more widely accessible in Finland, where survey evidence shows that younger cohorts have plenty of contact with English in their free time, often in the form of playing video games, chatting online, or interacting with electronic media (Leppänen et al. 2011).

Such use of English outside the traditional learning context of a language classroom – also known as 'extramural English' (Sundqvist 2009) – has been presented as a possible reason for why, contrary to other foreign languages in Finland, Finnish boys nowadays tend to do better at the English-language matriculation exam, which is sat at the end of upper secondary school. For example, in 2009 and 2010, the percentage of male students receiving any one of the top three grades (laudatur, eximia, or magna) was higher than the equivalent percentage of female candidates (Ylioppilastutkintolautakunta 2011a: 41–43, 2011b: 43–45). According to a popular lay theory, boys play more computer games, which, as it involves the use of English, increases their language proficiency (see e.g. Savon Sanomat 2012). In Finland, there is some survey evidence linking the amount of time spent playing video games and secondary school grades in English (Uuskoski 2011); moreover, in Sweden, which is in many ways a comparable society to Finland, Sundqvist (2009) found a significant positive correlation ($p < .01$) between time spent on outside-the-classroom activities involving English and vocabulary size as well as oral proficiency in secondary school students.

Differing from a somewhat simplified view of context as an environment where certain interactions takes place, conversation analytic work on (language) learning has highlighted the ways in which contributions to interaction are both context-shaped and context-renewing. This line of research emphasises the contingencies for possible learning of local, sequentially-developing interaction (see e.g. Hellermann & Doehler 2010; Lee 2010; Mori 2007) instead of considering context as an a priori, independent macro-level variable, or 'something only embedding a learning event' (Martin 2009: 134). Following such work, this article wishes to problematize a conceptualisation of 'formal' and 'informal', or 'naturalistic' and 'instructed' contexts as given states of affairs, and focus more on what kinds of contextual features students make relevant when producing action in classroom. Theoretically, it draws on the notions of contextual configuration (Goodwin 2000) and affordances, the latter having originally been introduced by James Gibson (1979) and later utilised by Leo van Lier in his ecological theory of language learning to refer to the relationship between an organism and the environment as an alternative for linguistic input. According to van Lier (2000: 253, 2002: 147, 2004: 91–95), the environment is full of language in the form of 'pre-signs' and 'action potential' that provide opportunities for individuals to relate to the world once they are perceived.

Although affordances in van Lier's work refer to a relationship between what appears as a 'fixed' environment and the language user, the concept has also been interactionally elaborated. Drawing on conversation analytic work, Forrester (1999) argues that talk contains important affordances which make possible the co-ordination of human action. As opposed to 'natural constructs' (ibid., p. 41), these social affordances are in the form of sequential and structural properties of talk for accomplishing talk itself and its communicative aims. To give an example, by virtue of the turn-taking organisation, speakers are able to recognise typical first pair-part actions, such as questions and invitations, to be making relevant a particular range of participation categories, such as answering or accepting in this case. Thus, when speaking a language we do not know particularly well, we may still be able to understand that our co-conversants are asking a question from us even if we do not understand the exact words being conveyed. It is in this sense that the contingencies of talk, together with physical properties of the environment, can be seen to afford subsequent action and participation.

Examples of affordances, as discussed by van Lier tend to at least implicitly refer to situations in which one single organism, be it a human being or an animal, is conducting some sort of action on its own in the 'environment'. However, often when we do something, we do it together with other humans, whether that something is gossiping, watching a football match or teaching a foreign language in classroom. It is in this sense that interaction is the 'primordial site of sociality'(Schegloff 1992) through which social life and its institutions, such as formal education, are enacted. To this end, another perspective on how the environment figures into the organisation of multi-party human action is offered by Charles Goodwin (2000), who argues that speakers build action by continuously co-ordinating multiple semiotic fields, i.e. 'different kinds of sign phenomena instantiated in diverse media' (p. 1490). As they do this, they construct specific contextual configurations of semiotic fields which are the result of the speakers' orientation at any given moment in time – or their 'perceptual world' (p. 1503) – which Goodwin sees as the starting point for research on action-production. Although the two frameworks for human action in the environment discussed above certainly contain differences, there is common ground too. For example, Goodwin's (2000) account resonates with van Lier's (2000) view on affordances being created through an organism's perception, although it is not a point that Goodwin (2000) himself makes. A clear difference, however, seems to lie in the conceptualisation of 'environment': Goodwin (2000: 1519), by stating that 'context is not...presupposed', and Forrester (1999), by focusing on structural properties of talk, emphasise the role of interactants in constructing the specific context which can then afford action. Van Lier, however, seems to consider 'environment' as a more separate construct from the organism, as opposed to something that the organism can shape, although in later writings he (2004: 94–95) recognises that talk between language users and 'words' can become affordances. Drawing on Goodwin (2000) in particular, this article describes how students in a bilingual classroom actively construct their interactional context in which they perform particular actions by introducing semiotic fields that are not 'present' in the classroom environment before they bring them in. The argument is that when students are bringing into classroom language from their free time, they are making relevant experiences and domains that do not necessarily involve 'being a student', but instead portray the speakers as competent users of English-language entertainment industry.

Lastly, although research focused on learning in classroom interaction, both SLA and other paradigms, generally treats teacher-student exchanges as possible triggers for subsequent learning – whether 'learning' is conceptualised using the metaphor of acquisition or participation (Sfard 1998) – which can then be supported by some sort of evidence from a later point in time, the focus of this article is somewhat different. My claim is not so much that interactions such as excerpt 1 would be clearly definable moments where somebody begins to learn something, as implied by research on the acquisitional merits of corrective feedback by teachers. Instead, I view them as having more to do with previous learning experiences having created possibilities for action-production in a new context at a later point of time. Such connection-making across time and space can then be seen as instances of 'doing learning transfer' (Lobato 2006; Marton 2006), rather than the start of a completely new learning trajectory from scratch. Being a complex interactional environment, not all the actions produced in the language classroom making use of previous experiences necessarily orient to learning – the playful remark in extract 1 being a case in point. Even an explicit orientation to learning in students' group talk is often embedded in other activities, such as doing humour, which is in many ways similar to everyday conversation (see e.g. Kääntä et al., 2013). This discrepancy between the official business of classrooms – i.e. the production of knowledge and learning – and the often humorous language functions which students come across in their free time may be why it is sometimes suggested that the knowledge these two settings produce are somehow incompatible, or, as van Lier (2002: 158) puts it, the everyday knowledge is 'not "legitimate" in the language classroom'. However, as the data reported in this paper suggests, the 'everyday' is there, and it is being used by the students for a variety of purposes.

DATA AND METHOD

The data used in this article are video-recorded history lessons taught through English to 14–15-year-old students at a lower secondary school in Finland.2 The lessons represent an elective module that was offered as part of the school's bilingual programme to native Finnish-speaking students, taught by an experienced native Finnish teacher who is also fluent in English. During the course, the students were sitting in five fairly permanent groups of three or four students at each table, where they would work on their individual and group tasks as well as participate in regular teacher-led lesson activities. Both English and Finnish were used in the classroom: most of the time, the teacher maintained a monolingual English-only norm in the whole-class talk, however, the students would also use their first language, Finnish, in group talk alongside English.

The lessons were recorded with three classroom cameras and portable voice recorders at each table in order to capture students' group talk as fully as possible. From a database of 16 lessons, a loosely-defined collection was created where students appear to be using 'informal English'. From this collection approximately 30 cases were selected where speakers make explicit that they are using either language or knowledge that originates in popular culture. These interactions form the basis of this article.

The data extracts presented in this paper have been transcribed and analysed using conversation analytic (CA) methodology (see ten Have 2007 for an introduction). In addition to a standard Jeffersonian notation, the transcripts either verbally describe or illustrate through sketch drawings based on video screenshots those embodied actions which the speakers are treating as relevant for the on-going interaction (see Appendix for the transcript symbols used). Moreover, turns that contain Finnish language units have been idiomatically translated into English.

ANALYSIS

This article is concerned with sequences of talk in which students in an

English-medium classroom bring into classroom interaction language or knowledge from the domain of popular culture (such as films, music, etc.). Although my interest in analysing connections between formal and informal is somewhat broader, the analysis is limited to sequences in which students make the connection to informal language learning domain clear to other speakers, so that they hearably orient to a mutual shift in the current contextual configuration of semiotic fields (Goodwin 2000). This means that something in the interactional context is perceived in such a way that the introduction of the new language or knowledge is a possible and meaningful next action. In my data, these sequences tend to be quite playful and occur in group talk, often during task boundaries. As we shall see in this section, the language that students introduce into interaction can be used to do a variety of social actions, including, but not limited to, language play, affiliative teasing and accounting for knowing.

Using an English-Language song to do Affiliative Teasing

Excerpt 2 illustrates how students in a bilingual classroom may draw on their knowledge of popular culture to do teasing, in a manner similar to everyday interaction. It takes place after the students have arrived to the classroom, and are seated at their table having tea (as was customary in this particular class once a week) before the official lesson begins. One of the students, Konsta, has taken a fair amount of sugar lumps in his tea, which he announces to others at line 1 (näistä, 'these'). This gets a response from Mauri, who initiates a somewhat jocular teasing sequence, which culminates in a song about Spider-pig.

Extract 2. Spider-pig Konsta's

```
01 Konsta  toivottavasti mää en liikaa innostu näistä
           I hope I won't get too excited by these
02 Mauri   no e:thän sää.
           well no you wouldn't
03 Konsta  mm £hmhm[hm£
04 Mauri           [sää nyt jo juokset <seini[lle> ]
                   you're already bouncing off the <walls>
05 Juuso                                     [£hhh£]
06 Riku                                      [£hhh£]
07 Konsta                                    [£mhmh]mh£
08         [melkee.
            almost
09 Mauri   [♪spider pig spider pig does what[ever a spider pig does= ]
10 Riku                                     [♪ever a spider pig does=]
11 Mauri   [=can he swing (.) from a web (.) no he cannot=]
12 Riku    [=can he swing (.) from a web (.) no he can't =]
13 Mauri    [=♪he's a pig look o:ut he's a spider pig♪]
14 Riku     [=he's a pig look o:ut he's a spider pig♪ ]
```

Konsta's turn at line 1 conveys a possibility that something might happen as a result of his having all that sugar, and at the same time, makes him the centre of the interaction. He declares this possible course of events as undesirable, which, at line 2, receives a response that lexically appears to affiliate with Konsta's stance (no e:thän sää, well no you wouldn't). However, Mauri's turn is prosodically exaggerated; there is a marked stress on the first syllable of the word 'e:thän', making the turn hearable as an ironic statement, a mock-affiliation with Konsta's stance, which projects the beginning of a teasing sequence.

How do the speakers achieve this? The first two turns both contain off-record markers, which are regularly used to signal turns as doing teasing (Keltner et al. 2001). By describing a state of affairs that is generally perceived as positive (i.e. being excited) as something undesirable, Konsta indicates that nonliteral interpretations may apply to his turn. Mauri's turn at line 2, on the other hand, achieves 'off-recordness' by elongating the first vowel in the negation word (e:thän) as well as stressing the word-initial syllable. In terms of the sequential organisation, the evolving tease in excerpt 2 begins with – as teases in everyday interaction regularly do – a second position response to a previous turn that contains 'minor conversational transgressions' (Drew 1987). In this case, Konsta has made himself the centre of the attention for the group by toying with the idea of a forthcoming sugar-rush.

At line 3, Konsta receives the first teasing turn and goes along with it by providing a laughter particle, towards the end of which Mauri goes further in his jocular mockery (Haugh 2010) by delivering a blatantly exaggerated assessment of Konsta's current action (juokset seinille, bouncing off the walls). Interestingly, Mauri's playful assessment 'juokset seinille' (literally 'running on the walls') is not quite as formulaic as 'hyppiä seinille' (literally 'jump on the walls') would be in Finnish. Nevertheless, it is a typical tease insofar as it is 'recognizable as an exaggerated or extreme version' (Drew 1987) of the previous action. The last word of the turn is uttered more slowly, which makes it more salient than its environment. This second teasing turn is treated as humorous by the two other students at the table (lines 5–7), and Konsta, who plays along with the tease by accepting the assessment at line 8. As no-one else self-selects to take a turn, Mauri continues the teasing activity by switching from talk to singing at line 9. The song he initiates is a verbatim representation of the song Spider-pig, which features in the Simpsons Movie, and which itself is a parody version of the original Spiderman theme.3 Crucially, in order to be able to conduct the action this double-layered intertextual reference is doing – i.e. teasing – and be recognisable to the speakers as such, the song has to be part of a shared repertoire. And indeed, as Riku joins in the song at line

10, the duo proceeds quite fluently till the end of the sequence. What are the interactional affordances, or contingencies, that make the introduction of Spider-pig, a non-present semiotic field, relevant to the unfolding activity? By beginning the song immediately after his teasing assessment, Mauri makes it part of the humorous frame (Boxer & Cortés-Conde 1997) that has been set up. This sequential juxtaposition of the assessment turn and the song lyrics thus builds a similarity between Spider-pig, the protagonist of the song, and Konsta. That is, the song is designed to be heard as a song about Konsta. This connection begins to be established by the lexical choices of the assessment turn (line 4), which resonate with a scene in the Simpsons Movie in which Homer walks the pig along the ceiling in their house, which is not quite 'bouncing off the walls' but a comparable course of actions.

To summarise, extract 2 describes the students exploiting their cinema knowledge to perform a song to do affiliative teasing. Although classroom research tends to predominantly see students as 'learners', playful and teasing language use have an important role in the maintenance of the social relations in the classroom, as illustrated by Lehtimaja (2012: 128–139) in the context of Finnish as a second language teaching. Here, executing the song in English involves an orientation to other speakers not only as competent users of the language but also as aware of the intertextual references being made.

Drawing on Computer Games for Knowledge Construction

As suggested by Pennycook (2006: 6), the global transcultural flows involve the appropriation and use of English to construct and refashion various identities and imagined communities in a plethora of contexts. In the language classroom, knowledge of English that is acquired in an informal context, as opposed to being a result of conscientious 'studying', may be used to make relevant the kinds of identities which are favourable to social relations among peers. To illustrate this, consider the following extract in which three students are working independently on a written task when Inka misreads aloud a text that is somewhat illegibly printed (line 1).4 Consequently, she pronounces the word 'dagger' as 'dogger', which becomes a source of knowledge management in the ensuing interaction, as the students first resolve which word the text actually contains, and then establish a local meaning for 'dagger'.

Extract 3. Dagger

```
01 Inka     no s:chool-ar (.) shall wear a (.)
02          dogger or any other weapon ((READS ALOUD))
03 Susanna  dagger
04 Inka     QUICK GLANCE TO SUSANNA, THEN SHIFTS GAZE TO TEXT
05 Sakari   dogger (0.6) [dog
06 Inka                  [no täällä lugee
                          well it says here
07 Sakari   se [o dagger
            it is dagger
08 Inka        [oho
                whoops
09 Susanna  yes but it is (.) spelled like <dagger>
                      {INKA LEANS CLOSE TO THE TEXT
10          (0.8)
11 Inka     dagge:r
12 Susanna  [(yes)]
13 Inka     [onks ] se ↑dogger vai (.) [(dogger)] (.) [vai dagger]
            is it      dogger or        (dogger)     or dagger
14 Susanna                             [dagger  ]
15 Sakari                              [dagger  ] (.) da[gger    ]
16          <da[ggeri> ]
17 Inka        [what is] a dagge::r
               {GAZE TOWARDS SAKARI; SHIFT TO SUSANNA
18 Susanna  it is an (.) [err (.) th]at kind of,
19 Sakari                [knife     ]
                         {'STABS' WITH RIGHT HAND
20 Inka     [(net) ]
21 Susanna  [knife,] (0.4) err, (0.8) they-
22          there are err that [kind   of    in      R:unesca]pe
                                                {GLANCES AT SAKARI
23 Inka                        [>meat knife< (.) >meat knife<]
24          (2.0)
25 Susanna  I wouldn't know [it if I would not have not] err,
26 Inka                     [r::::::↑u↓ne:::           ]
                                             {GAZE TO TEXT
27 Susanna  played Runescape
```

As Inka has finished reading the text aloud, Susanna delivers an overt correction (line 3) of the former's pronunciation by uttering the noun 'dagger' with no explanation. The third member of the group, Sakari, also orients to 'dogger' by repeating it and engaging in a word association play (dogger-->dog). Inka then refuses Susanna's claim of knowing the pronunciation of the word better than her by making the text relevant to the interaction and using it as an epistemic authority (line 6). At this stage, there exists a 'reality disjuncture' (Pollner 1987), as the speakers have two competing versions of 'the objective world', i.e. whether 'dagger' or 'dogger' is the appropriate part of the sentence Inka has just read aloud. As Sakari aligns with Susanna to maintain 'dagger' as the correct word, Inka delivers the particle oho (line 8), which can be used to display surprise in Finnish (VISK § 1218), and which here – together with Inka's gaze being fixed on the text – appears to be 'doing noticing'. This action, together with Susanna's turn-initial yes but at line 9, which responds to Inka's claim that the text says 'dogger' (line 6), and which acknowledges the possibility of incorrect spelling being the reason behind the confusion, works to repair the disjuncture in the speakers' conflicting versions of reality and sustain the 'mundane reason' (Pollner 1987). The repair of the reality disjuncture manifests itself in Inka's downgrading of her epistemic stance (Heritage 2012) regarding the 'correct' form of the word in the text from line 6 to line 13, as she uses an alternative question format to request from the two other speakers whether the word in the text is 'dogger' or 'dagger', thereby positioning herself as unknowing and the others as possible knowers. Susanna and Sakari align with the initiated information-seeking activity by providing 'knowing' answers precisely at the point when Inka is projected to utter the 'correct' version of the word (dagger) over lines 14-15. Sakari makes the disputed word conform to Finnish morphological system by adding a word-final vowel to it at line 13 (see Pitkänen-Huhta 2008 for the same practice in EFL context).

At this stage, the speakers have come to an agreement that the illegibly written word in the text is 'dagger', not 'dogger'. As Susanna and Sakari have been established as knowledgeable speakers regarding daggers, Inka presents yet another information request at line 17, switching the code to English to enquire what the word means.5 Again, both speakers co-operatively construct an answer that claims to be knowledgeable. Susanna begins a turn (line 18), which breaks off and is marked with non-lexical perturbation err, something regularly used to show that a word search is on-going (M. H. Goodwin & C. Goodwin 1986; Helasvuo et al. 2004). This is attended to by Sakari, who provides a synonym (knife) for daggers at line 19, coupled with an embodied stabbing action, at a syntactically appropriate position with regard to Susanna's turn. Susanna then incorporates 'knife' into her phrasal response, and elaborates the definition of 'dagger' as a knife by saying they are the kinds of knives found in Runescape, an online role-playing fantasy game (lines 21-22). This action treats the semiotic field of computer games as relevant and essential to an understanding of what daggers are. Interestingly, the only time Susanna lifts her gaze from the desk is when she does this, as she uses it to address Runescape to Sakari, the other 'knower' in the group. This, and the later explicit account for knowing dagger at lines 25 and 27 on the basis of having played this particular game, may be ways of re-claiming epistemic primacy (Heritage & Raymond 2005) after the previous word search sequence.

Both Runescape and Spider-pig were within a shared territory of knowledge (Heritage 2012) between the students in question, insofar as the turns which used these semiotic fields were not only designed to treat these items of popular culture as unproblematic and familiar to the recipients, but were also received as such. Whereas Spider-pig was used to do teasing, Runescape was employed in matters related to knowing. In conversation, speakers not only display what they know and how they came to know it (see e.g. Glenn & LeBaron 2011; Heritage 2012; Sidnell 2012), but they may also manage issues of (classroom) social order, as illustrated in excerpt 3: in her account for knowing the word 'dagger' (lines 25, 27), Susanna treats her knowledge as a by-product of gaming, as opposed to owing to course books or other school texts. Treating the domain of gaming as a legitimate source of knowledge involves the mobilisation of out-of-school experiences, which may mitigate the risks of knowing 'too much' in the classroom, and of being perceived as a 'teacher's pet' or a 'swot' as a result.

Using Knowledge of Films to Explain an Unknown Word

The previous extracts have shown how students introduce semiotic fields (Goodwin 2000) that originate in popular culture into bilingual classroom interaction in a way that treats these fields as legitimate and shared sources of knowledge for the talk at hand. The final data extract describes how this knowledge may also be used by the teacher as a pedagogical device aimed at building connections between students' experiences in the everyday domain. It shows a situation in which a student (Konsta), who is not seated in the focal group, has been nominated to read aloud a text describing how Yorkshire puddings were cooked in Stuart time England. As the student is reading the text, teacher's gaze is on the overhead projector screen on which the text is also displayed. After the read-aloud is completed, the teacher checks whether the class understands a word ('rotating spit') which is mentioned in the description, and goes on to explain it by drawing on students' presumed knowledge of films.

As the read-aloud comes to an end, the teacher changes the focus of the activity from describing Stuart time food to explaining a possibly unfamiliar word. By addressing the class and checking whether they have understood 'rotating spit' over lines 6-8, she makes it a learning object (Lee 2010), and initiates a teaching action. This action orients to the previous cut-off and the subsequent 1.5 second pause (lines 1-2) in the student's read-aloud before he uttered the target word, which in itself was delivered at a slower pace than the surrounding talk, as being indicative of comprehension trouble.

The teacher's comprehension check invites an epistemic display from the students. More specifically, it calls for a display of a whether or not type of understanding (Koole 2010) of the word 'rotating spit' in this particular context, which the teacher constructs by attending to the overhead projector display of the text at line 8. At this stage, Inka provides an embodied claim of understanding (Mondada 2011: 543–544; see also Sacks 1992: 137–150, for the difference between claims and demonstrations) by nodding, being one of the two students in the classroom who visibly do this sequentially preferred action. These two claims are, however, not treated as sufficient evidence of the understanding of the whole class of 'rotating spit', as the teacher launches an explanation sequence at line 11, whereby she defines the problematic item using talk and gesture, as well as by drawing on the students' putative knowledge of films. This kind of framing of a learning episode as building upon something previously occurred can be seen as a way of producing learning transfer in the classroom (Engle 2006) by making opportunities to bring in everyday experiences.

Extract 4. Pirates of the Caribbean

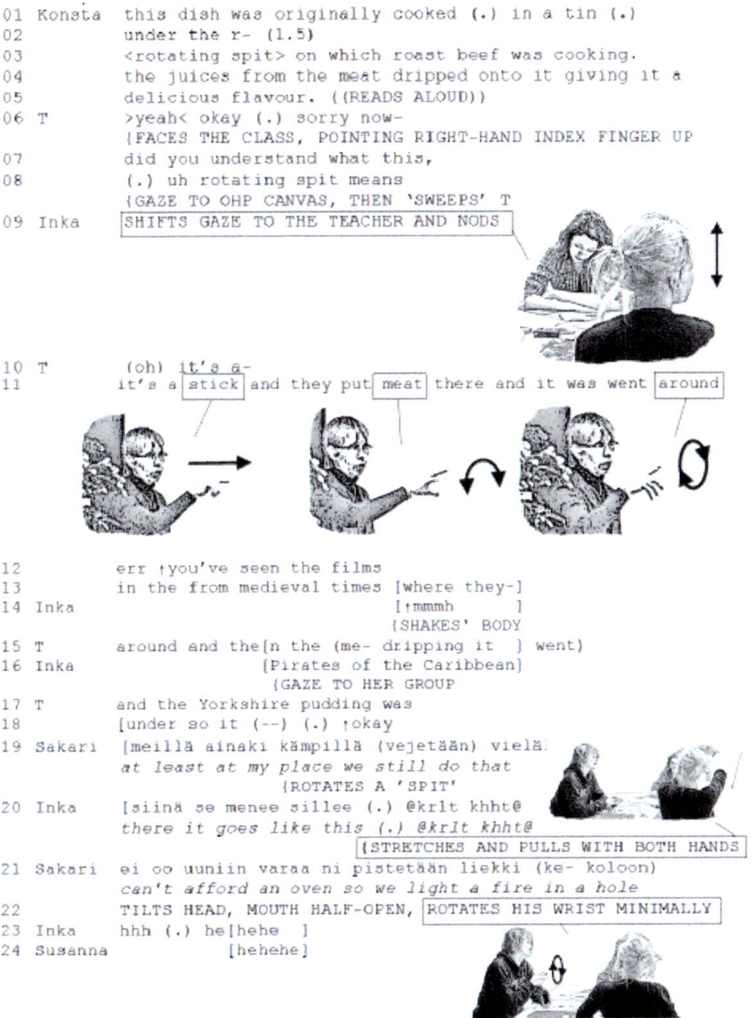

```
01 Konsta  this dish was originally cooked (.) in a tin (.)
02         under the r- (1.5)
03         <rotating spit> on which roast beef was cooking.
04         the juices from the meat dripped onto it giving it a
05         delicious flavour. ((READS ALOUD))
06 T       >yeah< okay (.) sorry now-
           {FACES THE CLASS, POINTING RIGHT-HAND INDEX FINGER UP
07         did you understand what this,
08         (.) uh rotating spit means
           {GAZE TO OHP CANVAS, THEN 'SWEEPS' T
09 Inka    SHIFTS GAZE TO THE TEACHER AND NODS
10 T       (oh) it's a-
11         it's a stick and they put meat there and it was went around
12         err ↑you've seen the films
13         in the from medieval times [where they-]
14 Inka                               [↑mmmh      ]
                                      {SHAKES' BODY
15 T       around and the[n the (me- dripping it  ] went)
16 Inka                  [Pirates of the Caribbean]
                          {GAZE TO HER GROUP
17 T       and the Yorkshire pudding was
18         [under so it (--) (.) ↑okay
19 Sakari  [meillä ainaki kämpillä (vejetään) vielä]
           at least at my place we still do that
                          {ROTATES A 'SPIT'
20 Inka    [siinä se menee sillee (.) @krlt khht@
           there it goes like this (.) @krlt khht@
                                {STRETCHES AND PULLS WITH BOTH HANDS
21 Sakari  ei oo uuniin varaa ni pistetään liekki (ke- koloon)
           can't afford an oven so we light a fire in a hole
22         TILTS HEAD, MOUTH HALF-OPEN, ROTATES HIS WRIST MINIMALLY
23 Inka    hhh (.) he[hehe  ]
24 Susanna           [hehehe]
```

Making 'rotating spit' an object of learning and relating the subsequent explanation to the semiotic field of films have created an affordance for the students to relate to, and indeed, Inka takes this up and introduces the film

Pirates of the Caribbean in the interaction (lines 14, 16). This is not designed to be a contribution to the teacher-led whole-class discussion, but rather a commentary on the topic of teacher's turn, addressed to her peer-group. After PoC has been made part of the contextual configuration of this group's talk, both Inka and Sakari do a rotating gesture but for different purposes: Inka appears to demonstrate how a massive spit was rotated in the film (line 20), whereas Sakari launches a self-denigrating mockery (Boxer & Cortés-Conde 1997) by telling a story of how rotating spits are still used in his home (line 19). This culminates in a somewhat unenthusiastic version of the teacher's original gesture, in which Sakari minimally rotates his wrist keeping the rest of his body unmoved (line 21) and adopting a very particular facial expression to entertain the other group members. Both Sakari and Inka thus relate in different ways to the same affordance for learning created by the teacher, which demonstrates the complex nature of interaction in classroom, particularly in interaction between students.

This section has investigated empirically how knowledge of English-language popular culture can be used for action-construction in content-based language instruction. Most of the time, references to popular culture are made relevant in students' talk to their peers, which is not necessarily preoccupied with 'learning', but often orients to social relations in the classroom. Nevertheless, as the final two extracts demonstrate, informal, out-of-school contexts can also be attended to for knowledge construction, not only in group talk, but also by the teacher in order to provide ways for the students to relate the pedagogic content to their everyday experiences. As extracts 3 and 4 illustrate, a focus on knowledge construction or learning does not mean joking and humour would necessarily be set aside, but rather playful undertones may provide a lamination to interactions which deal with the official business of classrooms.

DISCUSSION

This article has aimed to provide an initial, interactionally-grounded exploration of how everyday experiences with the target language may be used as a semiotic resource for producing action in the formal learning context of a bilingual classroom. The analysis has focused on sequences of talk where students make clear that they are bringing into classroom interaction either 'language chunks' or content knowledge they have previously acquired outside the classroom, usually in the form of intertextual references to popular culture. This involves a reconfiguration of the context to include new, non-present semiotic fields (Goodwin 2000) into interaction. Sequences involving this particular practice often have playful undertones, and as I have shown, are vehicles for various action categories, such as teasing and mockery, language play, as well as accounting for knowing something. In the data reported here, these turns appear not to be directed at the teacher but instead occur in group talk when the teacher is not present in the interaction (extracts 2 and 3), or are used to comment on whole-class talk to fellow students (1, 4). In this sense, extract 1, in which a student addresses Ghostbusters to another student is an interesting case, as it permeates the boundary between whole-class and peer talk: the teacher hears the comment and picks it up in her game-instruction. At the same time, it is the only extract in which the action (a humorous 'toss-out' attending to lexical similarity of two items) being done by the student is not recognised and aligned with by the teacher, who instead carries on with the game-instruction. It seems, therefore, that in this institutional context, the organisation of group talk offers a possibility to use a foreign language in a way that is not readily available in whole-class interaction, which appears to be reserved for more serious business. From a pedagogical viewpoint, it is important to be aware that these opportunities exist in content and language integrated (CLIL) classrooms, as proficiency and participation in what closely remind everyday interactional practices may be left unrecognised by teachers and exams in programmes which privilege academic genres of language use.

Besides describing a particular classroom practice in students' interaction, the aim of this article has been to problematize static notions of 'learning environment' and 'affordances' in a bilingual classroom context by analysing interactions which raise the question what exactly the configuration of a particular formal learning 'environment' is. As opposed to taking context as a given state of affairs in which affordances can be perceived, the analysis suggests context is something the speakers create in interaction by drawing on various semiotic resources (Goodwin 2000), some of which need not even be physically present in the location. It is in this sense that the particular learning context created by students and the teacher is a members' concern, or 'a result of our interpretation of that place', as suggested by Pennycook (2010: 2). As such, any particular 'formal' learning context may well involve the kind of language and topics, as well as patterns of turn-taking, which we might habitually associate with the 'informal' domain, such as films, gaming or everyday conversation, if they represent valid resources for the speakers to do specific actions. This raises an important question to which extent language learning processes – or conversely, social actions which are not about learning – in 'informal' and 'formal' settings may actually have something in common (Rampton 1999), even though research regularly treats them as dichotomous.

What do the sequences described in this article tell us about 'learning'? Recent conversation analytic work on learning (especially in CA-for-SLA) tends to conceptualise learning as changing participation of individual speakers over time (e.g. Hellermann 2011; Markee 2008; see also Martin 2009), which means longitudinal data is required in order to support claims concerning that change and its stability. As suggested in the introduction, interactions such as extract 1 and 2 are difficult to conceptualise as loci for new learning as an oriented-to phenomenon to begin to take place, at least in the sense of individual change. However, what this article has described is a classroom where speakers are actively establishing connections and creating relevance between semiotic resources in different domains and earlier experiences. This very production of similarities and differences across domains and time can be seen as an 'actor-oriented' (Lobato 2003, 2006; Marton 2006) – or in CA terms a participant's – perspective on learning transfer. From a learning transfer viewpoint, extracts such as 3 and 4, in which previous knowledge is employed to solve knowledge gaps concerning particular word meanings, shed light on the kind of interactional classroom work which 'permits the instruction to go on' (Macbeth 2011), and can be seen as part of learning as a social action (Sahlström 2011; see also Lee 2010) in its own right. Whether this is something any official pedagogy can systematically tap into is nevertheless a different matter: insofar as these playful associations represent a way of activating non-school related experiences, it may well be that when teachers begin referring to Spider-pig, it loses its appeal for students' identity work.

Most of the interactions presented in this article contain playful undertones, whether in the form of affiliative teasing, self-mockery or humorous remarks, which are phenomena that relatively rarely figure in theoretical discussions concerning the educational merits of language classroom interaction (although see Bell 2009; Cekaite & Aronsson 2005; Forman 2011). In fact, it appears that as Finnish students get older, their beliefs related to learning English as a foreign language at school appear to become more and more related to stereotypical school structures, such as textbook chapters and exams (Aro 2009: 114–116). Drawing comparisons between different research paradigms and learning contexts is obviously not straightforward, but it may well be that students in EFL or CLIL do not see playful language use as being 'language learning'. In other words, these kinds of events may go unnoticed but they are part of the social life of classrooms, even if their extent and interactional organisation may vary across pedagogic settings. For example, Nikula (2007) has suggested on the basis of a comparative analysis of whole-class IRF sequences in EFL and CLIL classrooms that CLIL students may have more 'space for interaction' around the three-part teaching exchange, as the way it was executed in CLIL lessons appeared less tightly-knit than in EFL. This article has not examined IRF sequences, nor has it compared any two settings, but the analysis portrays a picture of peer talk as a complex interactional environment where popular culture and curricular content co-exist, which may be part of global trends related to late modern schooling (cf. Rampton 2006) and the nature of English as a transcultural language (Pennycook 2006). Seen this way, key variables in making these kinds of interactions possible may be students' access to and interest in English-language popular culture, as well as a possibility to peer interaction in lessons, rather than whether the institutional context is EFL or CLIL. However, as most of the bridge-building sequences either completely take place in peer interaction, or are comments addressed to fellow students, it may be that the types of tasks (i.e. group work that is not preoccupied with linguistic form) which afford them are more common in CLIL than in EFL classrooms.

This article represents an initial exploration of how students learning English may use their informal language learning experiences in bilingual classroom context. What I have investigated here – i.e. sequences where speakers make clear they are referring to their out-of-class knowledge, such as popular culture – is likely to only represent the 'tip of the iceberg' of the effect of the informal context on students' all-round proficiency in English. Often in this classroom, students would use English in their group talk in a very idiomatic and conversational way, ranging from mild expletives (such as 'damn you') and frequent expressions ('oh my god') to repeating words such as 'awesome' with different accents. Although beyond the scope of this article, further research looking at these kinds of language use events may provide new and invaluable insights into how language learners make sense of their linguistic environments, not only at school but elsewhere, and at the same time, it can also tell a great deal about any specific environment.

ACKNOWLEDGEMENTS

This work was supported by the project ConCLIL - Language and content integration: towards a conceptual framework (2011-2014), led by Prof. Tarja Nikula, and funded by the Academy of Finland. I would also like to express my gratitude to Tarja Nikula, Leila Kääntä, and two anonymous reviewers for their insightful comments to previous drafts of this article. All remaining errors and omissions are mine.

ENDNOTES

1. Blockbusters was an American game show airing in the 1980s. A UK version followed shortly, and was shown during the late 1980s and early 1990s. Although the word 'blockbuster' is regularly used to refer to films and books that are commercial hits, the Oxford English Dictionaries (n.d.) suggest the etymological origin of the word is in massive WWII aerial bombs which were capable of destroying a whole block of streets. In this classroom, however, the

teacher does not introduce the cultural origins of the word; for the students, it is likely to simply be a name for the activity they are about to play, whereas the similarity of the activity to the TV series suggests it is at least to some degree familiar to the teacher.

2. The dataset was jointly collected by the Centre for Applied Language Studies and the Department of Languages, University of Jyväskylä during 2010-2011. The lessons were taught as an elective eight-week module to students registered in the bilingual programme (Content and Language Integrated Learning, CLIL) at the school. The names of the speakers have been anonymized.

3. A video of the original Spider-pig can be seen at: http://simpsons.wikia.com/wiki/Spider-Pig_(song)

4. The text contains a selection of Tudor time school rules, one of which is: 'No scholar shall wear a dagger or any other weapon. They shall not bring to school any stick or bat, only their meat knife.'

5. Notice how Susanna has been sticking to English throughout the sequence. It may be that Inka's code switch at line 17 is orientation towards Susanna's implemented language policy.

REFERENCES

1. Aoki, P. M., M. H.Szymanski, L. Plurkowski, J.D. Thornton, A. Woodruff & W. Yi 2006. Where's the "party" in "multi-party"? Analyzing the structure of small-group sociable talk. Proceedings of the 20th anniversary conference on computer supported cooperative work. Banff, Canada: ACM, 393–402.
2. Aro, M. 2009. Speakers and doers: Polyphony and agency in children's beliefs about language learning. Jyväskylä studies in humanities 116. Jyväskylä: University of Jyväskylä.
3. Bell, N. D. 2009. Learning about and through humor in the second language classroom. Language Teaching Research, 13 (3), 241–258.
4. Blommaert, J. 2010. The sociolinguistics of globalization. New York: Cambridge University Press.
5. Boxer, D. & F. Cortés-Conde 1997. From bonding to biting: conversational joking and identity display. Journal of Pragmatics, 27, 275–294.
6. Cekaite, A. & K. Aronsson 2005. Language play, a collaborative resource in children's L2 learning. Applied Linguistics, 26 (2), 169–191.
7. Churchill, E. 2007. A dynamic systems account of learning a word: from ecology to form relations. Applied Linguistics, 29 (3), 339–358.
8. Collentine, J. & B. F. Freed 2004. Learning context and its effects on

second language acquisition: introduction. Studies in Second Language Acquisition, 26 (2), 153–171.

9. Drew, P. 1987. Po-faced receipts of teases. Linguistics, 25 (1), 219–253.
10. Engle, R. A. 2006. Framing interactions to foster generative learning: a situative explanation of transfer in a community of learners classroom. Journal of the Learning Sciences, 15 (4), 451–498.
11. Eurostat 2006. Classification of learning activities - manual. Luxembourg.
12. Firth, A. & J. Wagner 1997. On discourse, communication, and (some) fundamental concepts in SLA research. Modern Language Journal, 81 (3), 285–300.
13. Forman, R. 2011. Humorous language play in a Thai EFL classroom. Applied Linguistics, 32 (5), 541–565.
14. Forrester, M. A. 1999. Reflections and projections of the developing self. Theory & Psychology, 9 (1), 29–46.
15. Foster, P. 1998. A classroom perspective on the negotiation of meaning. Applied Linguistics, 19 (1), 1–23.
16. Freeman, D. 2007. Research "fitting" practice: Firth and Wagner, classroom language teaching, and language teacher education. Modern Language Journal, 91 (5), 893–906.
17. Gass, S., A. Mackey & L. Ross-Feldman 2005. Task-based interactions in classroom and laboratory settings. Language Learning, 55 (4), 575–611.
18. Gibson, J. 1979. The ecological approach to visual perception. Boston: Houghton Mifflin.
19. Glenn, P. & C. LeBaron 2011. Epistemic authority in employment interviews: glancing, pointing, touching. Discourse & Communication, 5 (1), 3–22.
20. Goodwin, C. 2000. Action and embodiment within situated human interaction. Journal of pragmatics, 32, 1489–1522.
21. Goodwin, M. H. & C. Goodwin 1986. Gesture and coparticipation in the activity of searching for a word. Semiotica, 62 (1)–(2), 51–75.
22. Haugh, M. 2010. Jocular mockery, (dis)affiliation, and face. Journal of Pragmatics, 42 (8), 2106–2119.
23. Helasvuo, M.-L., M. Laakso & M.-L. Sorjonen 2004. Searching for words: Syntactic and sequential construction of word search in conversations of Finnish speakers with aphasia. Research on Language and Social Interaction, 37 (1), 1–37.
24. Hellermann, J. 2011. Members' methods, members competencies:

Looking for evidence of language learning in longitudinal investigation of other-initiated repair. In J.K. Hall, J. Hellermann & S. Pekarek Doehler (eds.), L2 interactional competence and development. Bristol: Multilingual Matters, 147-171.

25. Hellermann, J. & S. Pekarek Doehler 2010. On the contingent nature of language-learning tasks. Classroom Discourse, 1 (1), 25–45.
26. Heritage, J. 2012. Epistemics in sction: action formation and territories of knowledge. Research on Language and Social Interaction, 45 (1), 1–29.
27. Heritage, J. & G. Raymond 2005. The terms of agreement: indexing epistemic authority and subordination in talk-in-interaction. Social Psychology Quarterly, 68 (1), 15–38.
28. Higgins, C. 2009. Language in and out of the classroom: connecting contexts of language use with learning and teaching practices. Language Teaching, 42 (3), 401–403.
29. Howard, M. 2011. Input perspectives on the role of learning context in second language acquisition: an introduction to the special issue. IRAL - International Review of Applied Linguistics in Language Teaching, 49 (2), 71–82.
30. Hutchins, E. 1995. Cognition in the wild. Cambridge, MA: MIT Press.
31. Jefferson, G. 2004. Glossary of transcript symbols with an introduction. In G.H. Lerner (ed.), Conversation analysis: studies from the first generation. Philadelphia, PA: John Benjamins Publishing.
32. Keltner, D., L. Capps, A. M. Kring, R. C. Young & E. A. Heerey 2001. Just teasing: a conceptual analysis and empirical review. Psychological Bulletin, 127 (2), 229–248.
33. Koole, T. 2010. Displays of epistemic access: student responses to teacher explanations. Research on Language and Social Interaction, 43 (2), 183–209.
34. Krashen, S. 1976. Formal and informal linguistic environments in language acquisition and language learning. TESOL Quarterly, 10 (2), 157–168.
35. Kääntä, L., H. Jauni, S. Leppänen, S. Peuronen & T. Paakkinen 2013. Learning English through social interaction: the case of Big Brother 2006, Finland. Modern Language Journal, 97 (2), 340–359.
36. Lee, Y.-A. 2010. Learning in the contingency of talk-in-interaction. Text & Talk, 30 (4), 403–422.
37. Lehtimaja, I. 2012. Puheen suuntia luokkahuoneessa: oppilaat osallistujina yläkoulun suomi toisena kielenä -tunnilla [Directions of talk

in the classroom: students as participants in Finnish as a second language lessons in lower secondary education]. University of Helsinki.

38. Leppänen, S. & T. Nikula 2007. Diverse uses of English in Finnish society. Multilingua, 26, 1–46.

39. Leppänen, S., A. Pitkänen-Huhta, T. Nikula, S. Kytölä, T. Törmäkangas, K. Nissinen, L. Kääntä, T. Räisänen, M. Laitinen, P. Pahta, H. Koskela, S. Lähdesmäki & H. Jousmäki 2011. National survey on the English language in Finland: uses, meanings and attitudes. Helsinki: Research unit for variation, contacts and change in English.

40. Lilja, N. 2010. Ongelmista oppimiseen: toisen aloittamat korjausjaksot kakkoskielisessä keskustelussa [From problems to learning: other-initiated repair sequences in second language conversations]. Jyväskylä studies in humanities 146. Jyväskylä: University of Jyväskylä.

41. Lobato, J. 2006. Alternative perspectives on the transfer of learning: history, issues, and challenges for future research. Journal of the Learning Sciences, 15 (4), 431–449.

42. Lobato, J. 2003. How design experiments can inform a rethinking of transfer and vice versa. Educational Researcher, 32 (1), 17–20.

43. Long, M. H. 1983. Native speaker/non-native speaker conversation and the negotiation of comprehensible input. Applied Linguistics, 4 (2), 126–141.

44. Long, M. H. 1996. The role of the linguistic environment in second language acquisition. In W.C. Ritchie & T.K. Bhatia (eds.), Handbook of second language acquisition. San Diego: Academic Press, 413–468.

45. Lyster, R. 2004. Differential effects of prompts and recasts in form-focused instruction. Studies in Second Language Acquisition, 26 (3), 399–432.

46. Lyster, R. & L. Ranta 1997. Corrective feedback and learner uptake: negotiation of form in communicative classrooms. Studies in Second Language Acquisition, 19 (1), 37–66.

47. Lyster, R. & K. Saito 2010. Oral feedback in classroom SLA: a meta-analysis. Studies in Second Language Acquisition, 32 (2), 265–302.

48. Macbeth, D. 2011. Understanding understanding as an instructional matter. Journal of Pragmatics, 43 (2), 438–451.

49. Markee, N. 2008. Toward a learning behavior tracking methodology for CA-for-SLA. Applied Linguistics, 29 (3), 404–427.

50. Martin, C. 2009. Relevance of situational context in studying learning as changing participation. Scandinavian Journal of Educational Research,

53 (2), 133–149.

51. Marton, F. 2006. Sameness and difference in transfer. Journal of the Learning Sciences, 15 (4), 499–535.
52. Mondada, L. 2011. Understanding as an embodied, situated and sequential achievement in interaction. Journal of Pragmatics, 43 (2), 542–552.
53. Mori, J. 2007. Border crossings? Exploring the intersection of second language acquisition, conversation analysis, and foreign language pedagogy. Modern Language Journal, 91 (5), 849–862.
54. Nikula, T. 2007. Speaking English in Finnish content-based classrooms. World Englishes, 26 (2), 206–223.
55. Oxford English Dictionaries. "Blockbuster". Available at: http://oxforddictionaries.com/definition/english/blockbuster [accessed June 10, 2013].
56. Pennycook, A. 2006. Global Englishes and transcultural flows. New York: Routledge.
57. Pennycook, A. 2010. Language as a local practice. Milton Park, Abingdon: Routledge.
58. Piirainen–Marsh, A. & L. Tainio 2009a. Collaborative game-play as a site for participation and situated learning of a second language. Scandinavian Journal of Educational Research, 53 (2), 167–183.
59. Piirainen–Marsh, A. & L. Tainio 2009b. Other-repetition as a resource for participation in the activity of playing a video game. Modern Language Journal, 93 (2), 153–169.
60. Pitkänen-Huhta, A. 2008. Kielellinen leikittely oppilaiden teksteihin liittyvissä keskusteluissa [Linguistic play in students' conversations on texts]. In S. Leppänen, T. Nikula & L. Kääntä (eds.), Kolmas kotimainen: lähikuvia englannin käytöstä Suomessa [The third national language: close-up images of the use of English in Finland]. Helsinki: Suomalaisen Kirjallisuuden Seura.
61. Pollner, M. 1987. Mundane reason: reality in everyday and sociological discourse. Cambridge: Cambridge University Press.
62. Rampton, B. 1999. Dichotomies, difference, and ritual in second language learning and teaching. Applied Linguistics, 20 (3), 316–340.
63. Rampton, B. 2006. Language in late modernity: interaction in an urban school. Cambridge: Cambridge University Press.
64. Sacks, H. 1992. Lectures on conversation (Volume II). Oxford: Blackwell.
65. Sahlström, F. 2011. Learning as social action. In J.K. Hall, J. Hellermann & S. Pekarek Doehler (eds.), L2 interactional competence and development.

Bristol: Multilingual Matters, 45–65.

66. Savon Sanomat 2012. Pojat ovat tyttöjä parempia englannissa - syy: tietokonepelit [Boys are better than girls at English - the reason: computer games]. Available at http://www.savonsanomat.fi/uutiset/kotimaa/pojat-ovat-tyttoja-parempia-englannissa-syy-tietokonepelit/1218869 [accessed September 5, 2012].
67. Schegloff, E. 1992. Repair after next turn: the last structurally provided defense of intersubjectivity in conversation. American journal of sociology, 97 (5), 1295–1345.
68. Sert, O. 2011. A micro-analytic investigation of claims of insufficient knowledge in EAL classrooms. Doctoral dissertation. Newcastle University.
69. Sfard, A. 1998. On two metaphors for learning and the dangers of choosing just one. Educational Researcher, 27 (2), 4–13.
70. Sidnell, J. 2012. Declaratives, questioning, defeasibility. Research on Language and Social Interaction, 45 (1), 53–60.
71. Slotte-Lüttge, A., M. Pörn & F. Sahlström 2012. Learning how to be a tähti: a case study of language development in everyday situations of a 7-year-old multilingual Finnish child. International Journal of Bilingualism, 17 (2), 153–173.
72. Spada, N. 1997. Form-focussed instruction and second language acquisition: a review of classroom and laboratory research. Language Teaching, 30 (2), 73–87.
73. Sundqvist, P. 2009. Extramural English matters. Karlstad university studies 2009:55. Karlstad: Universitetstryckeriet.
74. ten Have, P. 2007. Doing conversation analysis. London: SAGE.
75. Uuskoski, O. 2011. Playing video games: A waste of time... or not? Exploring the connection between playing video games and English grades. Unpublished Master's thesis. University of Helsinki.
76. van Lier, L. 2000. From input to affordance: social-interactive learning from an ecological perspective. In J.P. Lantolf (ed.), Sociocultural theory and second language learning. Oxford: Oxford University Press, 245–259.
77. van Lier, L. 2002. An ecological-semiotic perspective on language and linguistics. In C. Kramsch (ed.), Language acquisition and language socialization: ecological perspectives. London: Continuum, 140–172.
78. van Lier, L. 2004. The ecology and semiotics of language learning: a sociocultural perspective. Boston: Kluwer Academic.

79. Varonis, E. M. & S. Gass 1985. Non-native/non-native conversations: a model for negotiation of meaning. Applied Linguistics, 6 (1), 71–90.

80. VISK = Auli Hakulinen, Maria Vilkuna, Riitta Korhonen, Vesa Koivisto, Tarja Riitta Heinonen ja Irja Alho (2004). Iso suomen kielioppi [Big Finnish grammar]. Available at http://scripta.kotus.fi/visk [accessed June 10, 2013].

81. Ylioppilastutkintolautakunta 2011a. Ylioppilastutkinto 2009: Tilastoja ylioppilastutkinnosta [Upper secondary school matriculation examination in 2009: statistics on the exams]. Sastamala.

82. Ylioppilastutkintolautakunta 2011b. Ylioppilastutkinto 2010: Tilastoja ylioppilastutkinnosta [Upper secondary school matriculation examination in 2010: statistics on the exams]. Sastamala.

Chapter 12

LANGUAGE IDEOLOGIES AND LEARNING HISTORICAL MINORITY LANGUAGES: A COMPARATIVE STUDY OF VOLUNTARY LEARNERS OF SWEDISH IN FINLAND AND HUNGARIAN IN ROMANIA

Attila Kiss

University of Jyväskylä

ABSTRACT

Language ideologies surrounding the learning of historical minority languages deserve more/closer attention because due to the strong nation state ideology, the relation between majority and minority languages has long been problematic, and native speakers of majority languages do not typically learn the languages of the minorities voluntarily. This article discusses the language ideologies of voluntary learners of Swedish and Hungarian in two contexts where these languages are historical minority languages. Data was collected at evening courses in Oradea, Romania and Jyväskylä, Finland on which a qualitative analysis was conducted. In the analysis, an ethnographic and discourse analysis perspective was adopted, and language ideologies were analyzed in their interactional form, acknowledging the position of the researcher in the co-construction of language ideologies in the interviews. The results show that the two contexts are very different, although there are also similarities in the language ideologies of the learners which seem to be significantly influenced by the prevailing historical discourses in place about the use and role of these languages. In the light of resilient historical metanarratives, I suggest that the challenges related to the learning of historical minority languages lie in the historical construction of modern ethnolinguistic nation-states and the present trajectories of such projects. At the same time, the learning of historical languages in contemporary globalized socio-cultural contexts can build on new post-national ideologies, such as the concept of learning historical languages as commodities.

INTRODUCTION

The language ideologies constructed by the learners are considered central to understanding issues involved in the learning and teaching of additional languages in general (see Wortham 2005, 2008; Spolsky 2010), even in the case of elementary school children (Martínez-Roldán & Malavé 2004). This applies in particular to the context of adults learning the language of a historical minority voluntarily (see Azkue & Perales 2005; Cenoz & Perales 2010; McEwan-Fujita 2010; Zenker 2014). In this article, I report the findings of an ethnographic research that I conducted about adult voluntary learners' language ideologies. The focus is on majority language speakers who learn historical minority languages, and more precisely on speakers of Finnish learning Swedish, and speakers of Romanian learning Hungarian in two sites: Oradea, Romania and Jyväskylä, Finland. I focus on two minority language contexts in the European Union, where the official policies and nation state ideologies show significant differences. I approach the issue from the vantage point of language ideologies, and I conduct a discourse analysis (see section 5 for details on methodology) on empirical data collected through interviews. Spolsky (2010) pointed out that the learning of minority languages first became popular during the 'ethnic revival' that flourished in Western Europe and North America in the 1960s. In practice, this phenomenon is related to the concept of language heritage, which means that the learners viewed/looked at the language that they were learning as their own, and this ownership and identification with the language can be seen as part of reclaiming their ethnic identity (e.g. Zenker 2014). However, recent developments in the theory and practice of language teaching have revealed that the contexts of learning historical languages are, in fact, manifold (e.g. Lynch 2003; Duff 2009). For instance, reviving languages, such as Gaelic or Welsh, are often learned by language enthusiasts (Zenker 2014: 64), who do not have anybody who speaks the language in question in their family (cf. McEwan-Fujita 2010). Most studies on linguistic minorities and language learning have been conducted in the traditional nationalistic framework. For example, heritage language learning studies usually focus on language as inheritance and the reproduction of native speakers, disregarding out-group learners (cf. Spolsky 2010; Guardado 2014; for exceptions see Pujolar 2007; Pujolar & Gonzales 2013; Oh & Nash 2014). My approach draws on current sociolinguistic theory and is not committed to the traditional perspectives. Similar emerging research on Western European settings focuses on new speakers in the broadest sense, referring to multilingual minority and immigrant language learners (e.g. Pujolar 2007). Parallel to such ventures (Pujolar & Gonzales 2013), my study concerns voluntary adult learners, which is a relatively under-researched area in general (but see Oh & Nash 2014). Studies on "new" Catalan-speakers have demonstrated that linguistic practices and language ideologies may change throughout life (Woolard 2013; for a similar case in South Tyrol, see Cavagnoli & Nardin 1999). In the contexts under examination, that is members of the titular group learning a minority language, May (2012) has directed the attention to the relations between the legal-political and the cultural-historical dimensions of nationhood. He argues that, in order to become a nation state in modern Western European terms, the hegemony of the majority culture and language needs to be secured. The projection of majority nationalism upon minorities is thus considered to be the naturalization of the nation state model with an integrative core language and core-culture. Greater representations of the minority language and culture, such as teaching a minority language to the titular group, "are viewed as parochial and destabilizing" (May 2012: 84), or in terms of historical development "essentially anti-modern" (May 2012: 27). Like most European countries, in Romania the ideology of the unity of nation, state and one language is normative and enshrined in the constitution, while in the case of Finland, Swedish retained its functions as a co-official language along with Finnish. As Kamusella (2009: 57) notes "this disqualifies Finland from the exclusive club of 'true' ethnolinguistic nation-states". I have chosen to compare these two contexts of language learning in order to explore whether the above approach has consequences for language ideologies with respect to the voluntary learning of the historical minority language. In the light of its historical dominance in relation to other East-Central European languages, the former imperial contexts of German bear a gross resemblance to the position of Hungarian in the multiethnic Hungarian Kingdom before 1920 (see Duszak 2006; Jaworska 2009; Nekvapil & Sherman 2009; Berecz 2013). German also serves as a basis of comparison in respect to the language policy developments of a privileged historical minority language in the present day because we can draw a parallel between Swedish in Finland and German in South Tyrol, Italy, where it has a similar position on a regional level (see Cavagnoli & Nardin 1999; Wolff 2000). In this article, I approach the study of the voluntary learning of minority languages by the majority by exploring the language ideologies of the subjects through interviews. Gal (2006a) conceptualizes the field of language ideologies as a form of discourse analysis. Language ideologies have been defined as "cultural, metapragmatic assumptions about the relationship between words, speakers, and worlds" (Gal 2006a: 388). In interviews, implicit and explicit statements as well as conceptions about languages occur (Laihonen 2008, 2009). My investigation mostly focuses on the transparent, explicit talk about languages, their value, and how and why they are learned. The implications for the learners can be far reaching since: "Ideologies, whether invited or imposed, normally come and go with a language" (Duszak 2006: 95). Following Gal (2006b: 15), in order to unfold language ideologies we need to analyze the configuration of these sometimes unconscious cultural assumptions and notions which serve as a frame for linguistic practices as well (cf. Blommaert 2006). Language ideologies also offer insights into "the microculture of communicative action to political economic considerations of power and social inequality, confronting macrosocial constraints on language behavior" (Woolard & Schieffelin 1994: 72). The language ideologies around the learning of historical minority languages deserve attention, especially since, in most cases, the relation between majority and minority languages has been asymmetric, as May stresses (2012), e.g. for many Western intellectuals majority languages represent modernity and progress whereas minority languages are tokens of cultural separatism and disintegration. From this perspective, it is no wonder that it is not a widespread practice that majority language speakers would embark on learning the languages of the minorities, if such an opportunity is offered at all (for a similar argument, see Nekvapil & Sherman 2009). In the analysis of research interviews, I subscribe to the tradition that illustrates how "talk about language is constructed to meet the expectations of the question, the general orientation of the interview and the amount of shared knowledge" (Laihonen 2008: 678). In the article I also point out how the "metalanguage is connected to the social situation" (Laihonen 2008: 671), as well as how "world views or social positions" are co-constructed together during interview interaction (Laihonen 2008: 671; see also De Fina 2009; Mori, 2012). That is, when a story is told, it is told for this interviewer (me) in the interactional context of the interview; for instance, because the interviewer asked a question and perhaps did not understand the answer, the interviewee ended up clarifying his answer with a narrative. My study is guided by the following questions: what are the language ideologies as displayed and co-constructed in interviews with the author, of the learners towards learning a historical minority language in voluntary courses? What underlying ideological considerations hinder or facilitate learning in both Romanian and Finnish contexts?

BACKGROUND: BASIS OF COMPARISON

Despite the relatively high proportion of the historical minorities of Finland and Romania (ca. 6 per cent in both countries, Official Statistics Finland 2010; Institutul Na□ional de Statistică 2011), the general perception in both contexts is that only few people voluntarily study Swedish in Finland and Hungarian in Romania. In the following, I present the contexts of two research sites, Jyväskylä and Oradea, placing them in the larger frameworks of the status of Hungarian in Romania and Swedish in Finland. In Finland, the status of Swedish is much different compared to the status of Hungarian in Romania. Romania defines itself as a nation state with Romanian as its sole national language (The Constitution of Romania 2003) while Finland is officially bilingual and Swedish and Finnish have equal status (The Constitution of Finland 2000). In the present territory of Finland, Swedish dates back to the first written sources of the 12th century. The area formed a part of the Swedish Empire before it became an autonomous Grand Duchy under Russia in 1809. Finland declared independence in 1917. Swedish and Finnish have been used and spoken by intellectuals and state officials for long, and it has not caused a problem for the elite to learn Finnish and later Swedish. After the general educational reform of 1968 (Palviainen 2010a), learning Swedish became compulsory for the masses. In Finland, education is conducted in Finnish and Swedish on an equal basis (Palviainen 2010a). Furthermore, the other national language is a compulsory subject in both Finnish and Swedish medium schools. Compulsory Swedish classes have been the subject of populist campaigns and have lately received some publicity in the Finnish media. The derogatory Finnish word pakkoruotsi, 'forced Swedish' (Palviainen 2013a: 4), designates Swedish as a compulsory subject in school. The idea of making Finland a monolingual nation state surfaces in populist political discourses, but so far it has been rejected by the majority of the educated Finnish speaking population. However, in a longitudinal survey carried out with the participation of altogether 1591 Finnish speaking students in 2006/2007 and 2010 (Palviainen & Jauhojärvi-Koskelo 2009; Palviainen 2010b), a significant decrease was observed in the numbers of those who expressed willingness to study Swedish if it were not compulsory in secondary education. In the context of the Austro-Hungarian Monarchy, the learning of each other's languages was a general practice that disappeared in the 20th century (Gal 2011: 32). In Transylvania, Romanian and Hungarian played out the 'dominated dominant' dichotomy as German and Czech did in the Czech lands (see Nekvapil 2000). In Transylvania, the end of the 19th century was characterized by the policy of 'Magyarization', which was carried out mainly through compulsory Hungarian education in state schools. Romanian speakers generally resisted this, and in Romanian villages, few used Hungarian outside of school (see Berecz 2013). In 1920, Transylvania was ceded to Romania. Since then, the Hungarian language has been perceived in terms of its former dominance, to be counterbalanced in a post-colonial venture to integrate the region into the emerging Romanian Nation State. From this background, the idea of learning the culture and language of the historical minority seems perhaps even bizarre for the members of the titular culture. The teaching of Hungarian for Romanian speakers is provided in the framework of supplementary classes in school education, provided demand for it exists. For example, in Oradea, there was only one occasion when a Hungarian optional language course was organized. Therefore, we can state that there is largely no formal Hungarian language teaching in the Romanian schools, such as there is Swedish in the Finnish educational system.

SITES OF RESEARCH

I conducted research in Jyväskylä and Oradea. Jyväskylä is an officially monolingual Finnish municipality in Central Finland. Founded in 1837, the city was chosen to host an education center for the first Finnish medium high-school and teacher education, partly due to the fact that the new capital Helsinki (Helsingfors) was predominantly Swedish speaking in the 1860s. The 19thcentury hamlet has grown into a major university city. Out of the 131,000 inhabitants, 312 are registered as Swedish speakers. In Finland everyone is officially registered at birth as a speaker of either Finnish/Swedish or a speaker of another language (Statistics Finland 2015). The existence of Swedish daycare and schooling indicate that there is Swedish bilingualism even in this overwhelmingly Finnish speaking city (see Palviainen 2013b). My second site, the city of Oradea (Hungarian: Nagyvárad, German: Grosswardein), is situated in Western Romania, 10 kilometers from the border of Hungary. According to the 2011 census, out of the total 184,861 inhabitants, the percentage of those who claimed Hungarian as a mother tongue was 23%. Before 1920 the city belonged to the Kingdom of Hungary. Generally depicted as a major center of Hungarian culture and literary life, Oradea is also significant to Romanian culture since it was an important site in the region for Romanian national awakening. The Hungarian-speaking Jewish population played an important role in the development and cultural life of the city (e.g. Mózes 1997). Nagyvárad was considered to be a cosmopolitan city despite the fact that Hungarian had the dominant position in administration and education, and Hungarian served as a lingua franca for the various ethnicities, even as late as the 1960s. In comparison to Jyväskylä, Romanian learners in Oradea frequently hear the historical minority language in everyday life. Next, I will take a brief look at the institutions where the voluntary learning of historical languages was investigated. In Finland evening classes have a long tradition. At Jyväskylä the classes were held at the local Community College (Kansalaisopisto), a nationwide network dedicated to adult education. Finnish interviewees often recall that they attend these classes because a good framework exists for it. After the 1968 educational reform in Finland, everybody has learnt Swedish on a compulsory basis in secondary education. Thus, there are no beginner courses offered at Kansalaisopisto, but only refresher courses, and the lowest level is intermediate. The study brochure of the institution advertises the courses as follows: "Did you forget the Swedish that you studied in school times? We will repeat the basic grammar structures and practice" (Jyväskylän Kansalaisopisto 2013: 36). This seems to resonate for example with the needs of participants of the third age1 in my data: "when I retired I think I must have some hobby (.) and then I thought I have three nights per week to study here something (.) so I began to learn Swedish because it isn't so difficult now. (...) I want to repeat what I learned before" (woman in her 60s). From another perspective, according to a teacher in Jyväskylä, it is more characteristic that participants attend the courses because they need Swedish for work purposes, or they moved to Jyväskylä from a Swedish speaking area in Finland and they want to maintain their language skills. The teacher recalled that among the learners there were employees in customer service, physicians, and nurses. In Romania there is no similar nationwide adult training network. Interviewees in Oradea were taking part in a course organized and taught by me under the auspices of the Debrecen Summer School in the building of a Hungarian medium high-school (see Kiss 2012). In Oradea, there was also interest on the part of the third age generation, but their numbers are not as significant as in Finland. The most numerous group in Romania were teachers who considered that Hungarian would be useful in their profession, which involves interacting with language minority students. In Jyväskylä there were also younger course participants as well as university students. For example, Jussi (all names are pseudonyms, Jussi was in his 20s) and Maiju (in her early 30s) were taking part in the course because they felt that they needed a basic course in order to be able to obtain the Degree Certificate of Studies in Swedish for civil servants (in Finnish often referred to as virkamiesruotsi) (see Palviainen 2010a). In Oradea, similar language courses were organized by the Municipality wherein members of the community police attended the classes on a voluntary basis, but no exams for civil servants in Hungarian exist in Romania.

DATA

The present article is based mainly on the findings of semi-structured interviews that were conducted by me in English in Jyväskylä, and in Romanian in Oradea. In the case of Oradea, being present as a teacher (for details see Kiss 2013), I documented three courses from 2010 to 2011. In Jyväskylä, I visited the Kansalaisopisto 10 times in 2013. Research diaries and institutional course brochures serve as sources of background information. The interviews in Romania were carried out after a period of around half a year when the participants were attending a second course. There were individual interviews and interviews conducted with two participants together. In Oradea my role in the field was foremost that of a teacher of Hungarian for the interviewees, a person who organized and taught Hungarian evening courses at the premises of a Hungarian high school, and a member of the ethnic Hungarian minority. As someone who lived most of his life in the city, I was looked upon as a person who did not need an introduction to the local situation. That is, I was treated as a person who possesses a great deal of emic and local knowledge. I had not known the course participants prior to the course, but due to our classes I had developed a closer personal relationship more with the Romanian interviewees than with the Finnish participants, whom I met for the first time when I solicited their interviews as a foreign researcher. Therefore, they looked upon me as an outsider not likely to be familiar with the ethnographic and political details of learning Swedish in Finland. I scheduled the interviews before or after their weekly Swedish classes at the Community College (kansalaisopisto). We usually sat down in the cafeteria of the City Library in Jyväskylä, or in the classroom where we would have our class in Oradea. I conducted interviews with 25 informants (12 in Oradea and 13 in Jyväskylä), and the interviews usually lasted from 30 to 90 minutes, resulting in a total of ca. 6 hours of audio material in both the Jyväskylä and Oradea cases. The interviewees were mostly college graduates, employed in education, or in the service industries. In Jyväskylä there were more third-age informants than in Oradea. I started the interviews by asking why they learnt the language, as well as how other people reacted to their decision to participate in a course on their respective minority language. I enquired about their trajectories as learners of Hungarian or Swedish and the areas of use of these languages as well as relations to members of the linguistic minority. Beyond the fact that the author conducted all of the interviews, the uniformity of approach and areas of interest resulted in comparable data sets.

RESEARCH METHODS

I use Discourse Analysis as complementary with ethnography. In approaching the language ideologies of majority language learners of historical minority languages, I adopt Geertz's (1973/2000) approach to ethnography, who considered it a viewpoint rather than a method. He suggested "thick description" in the study of the complexities and particularities of whichever social scenes are under scrutiny. The other two constitutive components of his approach were an emic, or insider perspective mainly in the Romanian context, and partly in the Finnish context, as well as the researcher's awareness that the researcher is a constitutive part of the research scene. The ethnographic approach stresses the open-ended nature of research and "getting quality from the actor's point of view" (Atkinson 2005: 50). This is especially relevant in the case of Language ideologies. In the analysis of the interview data I consider applied Conversation Analysis (CA) as a suitable method for its valuable practices and insights into analyzing spoken interaction. In comparison to the generally more static ethnographic accounts "CA portrays social behavior as dynamic, emergent and situated vis-à- vis the interactional contingencies of the moment" (Atkinson, Hanako & Talmy 2011: 88). I was interested in the ideas interviewees have about the historical minority languages they are learning, and what kind of explicit evaluations they make about the learning of said languages. I always include the questions and interviewer reactions to answers in the examination of interviewees' statements since I consider them relevant to the form and occurrence of metalinguistic comments. Another interviewer, posing other questions and reacting differently to the answers, would have received different accounts on learning a historical language. Interactional data is also used in Jaffe (1999) and Heller (2011) largely from the discourse analytic perspective of analyzing the content of turns by different actors, however, Laihonen (2008; see also ten Have 2004) brings together insights from Language Ideologies and Conversation Analysis in order to show how the contents and details of shifts in interaction are actually coconstructed and how language ideas are intertwined with the interactional structure in interviews. I analyze semi-structured interviews (see ten Have 2004 for different interview types). I approach the Second Language Acquisition of historical minority languages from the perspective of anthropological sociolinguistics applying ethnographical data collection and analysis methods as outlined by Heller (2008) and Blommaert and Dong (2010). Therefore, I take the interpretivist stance of linguistic ethnography, describe practices and address questions to shed light on language ideologies. In the analysis of the interviews I also look at "patterns of discourse as they emerge in interaction", and as "primary acts of meaning-making" (Heller 2001: 251). I use an integrative approach (Heller 2008) and look at larger social and historical processes and structures beyond the interaction, too.

LANGUAGE IDEOLOGIES: INSIGHTS FROM THE INTERVIEWS

Why People Learn a Historical Minority Language?

I started each interview by asking about the reasons for the interviewees' learning Hungarian or Swedish in order to map the most important factors that prompted interviewees to enroll in the voluntary learning of these two languages. One of the Finnish research participants in Jyväskylä, Leila, is a pensioner in her 60s, and beside from helping out her family dedicates two evenings to herself:

Excerpt 1*

1. 1 AK: what makes you study Swedish in your free time?
2. 2 Leila: I thought that I would love to have a language course as a
3. 3 hobby and I liked Swedish (.) it is easy (.) but I never had the chance
4. 4 to speak it in natural circumstances (.) I went to the discussion course
5. 5 for the second time (.) first I was surprised that there are so many
6. 6 people (.) first, I thought that it would not be a popular choice (.)
7. 7 in general people were not that interested in Swedish (.)
8. 8 you probably heard already that it is not a popular topic in school (.) or
9. 9 people don't need it in work life being in Central Finland (.)
10. 10 but anyway (.) the course it was almost full (.) it was 20 people.

* (.) denotes micro pauses less than 0.2 seconds. In the transcription of the interviews a simplified version of transcription conventions of Conversation Analysis is used. The list of transcription symbols can be found at the end of article. The interviewer in this question positions adult language learning as a free-time activity. Further, the question explicitly concerns learning Swedish in one's free time. Learning Swedish is an ideologically loaded question in Finland as the informant also mentions later (in line 8). In comparison, an alternative format would have been a general question (e.g. 'what makes you study languages in your free time?') or an ideologically more neutral 'hobby language' in this context, such as Italian or Spanish. Leila's answer implicates the ideological encumbrance of learning Swedish as a free time activity. First, Leila accepts the stance about learning languages as a hobby, which she explicitly states in her answer ("I would love to have a language course as a hobby"), then, in her next remark, she evokes ideological images of learning Swedish as a subject at school. That is, the informant presents an image of herself as a Swedish learner who liked the language in school, and finds it easy despite the fact that she did not have a chance to use it in "natural circumstances". This reflects the conception that Swedish is not used in this part of Finland. It was voiced in other interviews as well that Swedish is not needed in the region of Central Finland because it is a Finnish-speaking region

(see also Palviainen 2012: 20). However, other interviewees claim seeing both private sector and government job advertisements where Swedish skills were a requirement: “Swedish is still strong (.) or in demand in customer service (.) Swedish, it is required on a level to get by” (Tuija). In sum, there are contradictory evaluations, sometimes even within the same interview, as regards to the usefulness of Swedish in Central Finland. Leila is “surprised” (line 5) that there were many people attending the course, and recalls that her presumption was that “in general people were not interested in Swedish”. The next sentence introduced by “you probably heard” shows that the remark is clearly addressed to the interviewer, who is thus depicted as an outsider who might not have basic knowledge of the discourses on learning Swedish in Finland. In this way the interviewer’s position as a foreigner was reflected in other interviews with Finns as well, but not in the interviews with Romanians, where he had the position of a local, an issue to which I return later. Leila voices the stereotype “not a popular subject in schools” (line 8), introducing the interviewer to the widely circulated language ideologies in Finland. She explains this with the remark that “people don’t need it in work life being in Central Finland” making the instrumental connection between learning a language and acquiring a job. She also points out the different approaches to language learning. That is, the conversation course is different from the school education that she had experience with. Romanian informants from Oradea reflected upon the fact that they learned the language in informal settings through interacting with Hungarians. For reasons of space I present only the English translations of the interviews carried out in Romanian:

Excerpt 2

1. AK: how typical do you think your experience is? that er (.) you learned
2. Hungarian by (.) being in touch with the Hungarians from here?
3. Liliana: so (.) that most of the Romanians learn the language due to the
4. contacts that they have?
5. AK: yes
6. Liliana: I think that quite many (.) I don’t know but I have always been in
7. touch with (---) if it was neighbours (.) or family friends (.) or
8. acquaintances in general (.) and for me (.) at least it was like a game that I

9. can say something (.) or I could understand (.) to be able to understand (.)
10. to be able to say a few sentences in the language of the other one and he
11. she could understand (.) you I think it has to do with respect that you want
12. to show towards the other one (.) to show him=her that you know the
13. language he uses.

The interviewer introduces the idea that Romanians from Oradea acquire some Hungarian through interaction with Hungarian speakers. Aligning to this conception, the informant (Liliana, a Romanian in her late 30s) presents her personal experience, which sees language as a tool for communication among co-inhabitants (neighbors, friends). As this excerpt shows, proficiency in the language may not be very high, or go beyond a few sentences, but it serves the purposes of indexing respect. Liliana also introduces the idea that language learning was a game for her "and for me (.) at least it was like a game that I can say something (.) or I could understand" (line 8, 9). Due to the lack of formal language teaching, the learners often express that they were not acquainted with Hungarian grammar, and their knowledge is based on what they picked up from natural interaction with Hungarians, or from Hungarian television. Later in the interview she also refers to occasional job advertisements in the local newspapers that list Hungarian as an additional advantage. In other interviews, Romanian learners also mention that it could be useful to speak Hungarian in customer service. Here the instrumentality of Hungarian appears as a potentially useful tool for future possibilities and it is opposed to the traditional ideologies of ethno-linguistic group membership, or political division. From a comparative perspective, we can sum up that Finns in Jyväskylä acquire the basics of Swedish in the framework of formal school education whereas Romanians in Oradea acquire it from their environment. Finns can build on their school language courses at a later stage of their life when they decide to voluntarily study the language. Refreshing knowledge resulting from the previous formal training and knowledge is given as the reason for continuing their voluntary Swedish learning. Many Romanian learners could fall in the heritage learner category, and they too have surpassed the basic level of proficiency in Hungarian – mostly through picking up different elements of the language from the environment (see Kiss in press for details). In this respect they are different to most Finnish speakers. In sum, learners in both interview groups expressed that they feel they have the survival skills and feel able to perform simple touristic or border crossing tasks in their respective target languages.

Ideologies of Transnational Communication

Olli is a Finnish speaking man in his 60s who started studying Swedish both for personal and professional reasons. A significant part of the next interview is concerned with the areas of use of the languages as well as transnational communication. In the following excerpt the informant describes in detail his ambivalence regarding language choice at academic conferences:

Excerpt 3

1. AK: how often does it happen that Swedish is a common language?
2. Olli: when Scandinavians meet at conferences we have a feeling that we
3. belong to the same group of people: Finns, Norwegians, and so on, and
4. quite often when nations are grouped together (0.2) it is not nice when I
5. am not able to speak Swedish, because then all other people will speak
6. Swedish (0.2) Norwegians, Danes, Swedish people, and so this happens
7. quite often to me that I participate in a conference and we should have a
8. geographical meeting.
9. AK: mhm
10. Olli: and then Swedish, Norwegians and Finns we are put together. and
11. then it is a real, real problem, because Swedish people they know that we
12. do not want to speak Swedish
13. AK: mhm
14. Olli: and there is always discussion that er we have Finns there should we

15. speak Swedish or something else, and very often the solution is that all
16. Scandinavians just start to speak English.
17. Interviewer: mhm
18. Olli: and it would be very nice if we could say that just speak Swedish
19. AK: mhm
20. Olli: they know that they don't like or cannot speak very well Swedish
21. and then it is not nice for Scandinavian people that they cannot use their
22. language but this is quite common this happens almost every year
23. somewhere to me.

Some interviewees state that they feel too insecure about their Swedish skills to use it in a business context, and therefore, English is used. Based on another part of the interview where Olli mentioned Swedish as his lingua franca, the interviewer in line 1 requests clarification about the idea that Swedish could act as a lingua franca. I enquire into the frequency of such cases, and Olli answers with examples of situations where such a thing happens, and what problems it involves. Olli constructs an ideology that Finns are either "not able", or "do not want to" speak Swedish in international contexts, and this "is not nice for Scandinavian people that they can not use their language" (line 4,5). In this ideology, Swedish is the transnational language of Scandinavia, or the regional language of access for cooperation. Olli builds his answer on the ideology that there is solidarity between the Scandinavian people and that Scandinavian languages are mutually comprehensible, therefore the Finns should use Swedish in those situations. However, due to the lack of skills in Swedish, some Finns are of the opinion that using Swedish as a Scandinavian lingua franca is best, but the use of Swedish is problematic and fraught with many challenges. In the Finnish data we encounter many formulations about the usefulness of Swedish as the common language of Scandinavia. Swedish appears as a Scandinavian lingua franca in the eyes of interviewees. This seems to be in line with a common ideology in favor of Swedish in school education. In current debates one of the arguments is that Swedish skills enhance Nordic cooperation and may contribute to a sense of unity with other Nordic nations (cf. Palviainen 2011: 18). The common counter-argument is that English might be the de facto lingua franca of Scandinavia. In excerpt 3, and in other interviews, it was voiced, however, that knowledge of Swedish could be expected from Finnish speakers because of their school education. In Oradea interviewees also reflect upon the proximity of the border and language contacts.

Excerpt 4

1. AK: do you think that learning Hungarian will give you a chance to
2. meet more Hungarian speakers
3. Maria: […] not necessary for this […] to be able to speak a language (.)
4. it opens up the path to another culture, another civilization (.)
5. it is very important (.) for me by any means
6. it is important to be able to understand some neighbors (.) because I do not
7. know if you realize that Romanians know very little about Hungary and
8. Hungarians, not counting their daily experiences (.) but they do not know
9. anything about civilisation, history (.) I do not know whether this is a
10. mutual problem (.) probably not because (0.3) so
11. AK: what is the reason for that?
12. Maria: there are prejudices here (.) they do not have the inclination (.) and
13. for me it is most curious for one to learn German first, because Hungarian
14. is the first language that you bump into in our region.

This sequence starts with the interviewer's question as to whether the interviewees learn Hungarian in order to meet more Hungarian speakers. First, the informant develops a more general approach by saying that the more languages one knows the better it is: Maria (Romanian woman in her 50s) argues that she is learning Hungarian for more general reasons than just "meeting Hungarians", but in fact "to be able a language (.) it opens up the paths to another culture, another civilization"(lines 3, 4). That is, she builds a discourse that resonates with the late-modern and neo-liberal entrepreneurial project of self-improvement (see Giddens 1999). The informant says that she became interested in the language because she has Hungarian neighbors (line 6). The word has twofold significance because on the one hand it refers to her next-door neighbors, and on the other hand to the neighboring country, for the close proximity of the border and cross-border commerce is significant in the case of Oradea. Many Romanian speakers may regularly go shopping in Hungary, and some would even purchase a house, or weekend house, with possessing just basic knowledge of Hungarian. Some interviewees say that they do not intend to learn more than necessary to conduct these activities. Maria points out that there is a discrepancy between these dayto-day language contacts and a deeper knowledge of civilization and history. She says that "Romanians know very little about Hungarians" (line 7, 8). She explains this with the existence of prejudice and a lack of disposition (line 12) to language learning. By recalling prejudice as a politicized stance Maria references here the larger socio-cultural framework, describable as traditional ethnonationalist discourse, which typically works against the learning of historical minority languages. Just like in the case of Finland and Sweden, tourism and visits to each respective country are of the highest number between the citizens of Romania and Hungary. In the Romanian data we also find examples of trans-border communication:

Excerpt 5

1. AK: and how do you evaluate, are Romanians from Oradea interested
2. in Hungarian language and culture (0.2) do they get necessary information to
3. be interested (0.2) to bring it to their (0.2)
4. Corina: [here the worlds
5. AK: [attention?
6. Corina: [are really split (0.2) linked to the ↑real identity er of each one
7. (0.2) they have a lot of contact (.) and they are appreciative (.) of Hungarian
8. ↑civilisation (.), and in relation to what happens there

The interviewer asks the interviewees to speak about whether they think Romanians from Oradea are interested in Hungarian language and culture. Considering that the interviewer is a Hungarian from Oradea the interview can be looked upon as a kind of intercultural encounter with Romanians who gained intercultural experience by being bilinguals, and by taking part in Hungarian language courses. The informant, Corina (a Romanian woman in her 50s), resists the interviewer's generalizing category of "Romanians from Oradea". She begins speaking of other Romanians by consequently using the third person plural pronoun "they", instead of using the pronoun we, which would signal in-group affiliation: e.g. "they have a lot of contact (.) and they appreciative" (line 7). In this way she adopts the discursive role of an intermediary and positions herself as knowledgeable about both categories. She rejects the negative stereotypes and says that there is more communication and contact between the speakers of these two languages than may be evident from a superficial glance.

Negative Stereotypes on Learning a Historical Minority Language

The next interview excerpt is typical of how many interviewees refer to widely circulated negative discourses about Swedish in Finland:

Excerpt 6

1. AK: and what was the first reaction of your acquaintances when
2. you told them that you learn Swedish in your free time?
3. Tuija: first reaction is @WHAT? WHY?@ (everybody laughs) @ WHY@
4. would you do such a thing? it is because Swedish language is so hated
5. when we grow up in high school.
6. Mari: because you have to learn it
7. Tuija: you have to, so it becomes hated, and it is mandatory to hate it and
8. if you do not hate it you are discarded from the community so you have to
9. hate it (.) that kind of thing.
10. Tuija: it is a really ancient rivalry between Finnish and Swedish because
11. Sweden used to be our mother nation (---) for six hundred years (0.2) they

12. were the better people at the time (.) so all the nobles were Swedish
13. AK: does this still live on?
14. Tuija: yeah, yeah […] it lives on. it is kind of (.) not a real hatred it is a fun hatred (0.2)
15. you know it's like ice hockey
16. Mari: ice hockey is a good example

Even though not elicited by the interviewer, almost all Finnish informants speak about their school experiences as Swedish learners. Tuija and Mari, participants who belong to the younger generation (in their late 20s), reflect on the idea of the "compulsoriness" of Swedish in school. Tuija distances herself from this negative view of Swedish by ironically quoting some stereotypical voices. She enlists the negative stereotypes against Swedish, which include that it is not popular, moreover that it is "hated" because it is compulsory. Quoting the voices of others, laughter, and the use of the words "mandatory to hate it" (line 7) signals that she uses irony and constructs a subversive critique of the populist ideology, indexed through her deliberately choosing to study Swedish. Tuija takes this further by explaining that the relationship to learning Swedish is greatly influenced by generational peer pressure, which creates a culture of resistance among teenagers against the "compulsory" learning of Swedish. By giving a direct quotation (note also the change in voice) Tuija attributes these stereotypes held against Swedish to other people. The interviewee says that there is "ancient rivalry between Finnish and Swedish" (line 10), and the expression "they were the better people" (line 12) refers to a widespread historical stereotype in the Finnish data. When asked to reflect upon culture, some informants claim they know Sweden and Swedish culture quite well. Some stereotypes, however, seem to linger when one of the informant expresses that: "people in Sweden are *iloisempi* happier (.) more money" (Maiju, a woman in her 60s). In a reaction to this remark the interviewer asks: "do you think that you have a different persona when you speak Swedish? / Maiju: yes I think so." The interviewer introduces the ideology that language learning seems to go hand in hand with identity work, and the informant gives an affirmative answer. I interpret this coconstructed exchange, as an illustration how language "elicits subjective responses in speakers themselves: emotions, memories, fantasies, projections, and identifications" (Kramsch 2009: 2). Similarly, in the Oradea data, Ileana (a Romanian woman in her 50s) speaks of how her acquaintances reacted to the news when they learned that she studied Hungarian at evening classes:

Expert 7

1. AK: what did your acquaintances say when you told them that you study
2. Hungarian?
3. Maria: they found it funny (0.2) first of all they found it *cool* but how to
4. say it they were surprised (.) something like that
5. AK: weren't they wondering why?
6. Maria: yes first they asked why? @do you want to move to Hungary?
7. @but NOO. I say no (.) why should I?
8. AK: this was the first reaction?
9. Maria: this was their first reaction. (0.2) what is the hidden motive?

Learning a historical minority language, for instance Hungarian in Romania, and Swedish in Finland, as a subject of study in self-financed evening classes is a marked choice. In a manner similar to the analysis of the interviewer's questions in excerpt one, we can establish that inquiring into the learning of a historical language awaits some sort of denial of the negative stereotypes that go along with such languages due to the dominant nation state ideology in Europe. Here the interviewer can be seen to be probing for these stereotypes. That is, the question already implicates that whoever learns Hungarian in Romania has to take into account the reaction of the environment. The informant's (Maria, a Romanian woman in her 30s) response confirms that she has perceived this stance. In her response Maria relates that surprise was the first reaction of her acquaintances, and uses the English word "cool" in order to say that they found attending evening classes a novel and interesting activity. This is interesting since historical minority languages are often conceptualized as a thing of the past, and thus rather more "passé" than "cool". When asked to give details, she further clarifies that others in fact thought she might emigrate to Hungary. Ileana uses the same strategy of directly quoting the reaction of her acquaintances, and also her own answer. According to this stereotype in Oradea, language study must be instrumental and one is likely to study a language in order to move to the country where it is an official language. The general opinion is that one should learn a language of much wider circulation than Hungarian. A common trait in both the Western Romanian and Central Finland contexts are that the learners mention that their acquaintances were surprised when they mentioned their choice of language.

English, however, is generally accepted as a language to study in adult age both in Finland and Romanian, and Finns often mention Russian and Spanish as languages of choice in competition with Swedish.

Joint Histories, Common Traits, and Aspects That Hinder Language Learning

Informants, especially in the case of Romania, evoke the common historical past, which was often charged by episodes of conflict, and this may create resistance to learning these languages. As we could see previously, Finnish interviewees from the younger generation might express a critical opinion concerning the past. In respect to the recollection of stereotypes and historical grievances, there are even more marked examples in the Romanian data set. The popular oral histories between Romania and Hungary seem to have retained memories more of the offences of the earlier historical – and often more recent – conflictual periods:

Excerpt 8

1. AK: Did you speak Hungarian in the family?
2. Marcel: my father spoke the language (.) but did not support me learning it because
3. he had unpleasant memories of the Hungarian occupation.

Marcel (Romanian man in his 60s) recalls stories of his father that evoked the Hungarian rule during the Second World War. In Hungarian nationalist discourses, Nagyvárad was "liberated" and "returned" to Hungary in 1940, whereas from the Romanian point of view, the city was "occupied" by the Hungarian army. Next, I will present a longer interview excerpt in which two Romanian learners of Hungarian reflect upon Hungarian language and culture. Both interviewees are highly educated women in their early fifties and are interested in the arts and architecture:

Excerpt 9

1 AK: what motivates you to study Hungarian? lines 2-21 omitted [the interviewees, Ana and Corina, first develop their answers into a long reflection about Hungarian culture, especially in the context of arts, architecture and arts education]

1. 22 Ana: er for me (0.2) the area of the city and surroundings (.) is a matter of
2. 23 legitimacy (.) on a background where there are very many mixtures

(.) mixed

3. 24 families (.) friendships very (.) so it's a very well welded together area (.) existing

4. 25 (.) for many (0.2) with pa … with roots (0.2) with past

5. 26 Corina: so that of this tolerance?

6. 27 Ana: yes (.) so there is texture (.) inextricable (.) of families

7. 28 Corina: so it is

8. 29 Ana: [for generations there are mixed families (.) isn't it (.) so here you can

9. 30 not meddle (.) you can meddle in the zone (.) where I felt tension (.) even in my

10. 31 family (.) this rapport not ↑yet clarified (.) distorted and perverted between er

11. 32 masters and servants (.) so there exists this Romanian complex of the servant. of

12. 33 the serfs (.) while Hungarians are the noblemen (.) and er they've been masters all

13. 34 the time but (.) masters good or bad (.) well, it doesn't matter (.) so this complex

14. 35 of superiority and respectively of inferiority […]

At this point, she continues the interview by blaming politicians of manipulation of these feelings and by fueling these antagonisms. Here in the interview the informants tell two narratives in order to illustrate these points and continue by saying the following: Ana: so this er (0.2) how you said it. how did you say? (.) national fracture slit

1. 58 (sighs) and which touches the ethnic side (.) which is very sensitive especially in

2. 59 these areas it remained it remained (.) and it is ↑perpetuated now I think for

3. 60 political motives. and for interests to manipulate in all ways but it exists, it exists

4. 61 Corina: it seems to me
5. 62 Ana: [we grew up in it
6. 63 Corina: that here in this area where exercises of superiority are attempted, to be
7. 64 made. it is exasperating sometimes ones sometimes the others. it depends who the
8. 65 victim is and er (.) ignorance is: how to say it is at hand (.). so the history of the
9. 66 Oradea is not known. it is not known who the architects were who built the
10. 67 palaces on the main street (.) er and newly they are irritated if they have
11. 68 Hungarian names. yes? I think that this is a part of the history that has to be
12. 69 assumed it must be known for once and for all who build why they built (.) it is a
13. 70 building, an edifice that will stay there BUT it has its right for its own history […]
14. 71 Ana: yes, I know what ↑you are talking about, but I am telling you what ↑others are saying.
15. 72 So ↑others try to adjudge these values er (.) that are in a way already TRANSnational, and
16. 73 which are related to a history. but they try to rebuild a neoimperialist map through culture.
17. 74 namely, @we always dominated you through culture@. a kind of er intertextual message

In line 22 Ana (Romanian woman in her 50s) takes her turn. She starts out with the words “for me”. This and what follow shows that she has an alternative agenda for the discussion. The talk about Hungarian language in Oradea gives her a good platform to engage in two meta-narratives. First, she engages into a meta-story in a dialogue, not initiated by the interviewer, recounting the story of feelings of superiority and inferiority and inoculation against Hungarians and Hungarian language (lines 22–35). The second meta-story is that of cultural neoimperialism (lines 71–74), which she gives as an answer on the loss of identity and the history of the built heritage. Both of these stories have long trajectories outside the surface context of the interview and they can be interpreted only by taking into account the historical and social contexts. These stories contain numerous references to issues that are not explained to the interviewer, since it appears that a common understanding for the needs of the interview situation can be reached without such explanations, which are more typical in the Finnish data. The informants are well aware of and engage in complex discourses on Hungarian in Oradea. This is exemplified by the second meta-story about the use of names in the city and the topic of cultural neo-imperialism. Corina (Romanian woman in her 40s) relates how the history of Oradea is not known, and how a "newly they are irritated" (line 67) if the architectural structures have Hungarian names. She distances herself from this group, the dominant Romanian elite and states that history should be accepted. The last section of the excerpt (lines 71–74) is particularly interesting because of Ana's of the pronoun "they", which changes its reference multiple times: Ana first agrees with Corina and uses marked intonation and stresses in order to make her words more emphatic. The referent of "others" changes. The first "others" are Romanians who blame Hungary for engaging in a neo-imperialist cultural restoration. The second "others" in this reply, however, refer to the Hungarians who want to see the built heritage as their own. Ana argues in favor of transnational values, and by doing so she opposes such tendencies. The next "they" are the Hungarians who try "to rebuild a neo-imperialist map through culture" and there is "a kind of intertextual message". By evoking such discourses she voices typical Romanian resentment and the fears caused by these cultural attempts at reclamation. She seems to elaborate, and makes more concrete, the theme introduced by her in lines 29–35. In the quoted excerpts we see how the trajectories of historical discourses from the 19th-century Hungarian Kingdom are intertwined with the trajectories of local discourses concerning the preservation and naming of the built heritage of the city of Oradea in the second decade of the 21st century. In the next example, Olli, (see also section 6.2 and excerpt 3) reflects upon the historical background of Swedish in Finland:

Excerpt 10

1. AK: so the general public usually doesn't make this gesture (.) doesn't
2. make the gesture towards er the Swedish speaking Finns or it's not (.) common?
3. Olli: no I don't think so (.) and perhaps you are right that (.) it's not

very popular

4. to read Swedish (.) or to use Swedish this (.) for Finns (.) but I have some=some
5. (.) I have an intuition (.) or impression that (.) it's becoming perhaps not so
6. popular
7. Interviewer: ahm
8. Olli: the need of understanding Swedish (.) and we know that=that the history
9. (sighs) is long together with Swedish
10. Interviewer: mhm
11. Olli: to=to be in the same monarchy a:nd we know that the most important poems
12. is written in Swedish.
13. Interviewer: yeah
14. Olli: they were Finns but the most important literature was written in Swedish
15. Interviewer: I see
16. Olli: so it's quite important for Finns that we understand what our (.) Finnish (.)
17. Swedish speaking Finns wrote
18. Interviewer: ya
19. Olli: of course there are translations (.) but that's another thing
20. Interviewer: hmm
21. Olli: it's not the same that you read what Runeberg or Lönnrot or other Finns wrote

Based on previous interviews, the interviewer asks the informant whether or not he considers it common that Finns make a gesture toward Swedish speakers of learning the language. The interviewer already positions himself as someone who knows about the situation of Swedish in Finland. He constructs the idea that language study is a gesture toward the "Swedish-speaking Finns" (line 2). Olli then takes up this phrase and uses it throughout the entire interview. In a matter of fact statement, the informant refers to the joint history of Sweden and Finland by evoking the common monarchy. As opposed to other interviewees this gives him a reason to be interested in the language. Recalling the joint history does not seem to convey negative undertones to him. Also, later in the interview he says: "we were the same monarchy we were one country"

(Olli). Moreover, it seems to be an important aspect, or an added value, for him to learn the language. The informant here begins to build an ideology that the Swedish language belongs to Finland. Olli points out that there are similarities between the two countries and the two cultures. The "history is long together with Swedish" (lines 8, 9). History is evoked in a generally positive light. Next, he refers to the long joint-history of Finnish and Swedish speakers in the Swedish monarchy, and the lasting influence of literature in Swedish. He says that it is important that Finns should know the language in which significant pieces of Finnish literature was written. He gives Runeberg and Lönnrot as examples, and argues that Finns should know Swedish so that they can read their works in the original and not only in translation. Finally, we can recall how the informant talks about the 19th-century intellectual heritage of Swedish in present-day Finland, and that many outstanding Finnish intellectuals were speakers of Swedish. For example, Olli, in other parts of the interview not presented here, mentions Sibelius, and speaks of other prominent Swedish speakers, like Runeberg and Lönnrot, who had played a major role in the development of Finnish literature. The discourse is typical of an intellectual. In the Romanian context there are no similar Hungarian literary figures who would be accepted by Romanians.

CONCLUSIONS

The main objective of this analysis was to illustrate the diversity of discourses related to the learning of historical minority languages that circulate among the language learners. In the interviews, historical "metanarratives" and references to contemporary social/cultural contexts were frequent. This was fairly expected, since, for example, in the context of learning German in Poland (Mar-Molinero & Stevenson 2006) or South Tyrol (Cavagnoli & Nardin 1999), similar discourses are ubiquitous. Applying the qualitative interview format, I asked informants about their voluntary learning of the major historical minority language in Romania and Finland. Finding language ideologies in these interviews with learners of historical minority languages was easy. The language ideologies were clearly coconstructed in the interviews and the answers by the interviewees were clearly geared to my question interactionally, and in regards to my position as a researcher as well. In the interviews with Finnish interviewees, it was often made explicit that I was a foreigner in Finland, and certain things that would not be explained to other Finns were explained to me. In the Romanian context I was treated as a local and cultural references were often left open to interpretation (on my role as a teacher of Hungarian, see Kiss 2013). The voluntary adult learners not only voiced general stereotypes like children in other studies (Martínez-Roldán & Malavé 2004), but as adults they also reflected on them in detail and contested many of the widespread beliefs and ideas over the minority language and learning it in the majority communities. The adult learners provide a good example of what is required in regards to a language ideological reorientation—a possible change during the lifetime (Woolard 2013; Pujolar & Gonzales 2013)—to replace the common concept of minority languages as "parochial and destabilizing" (May 2012: 84) to a minority language as a resource ideology. As a conclusion, from a political perspective, there is a need to replace the one state one language idea, with the ideology of mutual linguistic accommodation toward cohabitating a state or a region. Following May, I find that "the retention of a minority language and culture is an enduring need for the majority as well" (2012: 186, emphasis in original). My main analytical goal was to compile the research results into themes and provide a discourse analysis of the themes that occur in both data sets in order to examine the similarities and differences of the two contexts. Learning Swedish at school is unanimously given as the basic reason for voluntarily learning Swedish. In comparison, Romanians had not previously attended language classes. However, family ties, geographical proximity, and economical interest as well as contact with the neighboring country were mentioned as reasons for learning Hungarian. Besides the mention of access to material goods (e.g. communication in tourism, shopping), both Hungarian and Swedish are seen as languages that are important tools to access spiritual and cultural goods like education, knowledge of fine arts, and poetry. Despite the very different backgrounds, historical discourses of the other bear resemblances in both countries. The grievance narratives have been handed down through generations and they obstruct openness towards the learning of the historical minority language. To some extent, both Swedish and Hungarian are still perceived by many interviewees as the language of the former elites. It is notable that even though Swedish learning is supported by the Finnish language policy, the stereotypes about the language still linger. In Finland, intellectuals express a cultural interest in Swedish language as the historic heritage and see it as part of Finland. In many interviews, the joint history offers a basis for a better understanding of other Scandinavian countries and of the history of the

Finns. In relation to meta-narratives about history, different approaches surface in the two data sets. In the Finnish data the learners who studied Swedish voluntarily expressed acceptance of the historical past and Swedish language as a part of Finnish history. That is, there are signs of mutual accommodation of Finnish and Swedish history, culture, and language in Finland. Perhaps this is a consequence of Finland not being a part of "the exclusive club of 'true' ethno-linguistic nation states" (Kamusella 2009: 57). In a clear contrast to the Finnish signs of mutual accommodation, we saw how Romanians learning Hungarian still struggle with the fact that common elements of history are neglected, or are outright rejected by both parties. One explaining factor can be that Finland was under Swedish rule as late as 1809, whereas Transylvania belonged to Hungary until 1920 and still in 1941–1944. That is, in Finland the 19th century Finnish linguistic nationalism was not a threat to the national unity of Sweden, and thus the Swedish speaking intelligentsia in Finland supported it to a certain extent. In contrast, the national movements of the Romanians in 19th century Transylvania were relegated to rebellious groups in the eyes of the emerging Hungarian nation state. The brief interlude of Hungarian rule in northern Transylvania during 1941–1944 is still referred to as "returning to home" ('visszatéres' in Hungarian) from the Hungarian point of view, whereas Romanian official and popular narratives refer to that period as "Hungarian occupation". The study in the two contexts shows that historical metanarratives about the joint historical past can hinder, or outright block, language learning of the respective minority languages, as we can witness in other contexts as well. The contemporary socio-cultural context, partly due to globalization and the spread of post-national ideologies (Heller 2011), is in both cases favorable toward the learning of the historical minority language. At first sight, it appears more favorable in the case of Finland, since learning Swedish is a part of the compulsory education for the majority. However, there is a paradox, for this both motivates and hinders the adults from learning the minority language. For those few capable of a language ideological reorientation free from the stereotype of pakkoruotsi ('compulsory learning of Swedish'), the previous experience at school motivates them to refresh their Swedish knowledge later on: "I didn't want to start a new language" as one of my interviewees put it. In general, the learning of historical languages can build on the contemporary socio-cultural context in Europe. At the same time, it is much harder to contest and change the historical metanarratives (e.g. that Hungarians "occupied" Oradea between 1941–1944, or that Swedish speakers form the "upper class" in Finland). For the future, where the learning of one another's language would also become standard for the majority, a general language ideological reorientation of these historical metanarratives is necessary. That is, by learning and acknowledging the other's perspective to history and linguistics belonging we can focus on shared history and multilingual practices instead of nation state antagonisms and monolingual preferences. Future research is needed to indicate general and context-bound ways to achieve such an ideological reorientation, which supports the voluntary learning of historical minority languages by the majority on a European scale.

ACKNOWLEDGEMENTS

I am grateful for the University of Jyväskylä, CIMO, and Svenska Kulturfonden for grants that have enabled me to carry out the research reported here. I would like to thank Petteri Laihonen, Åsa Palviainen, Sabine Ylönen and the two anonymous reviewers for helpful comments on earlier versions of this article. Any remaining shortcomings are solely my responsibility.

REFERENCES

1. Atkinson, D. 2005. Situated qualitative research and second language writing. In. P. Matsuda & T. Silva (eds.), Second Language Writing Research: Perspectives on the process of Knowledge Construction. Mahwah, NJ: Erlbaum, 49–64.
2. Atkinson, D., O. Hanako & S. Talmy 2011. Ethnography and Discourse. In K. Hyland & B.
3. Paltridge (eds.), Continuum Companion to Discourse Analysis. London: Continuum, 85–101.
4. Azkue, J. & J. Perales 2005. The teaching of Basque to adults. International Journal of the Sociology of Language, 174, 73–83.
5. Berecz, Á. 2013. The politics of early language teaching: Hungarian in the primary schools of the late dual Monarchy. Budapest: Pasts.
6. Blommaert, J. 2006. Language ideology. In K. Brown (ed.), Encyclopaedia of Language and Linguistics. Oxford: Elsevier, 510–522.
7. Blommaert, J. & J. Dong 2010. Ethnographic fieldwork: A beginner's guide. Bristol: Multilingual Matters.
8. Cavagnoli, S. & F. Nardin 1999. Second Language Acquisition in South Tyrol: Difficulties, Motivations, Expectations. Multilingua, 18, 17–45.
9. Cenoz, J. & J. Perales 2010. Minority Language Learning in the Administration: Data from the Basque Country. Jounal of Multilingual and Multicultural Development, 18 (4), 261–270.
10. De Fina, A. 2009. Narratives in interview: for an interactional approach to narrative genres.Narrative Inquiry, 19 (2), 233–258.
11. Duff, P. 2009. Indigenous, Minority, and Heritage Language Education in

Canada: Policies, Contexts, and Issues. The Canadian Modern Language Review, 66 (1), 1–8.

12. Duszak, A. 2006. Why 'New' Newspeak?: Axiological Insights into Language Ideologies and Practices in Poland. In C. Mar-Molinero & P. Stevenson (eds.), Language Ideologies, Policies and Practices: Language and the Future of Europe. Houndmills: Palgrave, 96–103.
13. Gal, S. 2006a. Language, its stakes and its effects. In R. Goodin & T. Charles (eds.), The Oxford handbook of contextual political analysis. Oxford: Oxford University Press, 376–392.
14. Gal, S. 2006b. Migration, Minorities and Multilingualism: Language Ideologies in Europe In C.
15. Mar-Molinero & P. Stevenson (eds). Language Ideologies, Policies and Practices: Language and the Future of Europe. Houndmills: Palgrave, 13–27.
16. Gal, S. 2011. Polyglot nationalism: Alternative perspectives on language in 19th century Hungary. Langage Et Société, 2 (136), 31–54.
17. Geertz, C. 1973/2000. The interpretation of cultures. New York: Basic Books.
18. Giddens, A. 1999. Runaway world: How globalisation is reshaping our lives. London: Profile Books. Guardado, M. 2014. The Discourses of Heritage Language Development: Engaging Ideologies in Canadian Hispanic Communities. Heritage Language Journal, 11 (1), 1–27.
19. Heller, M. 2001. Discourse and Interaction. In D. T. Schiffrin & H. E. Hamilton (eds.), The Handbook of Discourse Analysis. Oxford: Blackwell, 250–264.
20. Heller, M. 2008. Doing Ethnography. In L. Wei & M. Moyer (eds.), The Blackwell Guide to Research Methods in Bilingualism and Multilingualism. Oxford: Blackwell, 249–262.
21. Heller, M. 2011. Paths to Post-Nationalism: A Critical Ethnography of Language and Identity. Oxford: Oxford University Press.
22. Institutul Na□ional de Statistică (INS) 2011. Recensământul popula□iei □i al locuin□elor. [Retrieved February 18, 2014]. Available at http://www.recensamantromania.ro/rezultate-2/
23. Jaffe, A. 1999. Ideologies in action: language politics on Corsica. Berlin: Mouton de Gruyter. Jaworska, S. 2009. The German language in Poland: The eternal foe and the wars on words. In J.
24. Carl & P. Stevenson (eds.), Language, discourse and identity in central europe: The German language in a multilingual space. Basingstoke:

Palgrave Macmillan, 51–73.

25. Jyväskylän Kansalaisopisto 2013–2014. 2013. Jyväskylä: Jyväskylän kaupunki.
26. Kamusella, T. 2009. The Politics of Language and Nationalism in Modern Central Europe. Basingstoke: Palgrave Macmillan.
27. Kiss, A. 2012. Hungarian as a Second Language in Oradea/Nagyvárad: Cultural Reflexions and Language Ideologies. In K. Fenyvesi (ed.), Transition and difference: Hungarian Perspectives On East and Central European Studies. Budapest: International Association for Hungarian Studies, 279–293.
28. Kiss, A. 2013. A magyar mint második nyelv tanításának nehézségei **és** sikerei Nagyváradon.
29. [The difficulties and successes of teaching Hungarian in Oradea]. In O. Nádor (ed.), THL2: The Journal of Teaching Hungarian as a Foreign Language, (1–2), 97–115.
30. Kiss, A. in press. Teaching the Romanian neighbours Hungarian: Language ideologies and the Debrecen Summer School. Multilingua: Journal of Cross Cultural and interlanguage Communication.
31. Kramsch, C. 2009. The multingual subject. Oxford: Oxford University Press.
32. Laihonen, P. 2008. Language ideologies in interviews: A conversation analysis approach. Journal of Sociolinguistics, 12 (5), 668–693.
33. Laihonen, P. 2009. Language Ideologies in the Romanian Banat: Analysis of Interviews and Academic Writings among the Hungarians and Germans. Jyväskylä Studies in Humanities 119. Jyväskylä: University of Jyväskylä.
34. Lynch, A. 2003. The Relationship between Second and Heritage Language Acquisition: Notes on Research and Theory Building. Heritage Language Journal, 1–18.
35. Mar-Molinero C. & P. Stevenson (eds.) 2006. Language Ideologies, Policies and Practices: Language and the Future of Europe. Houndmills: Palgrave.
36. Martínez-Roldán, C. M. & G. Malavé 2004. Language ideologies mediating literacy and identity in bilingual contexts. Journal of Early Childhood Literacy, 4 (2), 155–180.
37. May, S. 2012. Language and minority rights: ethnicity, nationalism and the politics of language. New York: Routledge.
38. McEwan-Fujita, E. 2010. Ideology, affect, and socialization in language

shift and revitalization: The experiences of adults learning Gaelic in the Western Isles of Scotland. Language in Society, 39, 27–64.

39. Mori, J. 2012. Tale of Two Tales: Locally Produced Accounts and Membership During Research Interviews With a Multilingual Speaker. The Modern Language Journal, 96, 489–506.

40. Mózes, T. 1997. Evreii din Oradea [The Jews from Oradea]. Bucure□ti: Hasefer.

41. Nekvapil, J. & T. Sherman 2009. Czech, German and English: Finding Their Place in Multinational Companies in the Czech Republic. In J. Carl, & P. Stevenson (eds.), Language, Discourse and Identity in Central Europe: The German Language in a Multilingual Space. Basingstoke: Palgrave, 122–146.

42. Nekvapil, J. 2000. On non-self-evident relationships between language and ethnicity: How Germans do not speak German, and Czechs do not speak Czech. Multilingua, 19 (1-2), 37–54.

43. Oh, J. & A. B. Nash 2014. Attitudes and motivations of Adult Spanish Learners: A comparison of Heritage Language Learners and Second Language Learners. Heritage Language Journal, 11 (1), 29–44.

44. Official Statistics of Finland (OSF) 30.9.2011. Swedish-speakers› proportion of the population in 1900– 2010. [Retrieved February 18, 2014]. Available at http://www.stat.fi/til/vaerak/2010/01/vaerak_2010_01_2011-09-30_kuv_001_en.html

45. Palviainen, Å. 2010a. The Proficiency in Swedish of Finnish-speaking University Students: Status and Directions for the Future. Apples – Journal of Applied Language Studies, Vol. 4, 1, 3-23. [Retrieved February 2, 2014]. Available at http://apples.jyu.fi /article_files/Articles_2010a_Palviainen.pdf

46. Palviainen, Å. 2010b. Språkval och vägval – en valfråga 2011? Kieli, koulutus ja yhteiskunta.

47. [Retrieved February 18, 2014]. Available at http://www.kieliverkosto.fi/article/sprakvaloch-vagval-en- alfraga-2011/

48. Palviainen, Å. 2011. Frivillig svenska? Utbildningsrelaterade konsekvenser. Magma Finlands svenska tankesmedja. [Retrieved February 2, 2014]. Available at http://www.magma.fi /images/stories/reports/ms1103_frisv.pdf

49. Palviainen, Å. 2012. Lärande som diskursnexus: Finska studenters uppfattningar om skoltid, fritid och universitetsstudier som lärokontexter för svenska. Nordand Nordisk tidsskrift for andrespråkforskning, 7 (1),

7–35.

50. Palviainen, Å. 2013a. National identity and a transnational space: the strength of tradition in a time of change. Sociolinguistica 27, 1–18.
51. Palviainen, Å. 2013b. Att utveckla en Jyväskyläidentitet: Undervisning på svenska i en finskdominerad miljö. In Kieli, koulutus, ja yhteiskunta. [Retrieved February 18, 2014].
52. Available at http://www.kieliverkosto.fi/article/att-utveckla-en-jyvaskylaidentitetundervisning-pa- venska-i-en-finskdominerad-miljo/
53. Palviainen, Å. & C. Jauhojärvi-Koskelo 2009. Mitt i brytpunkten: Finska universitetsstudenters **åsikter** om svenskan [In the middle of a crossroads: Finnish university students› views on Swedish]. In L. Collin & S. Haapamäki (eds.), Svenskan i Finland 11. Föredrag vid elfte sammankomsten för beskrivningen av svenskan i Finland, **Åbo** den 16–17 maj 2008. **Åbo**: **Åbo** Akademi, 125–133.
54. Pujolar, J. 2007. The future of Catalan: language endangerment and nationalist discourses in Catalonia. In A. Duchene and M. Heller (eds.), Discourses of endangerement: Ideology and Interest in the Defence of Languages. London: Continuum, 121–148.
55. Pujolar, J. & I. Gonzales 2013. Linguistic "mudes" and the de-ethnicization of language choice in Catalonia. International Journal of Bilingual Education and Bilingualism, 16 (2), 138–152.
56. Spolsky, B. 2010. Second-Language Learning. In J. A. Fishman and O. García (eds.) Handbook of language and ethnic identity. Oxford: Oxford University Press, 172–185.
57. Statistics Finland 2015. [Retrieved June 28, 2015]. Available at http://pxweb2.stat.fi/Dialog/Saveshow.asp
58. ten Have, P. 2004. Understanding qualitative research and ethnomethodology. London: Sage Publications.
59. The Constitution of Finland 2000. [Retrieved February 18, 2014]. Available at http://www.finlex.fi/en/laki/kaannokset/1999/en19990731.pdf
60. The Constitution of Romania 2003. [Retrieved February 18, 2014]. Available at http://www.cdep.ro/pls/dic/site.page?id=339&par1=1&idl=2
61. Weiss, R. S. & S. A. Bass 2001. Introduction. In R. S. Weiss & S. A. Bass (eds.), Challenges of the third age: Meaning and purpose in later life. New York: Oxford University Press, 3–12.
62. Wolff, S. 2000 (ed.). German minorities in Europe: ethnic identity and cultural belonging. New York: Berghahn.

63. Woolard, K. 1998. Introduction: language ideology as a field of inquiry. In B. Schieffelin, K.
64. Woolard & P. Kroskrity (eds.), Language Ideologies. Oxford: Oxford University Press, 3–47.
65. Woolard, K. 2013. Is the personal political? Chronotopes and changing stances toward Catalan language and identity. International of Bilingual Education and Bilingualism, 16 (2), 210–224.
66. Woolard, K. & B. Schieffelin 1994. Language ideology. Annual Reviews Anthropology, 23, 55–82.
67. Wortham, S. 2005. Learning Identity: The Joint Emergence of Social Identification and Academic Learning. Cambridge: Cambridge University Press.
68. Wortham, S. 2008. The Political Matrix of Linguistic Ideologies. In B. Spolsky & F. M. Hult (eds.), The handbook of educational linguistics, London: Wiley–Blackwell Publishing, 83–98.
69. Zenker, O. 2014. Linguistic Relativity and Dialectical Idiomatization: Language Ideologies and Second Language Revival of Northern Ireland. Journal of Linguistic Anthropology, 24 (1), 68–83.

CITATION

CHAPTER 1

Angela Chambers, integrating corpus consultation in language studies, ISSN 1094-3501.

CHAPTER 2

Ogenyi, L. (2015) Strategy Use and Language Performance by Second Language Learners in Nigeria. Advances in Literary Study, 3, 65-78. doi: 10.4236/als.2015.33011.

CHAPTER 3

Thomas Roche and Michael Harrington, Recognition Vocabulary Knowledge as a Predictor of Academic Performance in an English as a Foreign Language Setting, DOI: 10.1186/2229-0443-3-12.

CHAPTER 4

Ziegler: Multilingualism and the language education landscape: challenges for teacher training in Europe. Multilingual Education 2013 3:1.

CHAPTER 5

YougenLou, (2015) An Empirical Study of Content-Based Instruction Applied in Non-English-Majored Graduate English Teaching in the Post-Massification. Creative Education,06,1578-1583. doi: 10.4236/ce.2015.614158

CHAPTER 8

Megawati Soekarno, Su-Hie Ting, Communication Strategy Use By Healthcare Trainees In Monologues And Dialogues During Strategy Training, file:///C:/Users/tri/

Downloads/communication-strategy-use-by-healthcare-trainees-in-monologues-and-dialogues-during-strategy-training.pdf.

CHAPTER 9

Omid Arast, Bahman Gorjian, The Effect of Listening to Comic Strip Stories on Incidental Vocabulary Learning among Iranian EFL Learners, doi:10.5923/j.jalll.20160201.01.

CHAPTER 10

Laleh Kohandel Jahromi, Amin Marzban, A Critical Review of Common Vocabulary Learning Strategies in Iranian EFL Classrooms doi:10.5923/j.jalll.20150101.05.

CHAPTER 11

Jakonen, T. (2014). Building Bridges - How secondary school pupils bring their informal learning experiences into a Content and Language Integrated (CLIL) classroom. APPLES : journal of applied language studies, 8 (1), 7-28. Retrieved from http://apples.jyu.fi/ArticleFile/download/421

CHAPTER 12

Attila Kiss, Language Ideologies and Learning Historical Minority Languages: A comparative study of voluntary learners of Swedish in Finland and Hungarian in Romania,http://dx.doi.org/10.17011/apples/2015090105

INDEX